MAKING MARTYRS EAST AND WEST

MAKING MARTYRS EAST & WEST

Canonization in the Catholic and Russian Orthodox Churches

CATHY CARIDI

NIU Press / DeKalb, IL

Northern Illinois University Press, DeKalb 60115
© 2016 by Northern Illinois University Press
All rights reserved

25 24 23 22 21 20 19 18 17 16   1 2 3 4 5

978-0-87580-495-8 (cloth)
978-1-60909-188-0 (ebook)

Cover design by Yuni Dorr
Book design by Shaun Allshouse

Library of Congress Cataloging-in-Publication Data
Names: Caridi, Cathy.
Title: Making martyrs East and West : canonization in the Catholic and Russian Orthodox churches / Cathy Caridi.
Description: First [edition]. | DeKalb : Northern Illinois University Press, 2015. | Includes bibliographical references and index.
Identifiers: LCCN 2015039179| ISBN 9780875804958 (cloth)
 | ISBN 9781609091880 (ebook)
Subjects: LCSH: Christian saints. | Rites and ceremonies. | Canonization.
 | Russkaia pravoslavnaia tserkov'. | Catholic Church.
Classification: LCC BT970 .C28 2015 | DDC 272—dc23
LC record available at http://lccn.loc.gov/2015039179

Contents

Acknowledgments ix

INTRODUCTION 1

CHAPTER ONE
Christianity's Unified First Millennium (until ca. 1054) 10
Introduction: Preliminary Remarks 10
A. Development of a Theological Concept of Martyrdom 12
B. Development of a Process by Which a Martyr Was Officially Recognized 17
    1. Prelude to a Process: Initially, Spontaneous Local Recognition by the Faithful 17
    2. Historical Elements Leading to a Future Process 19
        a. Liturgical Commemorations: Diptychs and Calendars 20
        b. *Passiones/Acta Martyrum* 28
        c. *Elevatio/Translatio* of the Relics to a Church Dedicated to the Martyr 31
C. Local Bishops, Civil Officials, and the Need for Authority 36
Preliminary Conclusions 43

CHAPTER TWO
Russian Orthodoxy from the Conversion of Rus' (ca. 988) to Today 46
Introduction: Lacunae in Russian Historiography and Some Consequent Methodological Issues 46
Part 1: From the Conversion of Rus' (ca. 988) until the 1917 Bolshevik Revolution 49
    A. Theological Concept of Martyrdom 49
    B. Process by Which a Martyr Is Recognized as a Saint 53
        1. Spontaneous Recognition by the Local Faithful 53
        2. But Simultaneously, a More Official Process Exists 54
            a. Liturgical Commemorations—Local Calendars 54
            b. Writing the *Zhitie*, Composing a *Sluzhba* 58
            c. *Elevatio/Translatio* of Relics and Two Requirements that Subsequently Develop from It 62
                i. Requirement 1: The Need for Miracles 62
                ii. Requirement 2: Incorrupt Relics 69

C. Authority: Who Makes the Decision to Canonize a Saint?   71
    1. The Earliest Russian Martyrs in the First Centuries in the Life of the Church   71
    2. The Unprecedented Canonization Councils of Metropolitan Makarii, 1547 and 1549   74
    3. The Holy Governing Synod as the Supreme Authority in the Russian Church   78

Part 2: From the Bolshevik Revolution in 1917 to Today   79
    A. The Restoration of the Patriarchate and the Beginnings of a Procedural Shift   79
        1. A Sidebar: The Possibility of "Decanonization"   82
    B. From the Collapse of the Soviet Union (1990) until Today   83
        1. Theological Concept of Martyrdom Revisited   83
        2. The Process by Which a Martyr Is Now to Be Recognized, according to the Canonization Commission   84
        3. Church Authorities Competent to Canonize: A Return to Prior Praxis   91
Preliminary Conclusions   93

CHAPTER THREE

The Catholic Church from the Great Schism (ca. 1054) to Today   100

Introduction   100
A. Theological Concepts of Sainthood/Martyrdom: Refining the Definitions   102
B. Elements of the Process by Which a Martyr Is Recognized   106
    1. Liturgical Commemorations: Calendars   107
    2. *Translatio*   111
    3. Writing a *Vita* and the Evolution of an Investigatory Process   113
        a. Development of a Detailed Evidentiary Process   117
        b. Proofs of Sanctity: Do Martyrs Need Miracles?   120
            i. Miracles and Incorrupt Remains   126
C. Authority: Who Makes the Decision to Canonize a Saint?   128
    1. Centralization of Authority, Originally as a Response to Local Abuses   128
        a. Decretalists and the Evolution of a Canonical/Theological Justification for Papal Canonization   132
        b. Can a Catholic Saint Be "Decanonized"? The Case of Philomena   133
    2. Canonizations with Territorial Limitations: The Development of Beatification   135
        a. Urban VIII's *Caelestis Hierusalem Cives* as Another Response to Local Abuse   136
    3. Bypassing the Bureaucracy: The Recent Trend of Pope Francis   140
Preliminary Conclusions   141

CHAPTER FOUR
Comparisons and Conclusions   145
A. Can Saints Canonized in the Russian Orthodox Church Be Accepted as Saints by the Catholic Church?   145
B. Can Saints Canonized in the Catholic Church Be Accepted as Saints by the Russian Orthodox Church?   154
C. Theological Differences or Cultural/Political Ones?   157
Final Thoughts   160

List of Abbreviations   163
Notes   165
Selected Bibliography   189
Index   197

Acknowledgments

A lot of people generously gave a lot of their precious time, and shared a lot of their priceless expertise, in the making of this book.

Vincenzo Criscuolo, O.F.M. Cap., the Relatore Generale of the Vatican's Congregation for the Causes of Saints, spent countless hours sifting through historical evidence with me, seeking in exchange only the opportunity to practice his English. (What a deal!) Norman Tanner, S.J., of the Gregorian University, and Rev. Constantin Simon, formerly of the Pontifical Oriental Institute, patiently poured through footnotes and constantly offered their encouragement.

Speaking of offering, Ilya Semenenko-Basin of Moscow has earned my eternal gratitude for sharing his then-unpublished research with me. John Burgess, of Pittsburgh Theological Seminary, pointed out important evidentiary sources which I would otherwise have missed; and James Muldoon, Professor Emeritus of Rutgers University, made astute observations about current events which helped me tie the research together.

Professor Emeritus Paul Steeves, of Stetson University, probably doesn't even remember by now his reply to my general queries before undertaking this project—yet his answers were more helpful than he could possibly have imagined. The input of Elina Kahla, Director of the Finnish Institute in St. Petersburg, was likewise far more valuable than she knows.

Спасибо большой! Господь воздаст вам!

INTRODUCTION

We generally communicate with each other by using words, but communication is impossible if we do not all understand and agree about what the words actually mean. It's not just a question of translating from one language to another; even though we are fluent in our mother tongue, we still need occasionally to check a dictionary to get the precise meaning of a word. We cannot work together if we don't have the same correct understanding of the meanings of the words we use.

Sometimes it's perilously easy to assume that we are all using a word in the same way, when in fact no universal definition of the term even exists. Well do I remember my first day in a course on Balkan politics in the government department of Georgetown University, surrounded by classmates who all were both much younger and much more attuned to current political events than I was. When a heated discussion erupted about Bosnian "genocide," I finally had to interject a humble admission that I was ignorant of that word's official, internationally accepted definition. Only at that point did the entire class discover that no universally accepted definition of "genocide" exists—thereby rendering our entire debate instantly meaningless.

As in politics, so in religion, the need to be absolutely sure that the words we use have identical meanings in the minds of all concerned is vital. Within the Catholic Church, this is the primary justification for retaining the use of Latin as its universal language: since Catholics speak literally every language under the sun, it is imperative that they all know exactly what they are talking about—and often enough one finds that when shifting from one language to another, some words simply don't translate.

In ecumenical affairs, when one Christian denomination discusses issues with another that shares so many of the same beliefs, they frequently find that they are all talking "on the same page," using terminology in exactly the same way. But as the Spanish Inquisition found in the fifteenth and sixteenth centuries while investigating supposedly orthodox Catholic "mystics," it is entirely possible to use a word that everyone around you thinks they understand, the meaning of which you actually understand in a markedly different way. What superficially appears to be agreement may in fact be significant discord, if terms are not being defined uniformly by all.

In the Catholic and Russian Orthodox Churches, assumption is generally made that when they speak of "saints" and "martyrs for the faith," they mean essentially the same thing. But doubts first began to arise in my own mind when the Romanov family was canonized in the year 2000 by the patriarch of Moscow. Mainstream news reports, both Russian and American, indicated that they were now considered "martyrs of Orthodoxy," which immediately gave me pause. I had always taken it for granted that the tsar, his heir the tsarevich, and the rest of the imperial family were murdered for reasons that were entirely political rather than theological—but perhaps my assumption was factually wrong. Were the Romanovs actually killed by the Bolsheviks specifically because of their Orthodox faith? Or did the term *martyr* perhaps mean something different to the Russian Orthodox than it does to Catholics?

Genuine confusion about terminology continued, as I came across numerous public objections to the canonization by members of the Russian Orthodox Church themselves. Although I initially thought their concerns would likely echo my own, the issues they raised were altogether different. Their primary grievance was that Tsar Nicholas had been a weak ruler, indecisive, and therefore not good for Russia. How, they wanted to know, could such a man be canonized a saint?

In the Catholic Church, such a question would not normally even be raised. For Catholic saints are canonized because of their heroic sanctity, and consequently the decision is not based on their professional success or even on their intelligence. It is entirely possible to be canonized a saint—and even regarded as a great one—in the Catholic Church, and yet in the temporal sphere to be regarded as what the average American teenager would term a "loser." King Saint Edward the Confessor (1003/5–1066), undeniably both a holy man and a pitifully inept ruler, immediately comes to mind as an example.

I realized that what I was seeing might be an unintentional, and possibly even unrecognized, disconnect between the two churches, regarding the definitions of words that each church has been using for centuries. Could it be, I wondered, that they are speaking different languages, in more ways than one?

Answering this question constitutes more than just an abstract exercise, of the sort that might engage a roomful of theology professors attending an academic conference. As Elizabeth Castelli has observed, *any* theological decision that someone has been martyred will carry with it a broader social message:

> Martyrdom generates its own self-authorizing claims to a privileged status in relation to truth and public authority.... the figure of the martyr conjures a heightened sense of certainty about the righteousness of one's cause and the favor that God bestows on one's earthly projects.¹

A declaration that a person should be venerated as a martyr and saint, therefore, invariably reveals many of the moral teachings that ecclesiastical decision-makers believe the faithful should both value and imitate. Defining a particular kind of death, under particular circumstances, as "martyrdom" can show the world just what actions and attitudes the church hierarchy considers to be virtuous and heroic, and what it thus expects the faithful under their spiritual care to try to emulate. There's a flip side to the same equation, too: the canonization of a martyr carries with it a lesson that those who killed the martyr were/are enemies of both the church itself and the way of life that it embraces.

In short, canonizing martyrs as saints may not be the most central, pivotally important component of either Catholic or Orthodox theology; but focusing on how it's done, and what factors are taken into consideration when making this decision and why, can give us almost a "mini-lesson" in that church's teachings about putting faith into practice while living (and dying) in the real world. "Live as this person did," a canonization tells the faithful, "emulate this person's values and perseverance, and commit yourselves to refusing to cooperate with the enemies of the faith, even if you don't ever find yourself in exactly the same situation as this great saint." And it follows that if this sort of theological declaration is influenced—or even hijacked outright—by political interests at a given point in history, the implications can potentially have an outcome that is much farther-reaching than the mere addition of a feast-day into a church's liturgical calendar. It can affect the entire culture of the church.

Speaking of politics and culture, the practical, current implications of the cultural differences between the Catholic West and the Orthodox East have been visible in a brutally irreligious way since early 2014, in the political and military events taking place in and near Ukraine. Unluckily located directly on the geographical border between the worlds of Catholicism and Orthodoxy, Ukrainians in the war zone have been living the violent result of a chronic, centuries-old internal division between their ethnically Ukrainian Catholic population in the western part of the country, and their Russian-speaking Orthodox citizens living in the area of the nation bordering Russia. While the bombings, airline disasters, and floods of refugees might not seem to have anything directly to do with religion per se, the fundamental identity of the Ukrainian people is very much tied to their spirituality: Orthodox Ukrainians (mostly in the East) naturally identify with their counterparts in Russia, just as Ukrainian Catholics tend instinctively to want to ally themselves with the people of non-Orthodox, Western nations. The tragic cultural tug-of-war that has resulted cannot be addressed—let alone resolved!—without keeping the religious differences between the two sides firmly in mind.

And since religion and its cultural influences play such a fundamental role in the differences between the peoples of East and West, it follows too that Catholic–Orthodox theological rapprochement would naturally have enormous implications far outside the doors of the local parish church. Imagine, if you can, the political fallout from even a partial theological unification between Catholicism and Orthodoxy in the twenty-first century! While on the immediate surface such an event might seem exclusively to have resulted from the resolution of various theological intricacies, the unity would unavoidably have to go much deeper, and include commonalities in the way that the peoples actually *think*, and what they think is important and why.

This sort of unity may seem nothing more than a pipe dream—and yet it is precisely such unification in a previous century that has, paradoxically, given Ukraine its current cultural division. In 1595, the Orthodox faithful living in a huge swath of what is today Ukraine were united to Rome, with a declaration known as the Union of Brest[2]—in the process, of course, ending communion with the leadership of the Orthodox Church. The members of what is now known as the Ukrainian Greek Catholic Church are ethnically Ukrainian (and would unquestionably resent any suggestion to the contrary), but once they placed themselves under the jurisdiction of the Roman pontiff, their theological orientation necessarily shifted from East to West. The Catholic Church rejoiced at the ecclesial unification; yet it brought with it sufficient cultural rupture with those who remained Orthodox as to leave Ukrainians today with what many of them describe as an identity crisis. The results of this, as the world has seen, have been paid for in blood.

Meanwhile, back in the comparatively peaceful world of theologians and academics, talks are perennially being held between the Catholic Church and the Orthodox Churches as a whole, with the ultimate goal of determining their areas of true theological commonality and those of genuine difference. Ecclesiological issues (first and foremost among which is, of course, papal primacy), and fundamental Christological questions (as exemplified by the endless *filioque* debates) always take center stage, and rightly so. Discussion of the medieval martyr-saints who are commemorated on their respective liturgical calendars hardly carries with it a comparable urgency.

But as can be seen with the Romanov controversy, in recent years the issue of what it really means to be a "saint," and the criteria required in order to merit the appellation of "martyr," have come to the forefront within the Russian Orthodox Church. With the collapse of the Soviet Union, the much-heralded end of the Communist system of government, and a corresponding new freedom of religion in general and for the Orthodox Church in particular, the church in Russia is now able to assess the spiritual implications of seventy years of government persecution without limitations or fear of reprisals. It is only reasonable that it now wishes to commemorate publicly the thousands of clergy and other Orthodox faithful who were tyrannized—if not murdered outright—by the Communist Soviet regime. Suddenly, it matters very much whether the Russian church has an articulated and internally consistent definition of *martyrdom* and of *sainthood* that it can seek to apply to those killed in the twentieth century for their Orthodox beliefs.

And for Catholics who are sincerely convinced of the importance of the ongoing dialogue with the Orthodox Churches, this internal matter that technically concerns only the Russian Orthodox Church is of long-term concern as well. For someday, it is hoped, the church will once again be able to "breathe with both lungs," as Saint John Paul II so aptly put it; someday it will be able to fulfill the prayer of Christ Himself "that they may be one" (John 17:21). And if the churches really return to full communion some day, such a move will necessarily bring with it—in accord with Catholic canon law (CIC c. 205, CCEO c. 8)—a sharing in the same profession of faith, sacraments, and ecclesiastical governance.

At that time, among the many other issues that will have to be addressed will be the question of accepting or rejecting each other's saints, particularly those who lived or at least were canonized after the Great Schism in the eleventh century. Should a feast-day commemorating this or that Russian martyr be inserted into the Catholic liturgical calendar and should the Orthodox add feast-days commemorating Catholic ones? Should everybody be praying for the intercession of a saint who currently is venerated in only one of the two churches? Can everyone accept that canonizing a saint in either church ought at that point to be considered valid for them both?

And with regard to ecumenism, if the procedures for saint-making in both churches are identical—or at least substantively the same—this could be an indication that, spiritually, they are fundamentally on the same page. The flip side is also true, of course; if the respective canonization processes for martyrs are so radically different, it may be that the churches' definitions of *canonization*, *saint*, and/or *martyrdom* are far from synonymous. Or it may be that while their theological understanding is essentially the same, the procedural standards of one church are too low, or are otherwise flawed, in the eyes of the other.

Comparing the two churches' *current* systems of canonization, however, is not enough. For one thing, both the Catholics and the Russian Orthodox have been creating new saints more or less continuously since the Great Schism, for a period of nearly a thousand years. Examining the process of saint-making as it is today does not necessarily help us to determine the criteria in force in centuries past.

But more importantly, a simple snapshot of the procedures now in place in both churches would be misleading at best. In each church, the contemporary process can only be understood in its historical context. For Christians have been venerating martyrs since the earliest days of the church.

In the days of Emperor Nero's active persecutions, when Christians were being butchered by the thousands in every available circus, nobody sat down to compose a system for the canonization of martyrs as saints. In fact, in the beginning, nobody thought to articulate a theological rationale for the veneration of deceased Christians as martyrs at all! The practice developed naturally, spontaneously—or, to cite a term used frequently in similar contexts by the former Cardinal Ratzinger, "organically."[3] Any written system or theological justification, therefore, necessarily evolved later, as a means both of explaining the practice in spiritual terms and, on a more pragmatic level, of providing some concrete guidelines for future cases.

In the West, the Catholic Church has had the benefit of nearly two thousand years of continuous tradition upon which to base its contemporary theological understanding of sainthood in general and of martyrdom in particular, and its juridical procedure of canonizing new saints. One would presume that the modern process is the end result of centuries of development, refinement, and adaptation.

Russia, on the other hand, has been a Christian nation for slightly more than half as long as the West, and it basically inherited the saint-making system already in use by that time among the Greeks. But since the Greek church did not micromanage its new Russian converts once Christianity was solidly established among them, the Russian clergy—who were relatively new to the faith themselves—were left in charge of creating new Russian saints when they began to emerge. The Russian church did not, therefore, devise an entirely new set of definitions and processes ex nihilo; but at the same time, neither was it given an organized, written, codified system based on explicit, well-articulated definitions. At the end of the first millennium AD, Christianity's theological understanding of sainthood, and particularly of martyrdom, was still in flux even in those parts of the world that had already been Christian for centuries. Consequently, the Russian clergy did their fair share of developing and innovating—without any input from the West, from which it was soon completely separated in the ecclesiological sense.

It will therefore be entirely understandable already if we find that canonizing Russian Orthodox martyrs is markedly different from canonizing Catholic ones. But in evaluating the Russian church, there is of course an added twist, for as we all know, the rise of Communism in Russia in the early twentieth century soon brought with it the active persecution of the Russian Orthodox Church (and all other faiths as well) for nearly seventy years. Thousands upon thousands of clergy and lay-faithful were killed during this period by the Soviet government; yet it was only after the collapse of the Soviet Union in the 1990s that the Russian church was really free for the first time to assess the circumstances surrounding their deaths, to try to determine whether these victims of twentieth-century Soviet persecution should indeed be venerated as martyrs.

It is true that the Russian church already had its own theology of martyrdom, and its own canonization process, from the years preceding the Bolshevik Revolution in 1917; but the post-Soviet era was another world, far from the days when Russian Orthodoxy was the official state religion under the Russian tsar. The old system, which had more or less lain dormant for the better part of the twentieth century, needed rethinking and a new articulation.

Accordingly, what follows is a historical analysis of the development of a canonization process for martyrs, from the rise of Christianity to the present, in the Catholic and Russian Orthodox Churches. We are searching here for the criteria that have been and are used in each church, when determining whether a person should officially be declared a saint because he or she died a martyr's death. Note that no direct attention will be paid here specifically to legislation pertaining to the procedure of canonization of *non*-martyrs, except in those instances where the procedure is identical for all saints, or at particular points in history when elements of the procedure originally intended for non-martyrs affected that of martyrs (as did indeed happen, more than once).

Perhaps this is a good point to mention what this book is *not*. It is not simply a hagiographical work, providing stories of the lives/deaths of various martyrs in East and West, as interesting as such a book might be. Numerous stories of martyrs are indeed recounted here as examples; they have been selected, however, not because they necessarily have the most exciting biographies, or are the most historically or culturally significant—but rather because from the extant records of their canonizations we can glean specific information about how the church at that point in history regarded martyrdom and sainthood, and what it was doing procedurally during that period when it decided that someone should henceforth be venerated as a martyr-saint.

Similarly, there will be no particular focus in this book on nonprocedural elements, such as the manner in which the faithful have venerated and continue to venerate the martyrs,[4] burial practices, or societal factors of a given place/time that may have caused a person to die a martyr's death—unless these elements are found in some way to play a direct role in the martyrs' canonizations. As already mentioned previously, the criteria that a church chooses to employ in this process will invariably tell us a lot about how its members (or at least its hierarchy) think and what they believe to be important; but detailed discussion of the specific sociological conclusions that might be drawn from this information is best left to sociologists and others who are more well versed in that field than I.

The topic addressed in chapter 1 is Christianity in the first millennium—in other words, tracing the initial development of the notion of *martyr*, the concept of *sainthood*, and the evolution of a basically uniform set of procedures for what soon became known as *canonization*. Since these developments preceded the East–West Schism, they logically should (at least in theory) have been accepted by both churches.

Consistent with the manner in which these concepts evolved, the chapter is divided into three parts. First, there is a discussion of the development of the original concepts and definitions of the terms *martyr* and *canonize*. This is followed by an analysis of early practices regarding the veneration of martyrs, which would eventually solidify into a set process of canonization, with established rules and regulations. The final part traces the issue of competent authority, and examines precisely who it was that had the power to create new saints.

The second chapter, pertaining to the Orthodox Church in Russia, follows the same basic format, beginning with an examination of the definitions of terms, and the concept of *martyrdom* as Russia came to understand it; next, the procedural elements that became necessary to effect the canonization of a new martyr; and lastly, the church officials competent to canonize.

Chapter 3, in which the focus is the Catholic Church in the second millennium (after the Great Schism), is organized in the same manner: definition of terms, delineation of procedure, and then identification and discussion of the Catholic authorities possessing the power to create new saints. By this point, many similarities and differences between Russian Orthodox and Catholic praxis should become evident.

In conclusion, in light of the factual information presented in these three chapters, there will follow a comparative analysis of the canonization procedures, both historical and contemporary, of the two churches—the ecumenical and cultural implications of which, one hopes, will be obvious. It should by that point be possible to see whether the Catholics and the Russian Orthodox are actually doing the same thing, for fundamentally the same reasons, when they canonize someone because he or she has died a martyr's death. And if they aren't, by the end of our journey here we ought to be able to appreciate why not, and gain a better understanding of the theological and historical/cultural issues that, over the centuries, have led the churches down different paths.

At the same time, we'll be able to answer some of the juridical questions raised by the scenario of a Catholic–Russian Orthodox reunion. The related theological questions, of course, are best left to the pope and the patriarch of Moscow, who have far more competence—and, one hopes, divine assistance—to resolve them than does any canon lawyer.

CHAPTER ONE

Christianity's Unified First Millennium (until ca. 1054)

Introduction: Preliminary Remarks

In the first centuries of the church, the early Christians certainly never envisioned the existence of an established procedure to canonize martyrs as saints for the universal church, and anyone who expects to find such a system in early church history will search in vain. The Christian faithful could not have deliberately planned in advance a process for the official recognition of martyrs, any more than they could have foreseen the deaths of countless Christians as a result of the Roman Empire's persecution of the church for generations. Rather, the procedures that ultimately came into being developed organically, from the first Christian believers' entirely natural reactions to these persecutions. The concept of *martyrdom* arose spontaneously and gradually solidified into a set form, as did the practices intended to venerate those who were crowned with it.

Similarly, no one in the church's earliest days could have imagined that the recognition of a martyr as such would eventually become what is fundamentally a canonical process, for at its origins there is nothing specifically canonical about it. As we are about to see, acknowledging that a Christian had died a martyr's death initially required little more than some common sense and a right understanding of Christian theology. But rules and regulations gradually developed, for the precise reasons that all laws generally do: (a) gray, borderline situations arose that required both clarification and the development of official, consistent definitions of the terminology in use, and (b) perceived abuses cropped up that had to be checked. It was theology, not canon law per se, that required church officials to act.

For just as the faithful were presented with many cases of Christians who indubitably had to be acknowledged as martyrs, so they also encountered over time numerous examples of people who for a variety of reasons did *not*. It was the need to decide who belonged in which category that led the church to create a system to recognize martyrs in an official way. Terms had to be defined and consistent criteria had to be established. At the same time, many of the local solutions that were found were later adopted by Christians in other lands, ultimately leading to practices that were essentially uniform throughout the Christian world.

The end result was a more or less set legal procedure that cannot be found articulated anywhere in early church history, but that is firmly grounded in that history all the same. All the most fundamental elements of the system used to canonize new saints today, in both East and West, can find their origins right here, in the basic procedures that developed in the first centuries of Christianity. By the time of the great East–West Schism, traditionally dated to 1054 AD, the entire church was well familiar with the notions of martyrdom, the veneration of saints, and canonization, and there were already ample historical precedents to guide anyone seeking to canonize a new martyr for the faith.

Therefore, while the Catholic Church in the West and the Orthodox in the East each subsequently followed its own separate path of theological development, they obviously share the same historical roots. If we wish to examine the ways in which each church regards the concept of martyrdom today and canonizes martyrs as saints, we have to start at the very beginning—back in the earliest years of Christianity, when there were no divisions between East and West, Catholic and Orthodox. Only in this manner can we truly understand and appreciate that Christianity after the Great Schism may have evolved procedures that appear radically different—but the basic concepts underpinning those procedures were/are exactly the same.

What follows, then, is a history of the evolution of the Christian understanding of martyrdom, and the process of canonization of martyrs, up until the time of the Schism in the eleventh century. It is divided into several parts. First, we will look at the development of precisely what it meant to be a "martyr," in order to establish how the church ultimately arrived at its understanding of the definition of the term. Next will follow an examination of the evolution of the various practical elements of the church's veneration of the martyrs, for these elements would, each in its own way, eventually constitute procedural requirements for a martyr's canonization.

Finally, it must be noted that no terms can be officially defined, and no procedures can be authoritatively established or implemented, unless everyone involved is in agreement as to who exactly has the power to make such decisions. Consequently, the third part will trace the development of an understanding of which persons officially had the ability to set the rules and made decisions in individual cases.

Before beginning, however, a methodological caveat is in order. Because the church in its first centuries was not thinking in terms of an actual "canonization process," it also did not think to document in any formal, systematic way the elements of what would become that process. And since the development of a process was unintentional and unorganized, trying to trace that development can be a very messy business. On top of that, of course, there undoubtedly were many documents that did exist, but have since been lost to us. This is especially true of the church in the eastern parts of the Roman Empire, where we know that numerous writings were deliberately destroyed if they were written by persons perceived by their opponents to be heretics.[1] Obviously we can only work with the historical sources that we have. Tracing the development of the various aspects of what would become the process, therefore, requires us in many cases to piece together information from extremely disparate sources. The result is that at times, some of the findings might seem to resemble not so much patchwork as guesswork. Nonetheless, the amount of information that is still extant is both sizeable and concrete enough to allow us to see rather clearly what led to the canonization procedures for martyrs as they stood at roughly the end of the first millennium of Christianity.

A. Development of a Theological Concept of Martyrdom

Originally the ancient Greek word μάρτυς (or μάρτυρ, in western Greek dialect) simply meant "witness," a person who had seen something and could testify to its existence or veracity. As such it had no theological, much less specifically Christian, connotations. The Greek poet Aeschylus, for example, used the word when he wrote in the early fifth century BC, "I will show you evidence of what I say . . . a witness [μάρτυς] is here present."[2] And a century later, Plato noted in his *Gorgias* that "in the law courts . . . one side is supposed to refute the other side, when they bring forward multiple witnesses [μάρτυρας] to the things they have said."[3]

Even in the New Testament, in the context of the first members of the church explaining their beliefs, the terms μάρτυς and μαρτύριον were still used simply in the sense of providing witness. Matthew, for example, quotes Christ Himself prophesying to the apostles that they would be "dragged before governors and kings for My sake, to bear testimony [ἕνεκεν ἐμοῦ εἰς μαρτύριον] before them and the Gentiles" (8:18). Paul, meanwhile, calls himself "the least of the apostles," and then states that "we testified [ἐμαρτυρήσαμεν] of God that He raised Christ" (1 Cor. 15:15), which if anything would suggest that Paul is equating being a martyr with being an apostle.[4] While the specific object of a Christian's witness might have been novel, the fact remains that a Christian μάρτυς was still essentially a witness.

In the Apocalypse, John the Evangelist even uses the word to refer to Christ, Whom he describes at the very beginning as "the faithful witness [ὁ μάρτυς, ὁ πιστὸς]" (Apoc. 1:5). Later, the Voice dictating to John instructs him to write, "These things says the Amen, the true and faithful witness [ὁ μάρτυς, ὁ πιστὸς, καὶ ἀληθινὸς], Who is the beginning of the Creation of God" (3:14). There seems no other way to interpret the word μάρτυς here than in the usual sense of someone giving testimony.[5]

It is not until the Christian persecutions in the second century AD that we find the earliest examples of the terms μάρτυς, "martyr," and μάρτυρειν, "to be martyred," specifically referring to those who give their lives for Christ. The unknown author of the so-called Letter of the Church of Smyrna, from the second century AD, recounts the death of Saint Polycarp and others, noting that "We write to you, brothers, about the things that happened to those who were martyred and about the blessed Polycarp, who put an end to the persecution, having as it were ratified it through his own martyrdom."[6] The mere fact that the verb *to martyr* is in the passive voice shows us that it cannot be intended to mean simply testifying as a witness; something clearly was done *to* these Christians, and not merely *by* them.

Not many years later, this idea was echoed by Origen (ca. 185–254), who made a specific reference to this terminology. He explained that it had become customary that only those persons were called "martyrs" who had shown witness to the sacred mysteries by the shedding of their blood.[7]

But while the term began to acquire a more specific definition, its original meaning was not completely discarded. In the *Ecclesiastical History* of Eusebius of Caesarea (263–339), the word *martyr* and related terms retained the sense of witnessing to Christ, even if not necessarily resulting in loss of one's life for Him. Thus when writing of those who publicly professed their belief in Christ, Eusebius asserts, "Therefore they come and lead the whole church as martyrs, even those among the members of the family of the Lord."[8] Simultaneously, however, the term *martyr* and its derivatives were also being used in the more specific sense in which we understand them today. The same Eusebius notes in passing, for example, that "Sagaris suffered martyrdom at the time when Servilius Paulus was proconsul in Asia," referring here to a Christian who had lost his life because of his belief in Christ.[9]

We can also see that, gradually, the definition of the term *martyr* was developing in not just a strictly linguistic sense; it was also acquiring a precise theological meaning. An unintended yet major catalyst for additional qualification of the word arose unintentionally with the rigorist heresy of Donatism.

Having begun in the early fourth century, it took firm hold in northern Africa and existed there for centuries, despite its condemnation by Pope Miltiades in 313. Its enthusiastic adherents often deliberately stepped forward during the period of Christian persecution, announcing publicly that, in violation of the law, they possessed copies of the sacred books and would not give them up. In this way they frequently sought out and met death at the hands of the Romans—and were subsequently revered by like-minded Christians as martyrs.

In response, Mensurius, bishop of Carthage in the early 300s, formally condemned those Donatists who voluntarily turned themselves over to their persecutors.[10] Subsequently, his fellow African bishop Optatus castigated those who were venerated as martyrs but who, he declared, did not meet the definition:

> To no man was it said "Deny God"; to none was the commandment given "Burn the Scriptures"; to none was it said "Place incense in the censer"; or "Pull down the basilicas." These are the commands which give birth to martyrdoms. . . . Of the same class were those who, out of desire for a false martyrdom, hired men to strike and kill them to their own destruction. From among these also they were drawn who hurled themselves down headlong from the summits of high mountains, throwing away their vile lives . . . consider carefully whether it be not rash to call men, who experienced no war waged against Christians, by the name of martyrs.[11]

In the midst of this conflict, Gratus, presiding over the Council of Carthage in about 348, successfully argued that misuse of the word was causing suicides and those who had simply died a violent death to be venerated as martyrs. Canon 2 of this council thus helped to refine the definition even more, by indicating that someone who had killed himself, or who had been killed in the act of committing a sin, could not be considered, much less venerated as, a martyr.[12] In this way the early church enshrined in law the notion that the word *martyr* possessed a precise theological definition.

No less a personage than that great Father of the Church himself, Augustine of Hippo (354–430), essentially confirmed this several decades later, when he asserted that it was not simply the punishment, but rather the reason for it, that made a martyr. Otherwise, he noted logically, every prisoner and murder victim could be crowned as a martyr for Christ, saying, "I am a just man because I suffer!"[13]

And yet this definition, already quite narrow, continued to be honed even further when it came to the issue of the orthodoxy of a purported martyr's beliefs. Assuming that he did not turn himself in, and was killed for his sincerely held beliefs, could a *heretic* rightly be considered a martyr? The Council of Laodicea was held in the mid-fourth century in what is now Turkey, far from the geographic center of the Donatist controversy; but it nevertheless addressed in several of its own canons the necessity to avoid contact with heretics. Its Canon 9 forbade orthodox Christians from visiting the shrines erected to martyrs in the cemeteries of heretics;[14] while Canon 34 anathematized those who honored heretics who had been killed for the faith, describing them as "false martyrs" and "aliens from God."[15] Thus we see that being killed for one's faith was insufficient in itself; it was necessary also to possess the *right* faith.

As far as the church was concerned, the term *martyr* had developed far behind the original, generic sense of one who simply gives testimony as a witness. At the same time, however, the notion of witnessing to the faith remained ever present. We have seen that the early church quickly rejected the idea that a Christian could become a martyr by voluntarily seeking to die for his faith; but at the same time, the church found the opposite extreme no more acceptable. To be considered a true martyr, a Christian whose faith had been discovered had to knowingly and freely accept death from his persecutors for his beliefs. Once again, this was confirmed by Augustine, who noted the importance of the intention of the martyr as well as that of the one inflicting martyrdom in this concise summary of the criteria necessary for a real martyr: "In this glorious agony, we must consider two things in particular . . . the cruelty of the torturer (so that we can detest it); and the patience of the martyr (so that we can imitate it)."[16]

The picture is thus clarified even further. Not long after the end of the Christian persecutions and the subsequent legalization of the existence of the church in the fourth century, we already find a technical description of martyrdom that is well developed. A martyr must, as a rule, die at the hands of someone who specifically intends to kill him because of his orthodox Christian beliefs, and the martyr must freely and willingly accept (though not seek!) that death.

This is why we find Sulpicius Severus, writing during the same period in what is today western France, comparing Martin, the bishop of Tours, to the martyrs while acknowledging that he did not fit into that category:

> For although the character of our times could not ensure him the honor of martyrdom, yet he will not remain destitute of the glory of a martyr, because both by vow and virtues he was alike able and willing to be a martyr. But if he had been permitted, in the times of Nero and of Decius, to take part in the

struggle which then went on ... he would freely have submitted to the rack of torture, and readily surrendered himself to the flames.... But although he did in fact suffer none of these things, yet he fully attained to the honor of martyrdom without shedding his blood. For what agonies of human sufferings did he not endure in behalf of the hope of eternal life, in hunger, in watchings, in nakedness, in fastings, in reproachings of the malignant, in persecutions of the wicked, in care for the weak, in anxiety for those in danger?[17]

There was still some room for a broader interpretation of martyrdom, however; more than one Christian who died only as an indirect result of abuse and general physical hardships, endured because of his beliefs, was subsequently honored with the title of "martyr." Pope Marcellus I (d. 309), for example, is considered a martyr even though he was not actually killed for the faith. Condemned by Emperor Maximian to work in the horse stables, he died only after working there for many years.[18] Since Marcellus's death was presumably hastened by the harsh living conditions to which he was subjected, he was regarded as a martyr even though he did not die in a violent way. It is clear enough that, had he not been persecuted by the emperor, he would probably have lived longer, and so in this sense Marcellus can indeed be said to have died for his belief in Christ.

But at roughly the same time, particularly in the East, the definition of martyrdom was nevertheless open to still more figurative interpretations. Gregory Nazianzen (329–389/390), leading the church in Constantinople during more or less the same period as the developments taking place in northern Africa, did not hesitate to equate the life of the non-martyr Bishop Athanasius of Alexandria with "his fathers, the patriarchs, prophets, apostles, and martyrs, who contended for the truth."[19] It seems that in Gregory's mind, at least, the original notion that a martyr was a witness for the faith was still paramount.

Similarly, the great Eastern Father of the Church, John Chrysostom (ca. 349–407), asserted on numerous occasions during the course of his many sermons that one could achieve martyrdom without actually dying a violent death. Asceticism and mortification, for example, were equal to martyrdom, in his view: "Mortify your body, and crucify it, and you yourself will also receive the crown of martyrdom."[20] Chrysostom likewise indicated that service to the church was akin to martyrdom, for he equated the virtue of the bishop who strove to build a church for the relics of the martyr Babylas to Babylas himself.[21] It is clear that there were some significant figures in the life of the early church who resisted the trend toward a more rigid definition of the concept of martyrdom, preferring instead a more flexible application of the term to Christian life.

B. Development of a Process by Which a Martyr Was Officially Recognized

1. Prelude to a Process: Initially, Spontaneous Local Recognition by the Faithful

Rather than vainly seeking to determine the process by which early Christians officially canonized their martyrs as saints, one has to recognize that originally, there was no canonization process whatsoever. For those thousands of Christian martyrs killed during the Roman persecutions that preceded the legalization of Christianity by Emperor Constantine in 313, there was hardly an opportunity for a judicial process to recognize their status in an official sense. When a Christian was killed by Roman authorities for his beliefs, the local Christian community spontaneously began to revere him as a martyr for Christ. Put simply, they knew a martyr when they saw one.

So what was done in these cases when the Church spontaneously acknowledged a person to be a martyr, exactly? In the early centuries of the church, far from being the result of an official juridical investigation, the recognition of a martyr as such primarily involved a liturgical remembrance by the local church. Concrete, explicit descriptions by contemporaries of what actually was done are scarce, but what is clear is that local communities took note of the person's death-date—which they termed his *dies natalis*, in reference to the beginning of his life in eternity—and commemorated his martyrdom on an annual basis during the course of the liturgy on that date. The same second-century account of the martyrdom of Polycarp that was mentioned above provides perhaps the earliest specific example of this practice:

> And so we later took up [Polycarp's] bones, which are more valuable than precious stones and finer than pure gold, and we laid them in a suitable place; where the Lord will allow us to gather together ... to celebrate the birth-day of his martyrdom for the commemoration of those who have already fought in the contest, and for the training and preparation of those who will do so in the future.[22]

Cyprian, in the middle of the third century, gives us what might be the clearest, most concise description of just what was done to commemorate a martyr. His account would suggest that the practice had remained essentially the same since the death of Polycarp, a century or so before:

> And finally, mark the days on which they depart, so that we can celebrate their commemorations among the memories of the martyrs: although our most loyal

> and devoted brother Tertullus ... has written and continues to write and tell me the days on which our blessed brothers in prison cross over by a glorious death into immortality; and we celebrate oblations and sacrifices here as their commemorations, which, under the Lord's protection, we will soon celebrate with you.[23]

Of key interest to us here is the fact that records were kept of those who were recognized as martyrs by the local church. As early as the first century AD, it is said that Pope Clement I (d. 99) had charged seven notaries with the specific task of recording the "acts" of those Christians who died for the faith in Rome.[24] Considering that thousands of Christians were martyred in Rome itself during the first three centuries AD, it made sense to create a system whereby factual accounts of their deaths were accurately recorded.

But it is important to keep in mind that such records, at least at this stage in history, were local only, and far from being fully systematic. It would be anachronistic to suppose that Clement's action indicated a desire by the bishop of Rome to create some sort of centralized "database" of all the martyrs who were being killed throughout the entire Christian world at that time. Still less does it constitute evidence that the martyrs whose names were recorded had been acknowledged as such after some type of vetting process. Rather, it appears that local bishops—including the bishop of Rome—were, each in his own way and to the extent that persecution in each region was leading to the deaths of members of the local Christian faithful, simply keeping lists of the names of those killed for their belief in Christ and the dates of their martyrdom.

For non-Roman Christian communities were likewise keeping records of their own martyrs, as the fourth-century historian Sozomen indicates in his *Ecclesiastical History*, when describing the local churches in the Palestinian cities of Gaza and Constantia:

> They have now the same city magistrates, military officers, and public regulations. With regard to ecclesiastical matters, though, they should still be considered two separate cities. Each of them has its own bishop and its own clergy, and feast-days for their own respective martyrs and commemorations of their own bishops.[25]

If we are looking for evidence of the "canonization" of martyrs during the very first centuries of the church, this is all we will find. Fellow Christians simply took note of a person's arrest and subsequent execution for his beliefs and observed the date of his death—his *dies natalis*—on an annual basis. There was no "process," no investigation that had to be documented, no explicit set of rules to be followed, when determining whose names should be included.

On the contrary, if anything, there often seems to have been something intuitive about the spontaneous acceptance of a martyr by the faithful of his locale. Eusebius provides us with a good example of this communal instinct when he mentions two very different persons who met the same violent death for their faith:

> Among [those who died at about the same time as Polycarp] also was Metrodorus, a follower of Marcion's error, but who appears to have been a presbyter, and who was committed to the fire. A very celebrated martyr of those times was Pionius . . . we refer [readers] . . . to a very full account of his particular confessions, of the freedom with which he spoke, of his defence of the faith before the people and rulers.[26]

Eusebius continues to describe at some length the edifying conduct of Pionius, while in contrast, no further mention is made of Metrodorus. Kemp notes that there is definite evidence that Pionius was regarded as a martyr by the Christian community but that no such evidence exists for the heterodox Metrodorus, adding that, in general, "An orthodox martyr was at once accepted, a heretic rejected out of hand."[27] It would appear that during this period, at least, the local church did not need an official investigation in order to determine who was a true martyr and who was not.

2. Historical Elements Leading to a Future Process

We can already see that in the first centuries of the church, the veneration of martyrs developed as a matter of course. Gradually, imperceptibly, various facets of this veneration became established practices, and over time these practices would ultimately develop into law. What began as an unwritten "standard operating procedure" eventually evolved into a set process with rules and requirements.

Therefore we can only trace the history of canonization by tracing aspects of these original practices that were never intended to constitute a "process." Originally, the various components of the veneration of martyrs that follow were liturgical, historical, and devotional actions. None of them were deliberately developed by the church with the specific goal of canonization in mind; in fact, initially it may be difficult to see how they could possibly evolve into elements of a juridical system at all! Yet every one of them would in the end become a key component of what subsequently became known as the process of canonization.

a. Liturgical Commemorations: Diptychs and Calendars

We have just seen that local Christian communities carefully kept lists of names of the martyrs. But what did they actually do with these lists of names? As described in both the passage on Polycarp and that written by Cyprian (both cited above), the whole purpose of compiling names and dates of martyrs' deaths was to commemorate these persons in the liturgy on the anniversary of their death. During the liturgy on the anniversary day, generally an account of the martyr's death was read, and a panegyric was given in his honor. We find an official sanction of this practice already in 340 AD at the Council of Gangra (today in northern Turkey), which anathematized anyone who, "in his arrogance, condemns assemblies in honor of the martyrs, or the celebrations for them, and the commemorations of them."[28]

The lists of names and the dates for these assemblies were included in the *diptychs*, the tablets on which were written the names of those who were to be commemorated during the liturgy. In itself there is nothing particularly remarkable about this arrangement; but what may give one pause is the fact that the same diptychs also included lists of names of the living, who were likewise remembered during the same liturgy. The question naturally arises, then, as to the nature of this "commemoration," and the intention of the early Christians in remembering the names of the martyrs in the course of their liturgical celebrations. For while it may strike us as logical for Christians to honor a martyr, who has given his life for Christ and is presumed to be present with Him now in a glorious state in heaven, it seems anything but logical to accord the same sort of honor to someone, no matter how virtuous and devout, who is still alive on earth.

The question is further complicated by the fact that the lists of deceased persons found in the diptychs were not limited only to those who had died for the faith. In general, they also contained the names of other deceased Christian members of the local community, regardless of the circumstances of their deaths. In particular, the names of all deceased local bishops were included, whether they had been martyred or not.[29] So how were these varied categories of Christians from the local church all commemorated during the liturgy? What exactly was being done to "commemorate" the martyrs? And were bishops being commemorated in precisely the same way?

Taft points out that the confusion is not the result of any intentional ambiguity, but is rather an issue of theological development:

> In the first half of the third century, when the martyr-cult was not yet distinct from the veneration of the dead, extant paleochristian tomb inscriptions and

graffiti show Christians praying indifferently to the dead, martyrs or otherwise, to obtain their intercession. At the same time, they prayed to God *for* the martyrs, for whom funeral repasts were offered as for the ordinary faithful departed. And although it was common opinion among early Christians from ca. 150 on that the martyrs, ... attained heavenly bliss immediately upon the consummation of their passion, another, minority view nuanced this by insisting that the martyrs ... must still await the resurrection of the dead and the Last Judgment, when their fate would be decided, too. So Christians could pray both *for* and *to* the martyrs without contradiction.... [This terminology] disconcerts not because it is *wrong*, but because it is *old*.[30]

A separate, yet comparable distinction is found in the liturgy of Saint Mark.[31] After the deacon would read the names of the deceased, the faithful would pray for them, asking God to grant them eternal rest (*Horum omnium animabus dona requiem*). In contrast, when the deceased bishops were named, the people gave glory to God for them (*Gloria Tibi, Domine*).

The less-than-clear-cut difference between the nature of the prayers that are offered in commemoration of the martyrs and those offered for deceased bishops is entirely consistent with a remark found in the Catecheses of Cyril of Jerusalem (313–386). In the course of describing the Eucharistic celebration, he explains:

> We commemorate first of all those ... martyrs, that at their prayers and intercessions God would receive our petition. Then on behalf also of the holy fathers and bishops who have fallen asleep before us ... believing that it will be a very great benefit to the souls for whom the supplication is put up, while that holy and most awful Sacrifice is set forth.[32]

It would seem that, while a type of commemoration was definitely being made for deceased bishops, its purpose was quite different from that made in the name of the martyrs. The faithful were praying for the martyrs to intercede with God for them; while their prayers naming former bishops seem to have been intended rather to obtain the repose of their souls.

In his in-depth study of ancient diptychs, however, du Cange takes a somewhat different approach when attempting to interpret the specific nature of these commemorations of deceased bishops. He posits that, when their names were mentioned during the course of the liturgy, the priest was not praying *for* them, as he normally would for other deceased persons; rather, he was praying that they would be inscribed with the rest of the saints whose names were customarily invoked during the same liturgy. This prayer was, du Cange asserts, the beginning of what would eventually develop into the process of canonization.[33] It did not, however, constitute an assertion that these deceased bishops were already to be regarded as on an equal footing with the martyrs.

By the early fifth century, the lines between the various groups of names were being firmly drawn, and the theological differences between the nature of the prayers offered in the name of these groups were becoming more unambiguous. Augustine could not have been clearer: "We do not pray for the martyrs. But we not only do not pray for them; rather, we commend ourselves to their prayers."[34]

Today, in the West, Augustine's theological precision is taken very much for granted. We pray to the martyrs (and other saints as well), asking for their intercession before God, and we may give thanks to God for the graces granted to them while on earth; meanwhile, we pray to God for all the other departed, seeking the eternal repose of their souls; and we similarly pray to God for the living, for their well-being on earth and their ultimate eternal salvation. In contrast, however, we find that early Christians tended simply to give glory and thanksgiving to God on behalf of those faithful who had died, regardless of whether they believed that these departed Christians were definitely already enjoying the glory of heaven after shedding their blood for Christ. Prayers on behalf of the faithful (both living and dead) and prayers glorifying the martyrs were all included together. As Salig put it, the fact that all names were listed together in the diptychs indicated the communion and love that united all the members of the church, triumphant, suffering, and militant.[35]

As will be seen later, the liturgical practices in Russia even to this day frequently lack the sharp distinction that distinguishes the veneration of canonized saints in the West from a relatively early date. One occasionally encounters instances where prayers are formally offered *for* persons who are about to be canonized—a practice that logically should not hold up under theological scrutiny. But it shows us that in the East, vestiges of this early ambiguity between praying to, and praying for, a saint have never been entirely resolved.

An eyewitness account of the liturgical commemoration of an abbot on the anniversary of his death was left us by the monk John Cassian (d. 435), who visited the abbey on that day. He notes that a crowd of monks had gathered to solemnly celebrate the anniversary of the previous abbot's burial.[36] Was this the commemoration proper to a saint? or were the monks praying for the repose of their former abbot's soul? It is impossible to tell from Cassian's description.

We can see that in the first centuries of the early church, there were undoubtedly some failures to make distinctions that are commonly drawn in the West today, and that these omissions lead to undeniable bewilderment when we attempt to view the early texts through a twenty-first-century lens. And this is not merely a side issue of some historical curiosity: as will be seen shortly, the common tendency in the primitive church to intermingle intercessions for both the living and the departed, along with prayers honoring the martyrs, would inadvertently lead to eventual confusion—at least in some parts of the Christian world—regarding the accurate classification of early Christians as martyr-saints in centuries to come.

In general, however, it is possible to see that the names of martyrs contained in the diptychs eventually gave rise to the first ecclesiastical calendars; while the lists of other deceased members of the faithful—particularly of bishops and other members of the clergy—ultimately developed into separate necrologies.[37] The oldest extant example of this division is found in the so-called Liberian Catalogue (*Catalogus Liberianus*), which is a group of documents apparently compiled during the reign of Pope Liberius (352–366) and contained in the manuscript known as the Chronology of 354.[38] Among other things, the catalogue includes a calendar, commonly known as the *Depositio Martyrum*, as well as the *Depositio Episcoporum*, a chronology of all the popes from Peter to Liberius.

It is undeniable that the *Depositio Martyrum* was designed to show the days on which certain feasts were to be celebrated. Besides the feast-day of the birth of Christ on December 25, the calendar lists twenty-three other specific dates on which various martyrs of Rome are to be commemorated, noting also the part of the city where they were buried. Several of the names found in the *Depositio Episcoporum* are likewise included here: Peter, Sixtus/Xystus, Callistus, Pontian, and Fabian were all bishops of Rome who are also known to have been martyred. There are no names of bishops on the *Depositio Martyrum* who were not at the same time martyrs as well. It seems obvious, therefore, that the popes who were mentioned in the *Depositio Martyrum* were included solely because of the manner in which they died, and not because they were bishops per se.

It should be noted that the well-known Polycarp, martyred two centuries before, is not even mentioned in this calendar of martyrs; but this is unsurprising as the *Depositio Martyrum* was intended for the church in Rome, and Polycarp died far from Rome in Smyrna. What may surprise us, however, are two entries on this Roman calendar pertaining to other martyrs who, like Polycarp, were not Roman at all: both September 14 (for Cyprian) and March 9 (for Perpetua and Felicity) are feast-days for Christians who died for their faith not in Rome, but in Carthage. They constitute good examples of what would eventually become an extremely common practice throughout the Christian world: when a martyr was, for whatever reason, particularly well-known outside his own local Christian community, other local churches might freely choose to commemorate his *dies natalis* in their own diptychs and calendars. The localized nature of these commemorations thus began already in the first centuries of the church to give way to broader, more inclusive collections of martyrs included on local calendars.

And we can see that this localization gave way relatively quickly, when we examine the so-called *Martyrologium Hieronymianum*, named for Saint Jerome even though it was almost certainly not authored by him. This calendar, which appears to have had its start in Gaul (now France), was the basis for the earliest "universal" calendars in use throughout the church; and the fact that it is clearly a compilation of multiple calendars, with more feast-days added later, is presumably what leads to difficulties in dating the earliest versions. Duchesne, who collaborated in what is still the definitive work on this calendar today, established that it is, in great part, borrowed from an older Syriac calendar containing numerous martyrs from local churches very far from the medieval Gallic monasteries where it was copied and used. At the same time, it also includes names on specific dates found in other calendars from places farther west.[39]

Meanwhile, the calendar of Carthage, from about the fifth century AD contains feast-days primarily for local African martyrs, but it continues the trend by also including a large number of "outsiders."[40] These non-Africans include New Testament figures such as John the Baptist and Luke the Evangelist, but one also finds some martyrs from other regions, like Rome's Lawrence and Popes Clement and Sixtus, as well as the Spanish martyr Vincent.[41] At the same time, the local bishop-martyr Cyprian, found in the Roman *Depositio Martyrum*, is likewise found in the calendar of his native Carthage; but Perpetua and Felicity, the two other African martyrs included in the Roman calendar, are not. And this is not a lone aberration; countless examples of variations like this can be found in calendars from different local churches over the centuries. Christians in one region might decide to commemorate someone as a martyr, while in a different local church the same person might for some unknown reason fail to be included in their list of annual commemorations.

Insofar as the establishment of these liturgical observances was the closest thing to a "canonization process" in existence at the time, it would follow that certain martyrs were considered to be saints, but only within the geographic boundaries of a single local church. Other martyrs might be commemorated in multiple regions, yet unknown to the rest of the Christian faithful; and still others (including the apostles and other biblical figures) might be celebrated as saints in most, if not all, parts of the Christian world. It is a pattern that, as will be seen later, continues to this day in the East, and it was not until many centuries later that the process became centralized and more uniform in the West.

It is also important to note that there are numerous martyrs included in the early calendars about whom we know absolutely nothing today. In the calendar of Carthage, for example, one finds among others Septimia (May 25) and Sistus (June 5), who are not mentioned in any other extant documentation regarding the early church, and thus cannot be identified with any certainty.[42] At the same time, mention is made of a martyr named Januarius, who might be either the fourth-century African martyr or the martyred bishop of Naples—or perhaps he is neither.[43] While there is no reason to doubt the authenticity of this particular calendar, or to question the existence or actual martyrdom of any of the persons whose names it contains, the fact remains that in some cases they are simply that—names and no more. Liturgical commemorations of identifiable martyrs as historical figures, and acceptance of their martyrdom as documented fact, raise problems of history which, far from being localized in Africa or particular only to the first centuries of Christianity, continue to haunt the church in all parts of the world to this very day, as will be seen in the succeeding chapters.

But to complicate things even further, it seems that there are a number of bishops listed on this calendar of Carthage who were not known to have been martyred. Bishop Gratus of Carthage, who reigned after the Christian persecutions had ended, is commemorated on May 5;[44] while the feast-day of Bishop Nemessianus of nearby Numidia, who is known to have survived the persecutions, is observed in late December.[45] Why are their names here?

It may be that their exceptional holiness of life led the local church to decide to venerate them as saints, in an early example of the development of the notion of *confessors*, non-martyrs whose unusually virtuous lives caused the faithful to include them among the saints together with the martyrs. But if that is the case, it seems odd that there is absolutely nothing known about them and their lives, for not even an identifiable passing reference to their uncommon holiness appears to exist. While there is no direct evidence that can resolve this question for us, it may be that their names were taken from a now-lost *Depositio Episcoporum* of Carthage, and added, either accidentally or deliberately, to this calendar of martyrs. This may seem as unlikely as it was (at least to our knowledge) unprecedented; but given the apparent rationale for the inclusion of names of bishops in subsequent calendars, it may be the correct explanation.

For it is clear from later calendars that the patterns—and the uncertainties—that we can already begin to see in simplified form in these two examples of early calendars take firm hold in those of later centuries. The so-called marble calendar of Naples, incised on marble slabs no earlier than the ninth century, is a far more extensive list of feast-days than the calendars of previous centuries and contains many more martyrs from other regions of the Christian world. The fact that numerous persons (especially the apostles) have more than one feast-day leads one to presume that this is a compilation of several calendars, in which the same saints were being commemorated on different dates. While Naples's own martyred Bishop Januarius is included, as one would expect, Roman martyrs are also well represented; among many others we find Lawrence (August 10) and Chrysanthus and Daria (October 25) all mentioned. But the marble calendar also lists commemorations for martyrs from more far-flung areas of the Christian world, like Phocas (September 22), who was martyred along the Black Sea, and the martyred Bishop Paul of Constantinople (November 6). Clearly the church in Naples had chosen to accept a significant number of persons from outside its own locale as martyrs whose feasts were to be observed.

Less clear, however, is the rationale for the inclusion on the list of a number of Naples's own bishops. For it appears that among the names inscribed on the marbles are some taken from a *Depositio Episcoporum*, or a list showing all of Naples's former bishops. Among them we find "our bishop Stephen" (d. 799/800) on April 11, "our bishop Saint Severus" (or, "our holy bishop Severus," d. 408/409) on April 29, and "our bishop Pomponius" (d. 536) on April 30. Given both their death-dates and the lack of evidence to the contrary, they do not seem to have been martyred for the faith. Were the faithful of Naples commemorating these bishops as saints (and thus praying *to* them), or were they, as du Cange described above,[46] praying that they would ultimately be included among the saints (and thus praying *for* them, although not in the sense in which the church prayed for other, more ordinary deceased persons)? The marbles provide no clues that would help us to resolve this question, unless perhaps we choose to focus on the fact that Severus, unlike the others, is described as "sanctus." Does this imply that he was already considered to have been established as a saint, or is the word simply intended to emphasize his personal holiness in a more generic sense? At first the former seems most likely, because today the Catholic Church accepts Severus as a canonized saint; and since Bishop Stephen is not considered to ever have been canonized, this would appear to solve the mystery—until we realize that Pomponius, who is not described as "sanctus," is today considered to be a saint as well! The inconsistency here is thus all too evident; the only conclusion that we can safely reach is that not everyone on the marble calendar is a saint, although the overwhelming majority of persons are.

If we hold that an early Christian became officially accepted as a saint by the inclusion of his name on the diptychs/calendars, then we must acknowledge that there are persons being venerated as saints who do not seem to have been originally regarded as such. Put differently, there was initially more than one rationale for including people's names in the diptychs; but over time the lines became blurred, and at least in some cases it appears that persons ultimately became accepted as martyrs/saints when in fact their names originally were listed for another reason. There may be numerous persons commemorated as "saints" in the calendars who initially were included in the diptychs simply because they had died and the local faithful wanted to pray for them during the liturgy—not necessarily because they had been martyred, or had demonstrated during their lives an outstanding holiness that would otherwise warrant their veneration.

To complicate the matter even further, it appears that the exact opposite occurred simultaneously as well: persons who had been listed on the early diptychs were, for whatever reason, omitted from the list when the names were copied from diptychs into early calendars. Morcelli notes that on the oldest extant calendars of the church in Constantinople, dating from the seventh and eighth centuries AD, there are only about a hundred names listed, a number that is definitely much lower than that found on the diptychs on which the calendars were based. He posits that some were omitted from the calendars because they were considered to have fallen into heresy, which would imply that the list of names found on the calendar was of a more sacred nature than were the earlier diptychs. Morcelli also cites examples of patriarchs whose names disappeared when the lists were being transferred from the diptychs onto liturgical calendars.[47] Such omissions are completely consistent with what has already been observed here, namely, that the diptychs originally included lists of deceased bishops and other faithful, not because they were being recognized as saints, but because the local church wished to remember them and pray for them. It seems that at least in some cases, attempts were made to keep the names of such persons out of the liturgical calendars, since inclusion would imply their sainthood, which the church did not accept. We will never know, however, how thorough and successful these attempts were. There are many early martyrs/saints about whom the church today knows next to nothing, but whose names were nevertheless included on the calendars—perhaps because they fully merit inclusion, but possibly thanks to simple human error.

There are also many martyrs from one region of the Christian world who were commemorated in another, leading ultimately to their acceptance as saints by the entire church. The missionary Archbishop Boniface, who was martyred in the Frankish kingdom in the eighth century, was quickly accepted as a saint by Christians in faraway England. In the late 750s, the archbishop of Canterbury even sent a courtesy letter to Boniface's successor in Mainz, informing him that "in our general synod, we have decided to solemnly commemorate his *dies natalis* annually."[48] As word about various martyrs continued to spread, so too did their acceptance into the calendars of local churches far from the place of their martyrdom.

b. *Passiones/Acta Martyrum*

As the practice of accepting martyrs as such, and putting their names into the diptychs, eventually developed and solidified into liturgical calendars, so the practice of documenting the facts surrounding their deaths gradually became standardized as well. We have already seen that even in the first century AD, Pope Clement is said to have charged notaries with the task of recording the names and details of those Christians who were being persecuted to death for their faith. Diptychs and later calendars contained the martyrs' names and dates, but apart from possibly including a very brief mention of a particular martyr's locale and state in life, no other historical information was normally incorporated into them. This necessitated the development of a separate group of writings that provided more specific details about the life and death of each martyr commemorated in the liturgy.

Lives of the saints are, of course, routinely written today by both Catholics and Orthodox. They may be intended as formal, authoritative works justifying the canonization of a particular saint; or, more commonly, they are written for individual readers, perhaps to promote a certain saint as a role model whose life is worthy of emulation by the faithful. What may be surprising is the fact that such works generally had their origins in biographical accounts that were often—though not always—specifically compiled for liturgical use.

For as already seen above, it is clear that historically, during the liturgy on the anniversary of a martyr's *dies natalis*, some account of his death for the faith (known collectively as *acta martyrum* or *passiones martyrum*) was read to the faithful. The Council of Carthage in 397 enshrined this in law, when it declared that the *passiones* of the martyrs were permitted to be read when celebrating their anniversaries.[49] Nearly three centuries later, Gregory of Tours shows us that the practice continued when he describes the liturgy on the feast-day of the martyr Polycarp: "When the *passio* had been read with the rest of the readings . . . the time approached for the [Eucharistic] sacrifice."[50]

It seems reasonable to presume that those first-century notaries, who are said to have compiled information on Rome's martyrs at the behest of Pope Clement, were the source of many of these narratives used during the liturgical observances for the early martyrs of Rome. Elsewhere it appears that accounts were sometimes recorded by eyewitnesses in individual cases, but there is no evidence of any systematic, organized attempt to collect accurate *acta martyrum* in other areas of the Christian world. Nor does it appear that the non-Roman *acta* that do exist were originally intended by their authors to constitute some sort of "official" account of the martyr's life and death.

This does not necessarily imply that they were factually inaccurate, and/or that they were written by persons with no knowledge or information about the martyr in question. Delehaye notes that, in general, the earliest *acta* tend to be the most historically reliable; many of them are based on the official Roman court records of their judicial interrogations.[51] The *Passio Cypriani* (sometimes known as the *Vita Cypriani*) is a fine example, recording both the life and the martyrdom of one of Africa's greatest bishops in about 259 AD.[52] Written by the deacon Pontianus, Cyprian's contemporary and companion, it affords no particular reason to question its authenticity; it includes dialogue apparently taken from a transcript of the legal proceedings when Cyprian was brought before the proconsul. This *passio* provides us with a detailed description by an eyewitness of Cyprian's arrest, interrogation by Roman officials, and subsequent execution in Carthage. But the fact remains that a reliable contemporary account like this is the exception rather than the norm.[53]

It is even more exceptional that this account still even exists. For while there was a relatively small number of *acta* written to begin with, the number we have today is even smaller, because many of them have been completely lost. They seem to have disappeared only a couple of centuries after their composition—perhaps during the period(s) of Christian persecution[54]—because already in the 400s, there were very few extant *acta*. Augustine, for example, noted in passing the paucity of accurate historical narratives of the martyrs' deaths during his own day, while preaching about the protomartyr Saint Stephen: "Although for other martyrs we can scarcely find *acta* which we can read on their feast-days, his *passio* [contained in the Acts of the Apostles] is in a canonical book."[55]

While the church during Augustine's era may have been eager for *acta* that were suitable for reading during the liturgy, it was at the same time not content with accounts of dubious veracity, still less with openly fictitious ones. The Council of Carthage in 401 shows us that issues of factual accuracy were already causing concern, because the veneration of some persons as martyrs/saints had evidently begun without sound assurances that they had even existed. The Council reprobated altars that had been raised for any "saint" based on information obtained solely through anyone's dreams or other questionable revelations.[56] We can see that already at this early date, church authorities in northern Africa wanted to focus on the historical facts surrounding the life and death of a possible saint, rather than rely on questionable information allegedly discovered through supernatural means. Before approving of someone's veneration as a saint, the church wanted to see hard evidence to justify it.

Despite these concerns, all too many of the *acta martyrum* still extant today were presumably written well after the fact, and thus their historical accuracy is open to question. Dufourcq, writing about the martyrs of Rome in particular, comments that in the ninth century far more details were known about the early Roman martyrs than in the fourth century.[57] Yet no historical treasure-trove of factual information about the martyrs was unearthed during the interim, so it seems clear enough that in many cases gaps were filled by suppositions, perhaps paralleling the *acta* of other martyrs, perhaps imitating other known literary works written during the period when a particular martyr lived and died.[58]

It must have been sufficiently well known that inaccurate, historically unsound *acta* were being used during the liturgy, because more than one council actually condemned them. In 494, for example, the Council of Rome prohibited the reading of *acta martyrum*, not because it was difficult for believers to accept that the martyrs had indeed suffered torments such as those described but because their authors were entirely unknown and possibly were heretics or at least unlettered persons. Pope Gelasius I, writing an account of this council in a subsequent letter, singled out as particular examples of unacceptable *acta* those written for Quiritus and Julitta, as well as that of Saint George. He also noted that because these writings in general were so suspect and thus apt to cause derision among the faithful, they were not read in the church in Rome.[59]

But it was not only the Roman church that considered the reading of questionable *acta* problematic. Canon 63 of the Council in Trullo, held nearly two hundred years later, likewise specifically condemned the practice:

> We command that martyrologies which enemies of truth have falsified, so that they might dishonor Christ's martyrs and cause their listeners to lose faith, are not to be read publicly in churches, but should rather be consigned to the flames. And we anathematize those who receive them or accept them as truthful.[60]

Interestingly, however, the Roman church appears to have subsequently reacted against this blanket condemnation of the reading of *acta* during the liturgy. Pope Hadrian I, who reigned 772–795, may have been thinking of the permissions granted at that Council of Carthage held four centuries earlier when he wrote in a letter to Charlemagne that "the sacred canons decree that the passions of the holy martyrs are to be read even in church, when their anniversary days are celebrated."[61] Of course, it may also be that he was simply reacting against the positions taken by the Council in Trullo, whose canons Rome never officially accepted.

In the early ninth century, it appears that at least in the eyes of the hierarchy in Constantinople, the cautions found in the Trullo canons against spurious *acta* were still valid. Echoing the Roman anathema over three hundred years before, Patriarch Nicephorus (758–828) explicitly condemned the *passiones* of Saints George, Quiritus, and Julitta, as did other bishops of his era.[62]

It must be admitted that the later, often romanticized accounts of the martyrs' lives and deaths were not intended to constitute accurate, official records of their martyrdoms. Rather, in keeping with the fanciful literary style of the time in which they were written, they often make little or no effort at historical accuracy, striving instead to promote the notion of the saint as a heroic figure to be emulated by the faithful.

We can only accept that there were real martyrs and other genuine saints whose *acta*, written long after their deaths, are factually dubious and often badly written, because accurate *acta* were never written by their contemporaries.[63] This omission in no way lessens the reality of their holy lives; it merely reflects the fact that at the time, the writing of their *acta* was neither officially required nor expected by established tradition—yet.

Eventually, as will be seen later, biographies of Christian individuals (whether martyred or not) were compiled with the specific intent of presenting church hierarchs with a justification for canonizing a particular person. In other words, they ultimately would be written not simply for the spiritual edification of the faithful, nor in order to preserve a truthful historical account for posterity; rather, the purpose of writing the account would be to convince church authorities that the person in question did indeed deserve to be recognized as a saint. It represents a marked development in the whole concept of hagiography that simply did not exist in the first centuries of the church. The tradition of writing lives of saints would live on, but the actual role of such biographies in the overall process of canonization would change radically.

c. *Elevatio/Translatio* of the Relics to a Church Dedicated to the Martyr

The notion that a martyr's remains should be moved ceremoniously into a church or chapel intended especially for that person may have eventually become a formal part of the "canonization" ritual, but it is unquestionably a later innovation, developing only several centuries after the end of the Christian persecutions. Initially, of course, the bodies of those Christians killed for their faith by civil authorities were generally taken away by Christian friends for a quiet burial. The description of the martyrdom of Polycarp, seen earlier, shows us the tremendous veneration showed by surviving Christians to the remains of the martyrs, already in the earliest days of the church. But the very fact of the persecutions obviously precluded any lavish public demonstrations of respect shown to the bodies of those who had been killed for their Christian beliefs. Only with the official legalization of Christianity in the fourth century could this veneration be manifested openly.[64] Gradually this would lead to the construction of altars, chapels, and even churches specifically intended to give honor to the martyr by name—which eventually would become an important element in the developing process of canonization. It is still a common enough practice today for both Catholics in the West, and the Orthodox in the East, to visit shrines built specifically to house the remains of canonized saints, and the continuance of this practice shows that little has changed in this regard since the early Christians first sought ways to honor those who had given their lives for Christ.

The phrase "translation of relics" is frequently used of the saints in two separate senses. The first and more common usage is the one that does not directly concern us here: it involves giving a fragment of bone from a saint's burial-place either to an individual, for private devotional purposes, or perhaps to a church for inclusion in an altar or reliquary there, while leaving the rest of the relics in their original place. While this practice clearly indicates that the deceased is held in great veneration, it does not, in and of itself, constitute his canonization.

But the second, less common sense of the term eventually does. At issue here is the moving of a deceased Christian's remains from one burial-place into another, grander location, with the specific intention of honoring him thereby. It is in this sense that the translation of the body (often known also as the *elevatio corporis*) of a martyr or other saint comes to be connected to his official recognition as such.[65]

This practice clearly was a later development, and thus cannot be equated with the *depositio* mentioned in early calendars. It is evident that the term *depositio*, used in reference to the dates on which many bishops and others were to be commemorated in the liturgy, refers simply to the date of burial, which may very well have taken place without any fanfare whatsoever—and was certainly not always done inside a church or chapel specifically dedicated to the deceased. Eusebius mentions in passing that after Pamphilus, his teacher and mentor, was martyred along with his companions in 309, their bodies were taken up and given a decent burial, according to the "established custom."[66] These martyrs evidently were interred like everyone else at that time, without any special ceremonial attention.

When the relics of martyrs and other non-martyr saints first began to be moved from their original tombs to other locations, the primary motivation for doing so was to protect them from desecration by invaders. They were often brought inside the city, either to a chapel (or under an altar) that was constructed especially for them, or at least to a location that church authorities decided would be a safer resting-place. The main purpose of such *translationes* was the safety of the remains.

An example of this that involves martyrs of particular importance was the *translatio* of the remains of the Apostles Peter and Paul. During the Christian persecutions under the Roman Emperor Valerian (ca. 198–ca. 260), their bodies were moved from their original burial places (at the Vatican and in Via Ostiense, respectively) to the Catacombs along the Appian Way. Evidence for these *translationes* comes to us from a brief reference in the *Martyrologium Hieronymianum* discussed above, which notes on the feast-day of Saints Peter and Paul that the relics of both were "in the Catacombs."[67] With the legalization of Christianity under Emperor Constantine in the early fourth century, the relics were returned to their original locations, where they could be venerated openly without fear of desecration.

While no eyewitness account exists today, it is impossible to imagine that this transfer of the remains of these great apostles, precipitated as it was by a new round of persecutions by the pagan Roman authorities, was carried out with public ceremony and solemnity. Still less can it be considered a formal act of the church's recognition of Peter's and Paul's status as saints, since they obviously were being venerated as such already. Rather, it was a result of the emergency circumstances in which the Church of Rome found itself, necessitating the protection of what it acknowledged to be among its holiest relics. Thus this particular example of a *translatio* certainly cannot be construed as being connected to an act of canonization.

But in the case of other martyrs, whose cult had not been so decidedly established before the decision to move their relics was made, the end result of such a *translatio* was official recognition. Since the determination to move their remains was made in an authoritative way by members of the church hierarchy, such transferrals gradually came to be seen as a sort of formal approval of their veneration.

In the late fourth century, Bishop Ambrose of Milan located the bodies of the martyrs Gervase and Protase and, with great pomp, moved them into the main basilica. His stated intention was both to glorify these great men as martyrs for the faith, and also to consecrate his most important church by including their relics under the main altar. Ambrose described the ceremonies surrounding the event in a subsequent letter to his sister:

> We found two men of marvelous stature, such as those of ancient days. All the bones were perfect, and there was much blood . . . there was an enormous concourse of people . . . and as evening was now coming on transferred them to the basilica of Fausta, where watch was kept during the night. . . . On the following day we translated the relics to the Basilica Ambrosiana. During the translation a blind man was healed. . . . The glorious relics are taken out of an ignoble burying-place, the trophies are displayed under heaven. The tomb is wet with blood. The marks of the bloody triumph are present, the relics are found undisturbed in their order, the head separated from the body. . . . Let these triumphant victims be brought to the place where Christ is the victim. But He upon the altar, Who suffered for all; they beneath the altar, who were redeemed by His Passion . . . that place was due to the martyrs. Let us, then, deposit the sacred relics, and lay them up in a worthy resting-place, and let us celebrate the whole day with faithful devotion.[68]

This preplanned, formal *translatio* was a far cry from the hurried removal of martyrs already known and venerated to a place of safety during periods of persecution or military attack. Ambrose made a point of searching for, and finding, the relics of these two second-century martyrs, and carrying them in triumph to a new resting-place, beneath the altar inside a church. In this way, the local bishop was not only authorizing the cult of Gervase and Protase as true martyrs, but he was also declaring to the faithful of his church that these bodies were in fact the remains of the two saints. By interring the relics under the main altar, Ambrose was both sanctioning and encouraging their veneration.

Farther east, the relics of the martyr Sabbas (also known as Sava), a Goth who had been drowned after horrific tortures in 372, had initially been buried in Scythia (which today is part of Romania and Bulgaria), by the Christian duke of that region. But subsequently his body was sent to Cappadocia, today in east-central Turkey, "at the request of the priests," who are otherwise not identified.[69]

Over time, the fact that a *translatio* like this was being done by church officials—normally the bishop—automatically carried with it an authority that ensured that the relics being transferred were those of a true martyr/saint. This came to be the case regardless of whether the remains were being moved with the explicit intention of declaring the person worthy of veneration, or were merely being transported to a place of greater safety during a dangerous period. After all, if a bishop judged that it was appropriate to move the remains of someone who had reportedly given his life for Christ, that surely implied that the person in question was indeed a genuine martyr and worth venerating as such! Kemp concisely sums up developments in this regard over the course of subsequent centuries:

> It is hardly an exaggeration to say that more than half the translations of the eighth, ninth, and tenth centuries were made under the influence of invasion.... By the end of the eighth century it becomes apparent that the actual translation of a saint may be regarded as a formal act of canonization.... It comes to be considered improper that a saint's body should remain underground, and so it is removed to a position where it can more easily be an object of veneration to the faithful.[70]

A good example of a translation-canonization of this very period is that of Saint Jeron, a Dutch priest martyred in 856. His relics were found one hundred years later, after Jeron reportedly appeared in a dream to a Dutchman and told him where to dig. The local bishop was notified and convinced of the veracity of the account; whereupon he led a procession to transfer the relics to a church in which the relics of yet another local saint, Adalbert of Egmond, were already venerated. Jeron's remains were solemnly placed with those of Adalbert, and as the historical accounts add nothing further, it is clear that with this translation, the "process" of recognizing Jeron as a martyr-saint was completed.[71]

One might therefore be tempted to conclude that when a tomb is found from centuries past, about which little or nothing is known, the remains it contains might be those of a saint if the tomb itself is elaborate and/or in a central place within a church or chapel. In fact, Delehaye strongly cautions against drawing conclusions about a deceased Christian's status based on the grandeur (or lack thereof) of his tomb, noting that Origen, who was never regarded as a saint by any means, was buried in a fabulously ornate tomb in Caesarea in the third century AD.[72] At the same time, great martyrs who were quickly buried during the periods of persecution did not necessarily have tombs with any superfluous adornments at all; if they were never the subjects of a formal *translatio*, their relics might very well still be in situ, in a relatively simple burial place. No matter how tempting it may be, we cannot extrapolate about the deceased based purely on the grandeur of their ancient tombs.

In fact, there were many Christians who were acknowledged as martyrs for whom there is no tomb at all, because the body was destroyed at the time of their martyrdom. Eusebius describes in detail the fourth-century persecution of Christians who were wrongly believed to be responsible for a fire in the palace at Nicomedia (today in western Turkey), showing that even at this early date, the pagan world had already realized the honors that Christians paid to those who died for the faith, even if they were confused about their theological meaning:

> But the [martyred] imperial domestics, who after their death had been committed to the earth with proper burial, their legal masters thought necessary to have dug up again from their sepulchres, and cast into the sea, so that no one might worship them in their graves as if they were gods.[73]

The fact that the bodies of such martyrs could not be kept buried and accorded the veneration already established in the church did not of course alter the recognition of the reality of their martyrdom. Not only was it not required of a true martyr that he have a lavish tomb in a church; it was not even necessary to have his remains. Assuming that sufficient evidence existed to prove their martyrdom—in this particular case, it seems clear that eyewitnesses passed along an account of events as they transpired—it was entirely possible to venerate them as martyrs even though their bodies had been completely destroyed.

C. Local Bishops, Civil Officials, and the Need for Authority

The various components of what would ultimately become known as the process of canonization developed not as a result of any explicit, conscious desire to create such a system, but rather out of the perceived necessity to establish exactly who was to be venerated as a martyr, and who was not. At the same time, concurrent with the evolution of this collection of rules and requirements, decisions gradually had to be made establishing precisely *who* it was that had the authority to make these decisions. The notion that a fellow-Christian had died as a true martyr was, as we have seen, initially an intuitive, logical conclusion that was often reached almost instinctively by the local Christian community as a whole. But we have also seen that among the black-and-white cases of genuine martyrdom, there soon arose numerous shades of gray, and this led the church in various locales to gradually establish that an official finding that someone had indeed died as a martyr could only be made by someone in a position of authority.

Local bishops and regional councils could not legislate for the entire church, of course; nor did they intend to. In some cases, it seems clear that the rules they established were accepted and applied only in the specific church where they were decreed; in others, however, it is possible to see that over time, a regulation that may have originally been made for one particular locale was adopted by many others—and eventually found its way into church-wide legislation.

The earliest direct assertion by church authorities of the need for this sort of determination was given to us in passing by Bishop Optatus of Milevis, whom we already met above as a key figure during the period of the Donatist schism in northern Africa. Historians have seized on a single word that Optatus wrote in the late fourth century, when objecting to the devotional practices of a laywoman who had been one of the original instigators of the controversy. Noting that this woman was, during the course of the liturgy, in the habit of touching the bone of an unknown deceased person as if to venerate a "martyr," Optatus wrote that it was not known whether the person in question had indeed been martyred, since he had not yet been declared *vindicatus*, or "proven."[74] Optatus neither defines the word (not found in other extant Christian writings during this period in this specific context) nor explains why he asserts that this sort of "proof" is necessary; indeed, his failure to do either might suggest that this was an established concept with which Optatus presumed his readers were already familiar. If so, it may mean that by this relatively early date in the history of the church—at least in northern Africa—it was accepted that if a deceased Christian were to be venerated as a martyr, church authorities first had to give their approval.[75]

Questions may legitimately be raised about whether an approval process known as *vindicatio* had been established in order to recognize martyrs in northern Africa; but there is definitely no doubt that in the following decades, the African church asserted the authority of the bishops over this very issue, albeit in other words. The Council of Carthage in 401 unequivocally gave bishops the right and the duty to ban the faithful from venerating as martyrs those persons whose martyrdom had not been clearly established. It asserts that bishops are even to tear down roadside altars erected to martyrs, if it cannot be proven that these altars contain the relics of true martyrs. The new law combines concern for historical precision with pastoral sensitivity, however, for the canon immediately acknowledges the possibility that this might lead to protests among the faithful; some middle ground is found, for if these altars cannot be destroyed without causing an uproar, the canon notes that bishops are at a minimum obliged to warn the people that they must not visit them, and to explain that they should avoid superstition.[76] We can see that even at this early date, not only did the Council Fathers believe that the veracity of the circumstances surrounding the lives and deaths of alleged martyrs had to be proven, but they also agreed on exactly who has the authority to make this judgment.

During the same period, a bishop in a different part of the Christian world was in fact engaged in the very activity being mandated by this synod in northern Africa. In the late fourth century, Bishop Martin of Tours put a stop to the cult of an alleged martyr once he discovered that the person's purported martyrdom, already suspect, was untrue:

> There was . . . a place very close to the monastery, which an erroneous human opinion had consecrated, with the understanding that some martyrs had been buried together there. . . . But Martin, not inclined to immediately believe uncertain things, often asked those who were his elders, whether among the presbyters or clerics, to make known to him the name of the martyr, or the time when he suffered. He did so, he said, because he had great scruples on these points, since no consistent tradition regarding them had come down from antiquity. Having, therefore, kept away from the place for some time, by no means wishing to diminish the religious veneration with which it was regarded (because he was still uncertain), but at the same time not giving his authority to the opinion of the multitude, lest a mere superstition should obtain a stronger hold, he one day went out to the place. . . . There standing above the tomb itself, Martin prayed to the Lord that He would reveal who the man in question was, and what was his character.[77]

At this point, according to Martin's contemporary biographer, Sulpicius Severus, Martin had a vision of the man, who admitted to Martin that he had been a thief, executed as punishment for his crimes. And so Severus concludes the story: "Martin made known what he had seen, and ordered the altar which had been there to be removed, and in this way he delivered the people from the error of that superstition." Vision aside, one could almost think that Martin's handling of the issue in Tours had been the model for the Fathers in Carthage, who within only a couple of years of this event formulated the abovementioned Canon 14 on this very subject.

A century later, the church in Rome was apparently still concerned with the general issue of the burial of dubious "saints" in churches dedicated to them. Pope Gelasius I, who reigned 492–496, gives us what may be the first clear-cut instance of an attempt at Roman centralization of the approbation of new saints. After a synod in Rome in 494, he decreed that no churches were to be consecrated without the authorization of the Apostolic See.[78] It seems safe to assume that this was a classic example of legislation intended to curb abuses: in his *Religious History*, the fifth-century bishop and historian Theodoret describes numerous persons who built rival churches, all intended for the body of the ascetic Saint Marcian of Syria—a fact that might not have seemed so strange in itself, were it not for the fact that Marcian was still living at the time![79] While we do not know how typical these admirers of Marcian may have been, there is no particular reason to presume that Marcian's was a unique case. The fact that the pope insisted that permission for the consecration of new churches had to be obtained from Rome clearly suggests that, at a minimum, there were local churches whose bishops had allowed such consecrations for questionable "saints," and there may even have been instances where the faithful were building such churches without any church approbation at all.

The repeated intervention of popes in the affairs of local churches far from Rome, in an effort to combat perceived abuses on the part of the bishops of those churches, is a phenomenon that ultimately played a key part in the development of a very centralized ecclesiological structure within the Catholic Church—and not merely in matters pertaining to canonization. Much of the power that was eventually arrogated by the papacy was taken away from local bishops because of allegations of their mishandling of church affairs such as these. It's a pattern that, as we will see in chapter 3, continued in the Catholic Church well into the second millennium.

Meanwhile, elsewhere in the Roman Empire, a very different sort of authority was being exercised on more than one occasion during the same period, as we find cases in which civil authorities—the emperors themselves—made public declarations about the martyr-status of persecuted Christians. The historian Sozomen, describing a three-way controversy between pagans, orthodox Christians, and Arians during the reign of Emperor Theodosius I (379–395), notes that when a group of pagans in Ancyra (now Ankara, Turkey) reacted violently to the conversion of their temple into a church, the emperor himself seems to have decided the official status of those non-Arian Christians who died in the fighting:

> When the emperor was informed of the things that had happened, he declared that the Christians who had been killed were blessed, as they had been admitted to the honors of martyrdom, and had suffered on behalf of the faith.[80]

Sozomen's account of this particular period in the life of the church, which is extremely detailed, makes no mention of any collaboration with the local, orthodox Christian bishop in the issuance of this decree. Nor is there any evidence that church authorities took issue with either the substance of the decree itself or with the fact that it had been issued by a civil, rather than an ecclesiastical, official. What does appear clear is that in the complicated, ongoing, and obviously sometimes violent altercations between various religious factions in that part of the empire, the emperor felt it was necessary and appropriate to intervene, in order to show the public which group was to be regarded as theologically and morally in the right and thus worthy of honor.[81]

Far less ambiguous was a comparable declaration made by Theodosius's son and subsequent heir to the throne, the Emperor Honorius (384–423), regarding the martyrdom of Telemachus in the year 404. The historian Theodoret describes the circumstances leading to the emperor's decree:

> Honorius . . . put an end to the gladiatorial combats which had long been held in Rome. The reason why he did so was the following circumstance. A certain man named Telemachus . . . when the abominable spectacle was going on, went himself into the stadium, and, stepping down into the arena, tried to stop the men who were wielding their weapons against each other. The spectators were indignant, and . . . stoned the peacemaker to death. When the admirable emperor was informed of this he included Telemachus in the list of victorious martyrs, and put an end to that impious spectacle.[82]

Again, we find civil authority declaring that a certain Christian who has died violently should be regarded as a martyr; but in this case, there is no doubt that Emperor Honorius did more than simply exhort the people to consider Telemachus's death as martyrdom—he actually ordered that Telemachus's name be put on "the list of martyrs," an apparent reference to the liturgical calendar in use in Rome at that time. And the name of Telemachus is indeed found on the calendars, a fact that evidently is attributable directly to the command of the Roman Emperor.[83] There is no evidence that the bishop of Rome, or any other ecclesiastical authority, had a hand in this decision or even gave it subsequent approbation. True, it seems safe to presume that, had the bishop of Rome at that time objected to Honorius's decision, he could have taken steps to block its implementation. But the death of Telemachus was so public, and his martyrdom was so obvious to all, that it is difficult to imagine a reasonable objection to listing him among the church's martyrs. The church plainly accepted the decision of the emperor.

Less acceptable was a different decree of Honorius's father, Emperor Theodosius, who in 386 addressed what he plainly considered to be significant abuses of the tombs and relics of the martyrs. A law found in the Codex Theodosianus states that no one is to move the bodies of martyrs to a different location, to divide up the remains (to send them to separate churches or other places), or to sell the relics.[84] This law was written at precisely the same time as the *translationes* of Gervase and Protase by Ambrose in Milan, which were discussed above; there is no way to know whether the timing was a coincidence, or whether Theodosius was for some reason reacting to the occasion of this very public transfer of martyrs' relics from one location to another. Regardless, the countless examples of martyrs who were subsequently translated, and/or whose relics were sent to multiple locations for veneration in different churches, show us the extent to which this civil law was observed; and the fact that the instigators of these *translationes* were normally the local bishops themselves would indicate that church officials neither agreed with this absolute ban, nor felt the need to defer to civil authorities in this matter.

Further indication of the law's non-acceptance is provided by a subsequent decree of Emperor Leo I (457–474), which more or less nullified it. Leo declared that it was indeed permitted to move the bodies of martyrs—but into buildings designed for religious worship, not those constructed for secular purposes, and only with the prior approval of the bishop.[85] Perhaps the new civil law was simply an acknowledgment that the earlier outright ban on translating relics was not being observed, but now there is a new twist: instead of merely outlining the proper way to deal with the relics of the martyrs, we find here the civil authorities formally deferring to ecclesiastical officials, asserting that it is the bishops who have the power to decide whether and where a martyr's remains are to be transferred.

Some centuries later, in a very different part of the Christian world, we find the members of the Carolingian dynasty using much the same approach in the newly Christianized kingdom of the Franks. Over a period of several decades they passed decrees urging bishops to exercise authority to regulate the veneration of martyrs and other saints. In 742, for example, Carloman noted the need for the church hierarchy to be watchful lest "foolish men" engage in pagan rituals under the guise of venerating Christian martyrs and confessors.[86] And in 789, Carloman's nephew and eventual successor Charlemagne asserted that it was not permitted to venerate false martyrs and saints whose history was not clearly known,[87] making a critical reference to those who invent saints out of anyone who has died.[88] Assuming that abusive practices must have arisen impelling the Frankish civil rulers to advance these laws, the spiritual situation—at least with regard to the veneration of saints—in their newly converted kingdom seems to have been bleak indeed. Yet while these civil leaders clearly assert their own authority when demanding proper regulation of the veneration of saints, it can be seen here that they do not attempt to specifically regulate that veneration themselves, instead indicating that this was the specific responsibility of the church hierarchy.

We have already seen church legislation passed in fourth-century Carthage on the topic of the erection of roadside shrines to questionable "martyrs." It would seem that this problem persisted for generations, or at least it subsequently surfaced in other parts of the Christian world, for the wording of that very same Carthage canon was reused by the church in the Frankish kingdom three centuries later. In 794, the Council of Frankfurt, convoked by Charlemagne, used much the same wording when it decreed that no new saints were to be venerated or invoked, nor were memorials to be erected for them along the roads, unless church authorities first determined that they should be venerated, based either on authoritative *acta,* or on their holiness of life.[89] Once again, under Charlemagne the emphasis was placed on the authority of the bishops to make these determinations.

This repeated deference by Charlemagne to the authority of ecclesiastical officials is all the more reason that it is so surprising to find at the Council of Mainz in 813, toward the end of Charlemagne's life, a sudden shift in the placement of this authority. Canon 51 of this Council notes that bodies of the saints are not to be translated to another place without first consulting with "the prince, the bishop, and the holy synod."[90] Now, nearly twenty years after Frankfurt, the permission of "church authorities" (which in practice ordinarily would refer to diocesan bishops) was not sufficient; the bishop's synod also had to be included in the decision, and even if these ecclesiastical officials were all in agreement, their findings still had to accord with the opinion of the secular ruler as well.

The sources are silent as to the specific motivation for these additional requirements. But we may reasonably presume that cases had already arisen in Charlemagne's kingdom where the need to obtain the approval of the bishop had failed to prevent the bodies of demonstrably false "saints" from being solemnly transferred to churches for veneration—else there would hardly be any need for the involvement of even more people in the process that had already been established.[91] We find here an instance of a higher authority attempting to "crack down" on those bishops who had wrongly permitted abuses in the creating of new saints, but this time it was the civil leader, rather than the Pope, who took this new legislative action.

Meanwhile, much farther east, we find the other Roman emperor also engaged in what appears to be saint-making. Emperor Basil I "the Macedonian," who reigned 867–886, built numerous ecclesiastical buildings on what seems to have been entirely his own initiative, most of them hardly controversial: they include churches and chapels in honor of Christ the Savior, the Archangel Michael, and the Apostles Peter and Paul.[92] What was more questionable, however, was the church he built on the occasion of the death of his own beloved son Constantine, thereby declaring him, at least obliquely, to be a saint.[93] Since his name is not to be found anywhere in the calendar today, it seems clear enough that the church did not accept Basil's "canonization" of his son.[94]

Despite the church's evident resistance, Basil's son, Emperor Leo VI (ruled 886–912), continued the practice when he unilaterally canonized his two wives, Theofania and Zoe, building churches in their honor. Historians appear to agree that, while Theofania enjoyed a reputation for virtue, Zoe decidedly did not. This seems to have been the church's position as well, for while Theofania was accepted as a saint, Zoe was rejected, and the church Leo built in Zoe's honor was subsequently rededicated to all the saints.[95]

The church likewise rejected the decision of Emperor Nicephorus II Phocas (ca. 912–969) that his soldiers who died in battle would be venerated as martyrs. The patriarch of Constantinople, together with other members of the hierarchy, successfully objected, and this excessively broad definition of "martyrdom" was definitively nixed.[96]

By the tenth century, therefore, we can see that while there are definitely inconsistencies and even a few apparent contradictions, a general overall pattern of authority regarding canonization of saints had begun to emerge. The concept of canonization by popular acclaim had decidedly disappeared, and the church in various parts of the world had repeatedly asserted its authority to regulate the veneration of martyrs and other persons as saints. The ecclesiastical officials who exercised this power as a rule were diocesan bishops, although we have found one instance, that of the consecration of new churches, where the pope in Rome declared his sole authority in a matter touching the making of saints.

At the same time, however, we can clearly see numerous instances of secular powers involving themselves in elements of the process, declaring certain persons to be martyrs, and building churches dedicated to those whom these rulers asserted to be saints. In some of these latter cases it appears that the church accepted the decisions of civil authorities; in others, it obviously did not. It is interesting to note that whenever there was an evident disagreement between the church and the state, it was always the ecclesiastical authorities whose position took precedence—in other words, there is no known example of a dispute involving the making of saints in which the secular powers ultimately overruled the church. Still, there was at this point no explicit delineation of powers, in any region of the Christian world, that clearly explained to all that every aspect of what would come to be known as the canonization process was within the purview of the church. This would, as we will see subsequently, lead in the future to continued inconsistencies in decisions regarding various elements of saint-making, particularly in the East.

Preliminary Conclusions

As noted in the beginning of this chapter, there was never an explicit intention to develop a procedure for the formal declaration that a deceased Christian should be venerated as a martyr and saint. Nevertheless, we can see that roughly by the first millennium in the life of the church, specific elements of a process for what ultimately came to be known as *canonization* had definitely evolved. Practices had become established, and the authorities competent to make decisions in these matters were gradually becoming more and more settled (although there was definitely still some confusion with regard to the latter).

First of all, the term *martyr* had acquired a particular theological meaning. Through discussions regarding many of the faithful who had died in the persecutions raging during the first few centuries of Christianity, a precise definition was eventually developed. A martyr, in short, was one who died a violent death because of his or her belief in Christ. Such a person did not deliberately seek to die but, at the same time, did not run away from death when once faced with it, accepting it heroically as a means of publicly testifying to faith. And that faith had to be orthodox, for those who died for heretical beliefs could not be accepted as true martyrs. Ultimately, these requirements would lead as a matter of course to some sort of investigation by church officials into the circumstances surrounding a possible-martyr's death and the orthodoxy of his faith. In certain cases, the church acknowledged that it was possible to recognize as martyrs individual Christians who otherwise did not meet the definition: for example, persons could in theory die a natural death but be revered as martyrs, provided that death came as a result of sufferings endured for the faith; and it was acknowledged to be theoretically possible to accept as a martyr someone who had voluntarily sought death, if seeking it under divine inspiration. Nevertheless, these exceptions served to prove the rule.

Second, the notion that someone was declared a martyr carried with it specific implications for church worship and liturgical praxis. The primary result of a finding that a certain person had indeed died a martyr was that his or her name was inscribed in the liturgical books—first the diptychs, and later the calendars—so that a commemoration could be made annually during the liturgy, on the anniversary of the martyr's *dies natalis*. On this day the *passio*, an account of the martyr's life and death, was read as part of the commemoration; this led to the evolution of a particular literary genre, the *acta martyrum*, which ideally comprised factually accurate accounts, gleaned from eyewitnesses or at least from official documents—though the sad reality was that many of these *acta* were anything but historically reliable.

Additionally, once the public persecutions of Christians had ended and the church could worship freely, the practice developed of moving the relics of these martyrs into churches or chapels dedicated specifically to their honor. This was not an absolute requirement, as the tombs containing the bodies of many of the early martyrs have never been found, while the remains of others were definitely known to have been destroyed. But when possible, the relics were exhumed and transferred in a formal ceremony known as the *translatio*. The very fact that a person's remains were translated in this way came to constitute canonization, for this ritual was never carried out if the person was *not* determined to have died as a martyr/saint.

And finally, the development of this series of elements constituting a martyr's canonization naturally required the simultaneous evolution of an established authority who had the right to decide definitively whether someone was truly a martyr. Cases that involved gray areas in terms of orthodox beliefs or were factually dubious in some way needed to be determined by someone whom all agreed had competence in such matters. This authority soon devolved to the diocesan bishop, although numerous cases arose in which the civil authorities—generally the emperors—took this authority and made these decisions themselves. Still, there are also instances in which the secular rulers clearly declared that ecclesiastical officials had the right and the obligation to make these determinations; and in cases where there seems to have been some degree of disagreement between civil and church officials, the position of ecclesiastical authorities always appears to have taken precedence over that of the state.

Such was the state of the process for the canonization of martyrs during the period of history in which Christianity in the East and West were officially united. It remains to be seen now how things developed after the Baptism of Rus' in the late tenth century, shortly before the year 1054, the traditionally accepted date of the Great East–West Schism.

Chapter Two

Russian Orthodoxy from the Conversion of Rus' (ca. 988) to Today

Introduction: Lacunae in Russian Historiography and Some Consequent Methodological Issues

Traditionally, the conversion of Rus' to Christianity is believed to have occurred in or about 988, under Prince Vladimir, who (at least according to the account found in the chronicles) chose to embrace the liturgy and customs of Byzantium over those of the Latins. The Russians' knowledge of the basic teachings of the faith, their methods of celebrating the liturgy and the sacraments, and their understanding of the role of the hierarchy, were all garnered from the Greeks who taught them. Thus it is difficult, if not impossible, to imagine that the Russian church would have adopted either a theological understanding of sainthood in general and martyrdom in particular, or a procedural system to canonize new saints, that was fundamentally different from that of the church in Byzantium.

As we have seen in chapter 1, however, the division of Christianity at this early date into "Greek" and "Latin" would be anachronistic when it comes to the issue of the canonization of saints. True, external liturgical rubrics had already been developing in noticeably different ways in the East and West in preceding centuries, and common Christian concepts were often explained in East and West using markedly different terminology; but with regard to fundamental theological concepts, one would be hard-pressed to find significant substantive areas of disagreement. At the time of Russia's conversion, therefore, one could say that the differences between Eastern and Western Christians were more cultural than ideological. It seems reasonably safe to assume, then, that when the early Rus' first became a Christian people, they learned to regard both the veneration and the creation of saints—martyrs and non-martyrs—in the same basic way as did the faithful in any other part of the Christian world.

But this is only an assumption. For an actual fact, we have no historical documentation that explains the Russians' understanding of the process of saint-making (still less their theological rationale for creating a new saint who died a martyr) for hundreds of years. We can see from various historical accounts that Russian Christians were indeed being declared saints, sometimes after dying a martyr's death, so we know that in early Rus', the concept of canonization certainly did exist; but what is nonexistent is any explicit description in an official church document (or even an unofficial one, for that matter!) that could show us the criteria and the methods being used. Metropolitan Iuvenalii, until relatively recently the head of the canonization commission of the Moscow Patriarchate, admitted frankly the difficulties inherent in trying to trace the roots of Russian canonizations of centuries past: noting that the tradition is largely oral rather than written, he could only acknowledge the existence of large numbers of Russian saints of whose canonizations no written records exist—the only extant documents frequently being the liturgical propers for the saints' feast-days.[1]

To complicate matters further, even the records indicating precisely who was canonized where, and when, are replete with omissions, inaccuracies, and generally vague and confusing information. Not only is it unclear *how* saints were being canonized; in many cases it is equally unclear *who* was canonized. When this is coupled with what appear to be definite errors in the liturgical calendar (which will be addressed below), one quickly realizes that attempting to completely reconstruct the canonizations of centuries past is simply impossible. As the Russian scholar Vasiliev noted resignedly toward the end of the nineteenth century, "We are unable to *not* remark on the difficulty of arriving at uniform and precise conclusions" regarding the canonization of saints in the Russian church.[2]

At the same time, members of the church in Russia will affirm unhesitatingly that their system of canonization of saints is grounded in tradition. Since we have no extant documentation describing what that tradition really was, we are obliged to look to historical accounts of saints throughout the history of Christianity in Russia, since the conversion of Rus' over a thousand years ago. Our sources for the history of what is in fact a canonical procedure, then, are largely historical works, from which it is necessary to pick out the relevant procedural elements whenever they can be found.

Among the authors whose works are pertinent to this subject, an important place goes to Vasilii Vasiliev, who penned in the late nineteenth century what is, despite its undeniable imperfections, probably the earliest comprehensive history of the process for creating Russian saints.[3] In particular, his analysis of saints' feast-days on early Russian liturgical calendars, and their derivation from early Greek diptychs (which will be discussed in greater detail later in this chapter) remains perhaps the most masterful work on the subject even to this day.

But the undisputed master of Russian church history is of course Evgenii Golubinskii, who not many years before the Bolshevik Revolution wrote a historical work specifically treating of the canonization of saints in Russia.[4] Insofar as he successfully managed to collect information on hundreds of Russian saints ranging over a period of more than nine hundred years, often from medieval manuscripts of Russian historical chronicles and religious works that are difficult to access (if indeed they survived the tumultuous revolutionary years at all), church scholars are indubitably in Golubinskii's debt. There is no particular reason to question the overall accuracy of the huge mass of factual evidence that he compiled.

But what should give us pause, in the interests of accuracy, are the numerous lacunae in Golubinskii's historical narrative, which he does not hesitate to fill with his presumptions about what surely *must* have happened. All too often his rationale for the actions of a given hierarch in a particular situation is utterly unfounded in anything other than his laudable desire to defend the church. While his piety may be admirable and his intentions pure, Golubinskii's assertions about what *probably* happened must, from the standpoint of historical methodology, be treated with general suspicion. Consequently, there are some occasions on which it seems absolutely safe to rely on the information found in Golubinskii's work, and others on which it would definitely be imprudent, if not downright irresponsible, to do so.[5]

Another methodological issue concerns the translation of Russian terminology. While there often appears to be an undisputed correlation between a Russian term and a corresponding word in English (or some other Western language), this is not always the case and thus cannot be taken for granted. In fact, the very term *canonization* is not found at all in the Russian language until relatively recently, when it was borrowed, transliterated, from the West for use by Russian scholars themselves—who were, not surprisingly, having comparable difficulties translating Western terminology into Russian. Much more common in Russian hagiographical writings, at least in earlier centuries, are the terms *proslavlenie* (glorification), or the completely untranslatable phrase *prichtenie k liku sviatykh*, which might be equated to "raising someone to the altars," or "including someone in the ranks of the saints." Insofar as these terms were all used in the context of acknowledging that a deceased person was to be venerated as a saint—and it appears that they were, albeit with some nuances that will be addressed later in this chapter—translating them as "canonization" is often unavoidable, usually due simply to the structure of the

English language. More recent Russian writers have generally done the same in their native tongue, frequently replacing the older terms with the transliterated *kanonizatsiia*. It will become clear soon enough, however, that while accuracy of translation is important, it is in many cases the least of our worries.

Part 1. From the Conversion of Rus' (ca. 988) to the Bolshevik Revolution

A. Theological Concept of Martyrdom

Since the Russian church received its theological understanding of sainthood in general, and martyrdom in particular, from the church in Greece, it should surprise no one that they formally articulate their teaching on these concepts in fundamentally the same way. Saints are those who, based on their conduct during their lives here on earth, are now considered to be with God, and therefore willing and able to intercede for those Christians still living who pray to them for help.[6]

It follows naturally that of course the Russian church embraced the same notion of martyrdom held by Greeks and Latins both, as seen in chapter 1. Russians who truly died for their faith are thus labeled *mucheniki*, or martyrs, in essentially the same way as those Christians who were declared by the church to be martyrs in the first millennium.

But very early on, the newly Christianized Rus' developed a unique additional category of saints of its own: *strastoterptsy*, or passion-bearers. These saints are those who died a violent death, and their virtuous acceptance of the physical torments they foresaw rendered them similar to Christ.[7] Just as Our Lord displayed meekness and patience in the face of horrendous sufferings and death, *strastoterptsy* heroically accepted their sufferings for the love of God, patiently enduring death rather than attempting to defend themselves.

The examples par excellence of Russian *strastoterptsy* are Saints Boris and Gleb, two of the twelve sons of Grand Prince Vladimir. The earliest extant accounts of their life and death[8] (which we have no particular reason to doubt) indicate that despite their youth, they were the princes of Rostov and Murom, respectively.[9] At the death of their father in 1015, their elder brother Sviatopolk determined to kill his brothers in order to gain full control of Rus'. Historical accounts are consistent in asserting that these two brothers were killed because they stood in the way of Sviatopolk's full political control—and not specifically because of their Christian faith, which Sviatopolk presumably shared as well.

Our early Russian sources contain various speeches that are ostensibly direct quotations from the mouths of Boris and Gleb. They reveal that when Boris, who was killed first, discovered that Sviatopolk's assassins were en route to murder him, he did not attempt to run away, much less to resist. Rather, embracing suffering for the sake of peace, in imitation of the sufferings of Christ, he sadly but passively accepted the death that his elder brother inflicted on him.[10]

Intriguingly, the chronicler immediately asserts that Boris received the crown from Christ Himself and was included among the prophets, the apostles—and the martyrs.[11] It is an approach wholly consistent with the repeated statements of John Chrysostom centuries earlier (discussed in the previous chapter) that the virtuous life of a Christian can be equated to that of the martyrs, who shed their blood for the faith.

Gleb's death was evidently similar to that of Boris; after being warned by yet another brother not to go when he was summoned by Sviatopolk, Gleb disregarded the advice, and likewise meekly accepted death, as did Christ.[12]

While this concept of passive acceptance of violent death may certainly seem comparable to martyrdom, there is a significant difference in that the killer of a *strastoterpets* need not intend to kill specifically because of the person's Christian faith. Thus, while a *strastoterpets* by definition dies an unnatural death, such a death does not automatically constitute martyrdom as the term had come to be understood in the first millennium AD. At the same time, however, we could no doubt apply the title of *strastoterpets* to many of the early Christian martyrs who peacefully accepted death during the Roman persecutions. One might say that it was possible for a martyr to also be a *strastoterpets*, although a *strastoterpets* was not necessarily a martyr.

That having been said, however, even the most cursory examination of Russian hagiographic literature will immediately reveal that the terms *muchenik* (i.e., a martyr in the traditional sense of the term) and *strastoterpets* are frequently used interchangeably, as if synonymous. In his hagiographic entry for Boris and Gleb, to cite only one example, Barsukov cites multiple sources that repeatedly alternate between describing them as *mucheniki* and as *strastoterptsy*, suggesting that there was no distinction between the two terms.[13]

There are other Russian saints, of course, who are simply deemed to be *mucheniki*, or martyrs in the standard sense of the word. But even here, examination of the historical accounts of the deaths of many of these Russian martyrs indicates that they may not meet the criteria for martyrdom developed in the first thousand years of Christianity. A case in point follows.

Grand Prince Roman of Riazan' was killed in 1270 by the Tatars. An early historical account of the circumstances leading to his death indicates that he was brought to the attention of the Tatar khan because a "detractor" alleged (falsely?) that Roman had spoken derisively of the Tatars' pagan religion. Called to account, Roman is said to have declared to the khan that the Tatar faith was "filthy and loathsome," and he was consequently sentenced to death.[14] While Russian historians do not hesitate to describe Roman's death as "martyrdom," it is not clear from the original account whether Roman was killed because of the simple fact that he was a Christian, or because he had verbally attacked the Tatars' own faith, thereby provoking a deadly response.

Would the circumstances surrounding his death have led the early church to conclude that Roman was a martyr? It is of course impossible to be sure, but if we assume the factual accuracy of the narrative, it seems doubtful that Grand Prince Roman was actively sought out and killed for his faith as were the early martyrs during the Christian persecutions by Roman emperors. Before making any determination, it would be necessary first to ascertain whether the Tatar khan was killing all Christians indiscriminately, regardless of whether they had defamed the Tatar faith; or whether Roman was condemned to death only because of his verbal assault on the religion of the khan. If other known Christians were left by the Tatars in peace and Roman's taunting of the pagan Tatars was the primary cause of his death, it could logically be concluded that he was not in fact killed solely because of his faith. Alternately, if Roman sought to provoke the Tatars by his critical comments, one could apply to him the same principles employed by the church during the fourth-century persecutions in northern Africa, when it sought to determine whether a Christian had indeed died as a martyr. As was seen in the preceding chapter, the fathers present at the Council of Carthage in about 348 had declared that those who turned themselves over to their persecutors, voluntarily seeking a martyr's death by drawing attention to themselves, were not to be accepted as martyrs. The concept had become an established element in the gradually evolving definition of martyrdom throughout the church. But Grand Prince Roman is nevertheless listed as a saint of the Russian church specifically because he died a martyr's death.[15]

Thus far we have seen instances of deceased Russian Christians being declared saints and described as martyrs although their deaths do not necessarily seem to have met the definition of the term that had been more or less established in the first millennium. But at the same time, the Russian church has traditionally canonized saints who definitely died a martyr's death in the standard sense of the word, yet does not term them *mucheniki* if they also happened to be members of the hierarchy. A bishop, metropolitan, or other high-ranking member of the clergy who was truly martyred is typically labeled not as a martyr but as a *sviatitel'*, or sanctifier. Thus there are numerous *sviatiteli* who in fact suffered martyrdom but are not included among the martyrs, their status as members of the episcopacy "outranking" their status as martyrs.

An obvious example of this is Metropolitan Philip II of Moscow (1506–1569), who was chosen to head the Russian church by Tsar Ivan IV ("the Terrible"). Philip's opposition to Ivan's ruthless political killings, undertaken during the period known as the Oprichnina, led Ivan to persecute the metropolitan in turn.[16] After a protracted period in which the tsar vainly sought to publicly destroy Philip by falsely accusing him of immorality, Philip was imprisoned, deposed from office, and ultimately strangled to death by one of Ivan's hired assassins.[17]

There is little question that Philip's death would meet the traditional definition of martyrdom, for he was killed for repeatedly upholding the moral teachings of the Christian faith. But on his two feast-days, he is not listed as a *muchenik* on the liturgical calendar of the Russian church, but is simply referred to as saint, metropolitan, and *sviatitel'*.[18]

Another complicating factor in the Russian system of labeling saints is the fact that many are described simply as *chudotvortsy*, or "miracle-workers." The issue of requiring miracles before canonizing even those persons who died for the faith will be addressed below; suffice it to say here that describing someone who died a martyr's death as a *chudotvorets* often inadvertently masks the fact of his martyrdom. It has already been noted above that Boris and Gleb are described alternately as *strastoterptsy* and *mucheniki*; they are also at times referred to as *chudotvortsy*, as is the *sviatitel'* Metropolitan Philip II, whom we just met. It is, therefore, very evident that persons who die as martyrs are sometimes, but not always, identified as such by the Russian church.

What is equally evident is the undeniable fact that the theological orthodoxy of a person's beliefs has always constituted a sine qua non for canonization in the Russian church, just as it had elsewhere throughout the first thousand years of Christianity. We have seen in the preceding chapter that the early church declined to accept as martyrs/saints those Christians who indeed died for their beliefs, but whose beliefs were heterodox. The church in Russia continued firmly in this tradition; their rejection of the saints recognized as such by the sect of Old Believers, in schism with Moscow since the late seventeenth century, provides us with much evidence of this.[19] While there is no question, speaking historically, that many Old Believers did in fact die for their faith during the decades after they first rejected the liturgical reforms of Patriarch Nikon in the 1650s, they have certainly never been acknowledged by the official Russian church as true martyrs, worthy of veneration.[20] Thus while the church in Russia definitely is aware that the schismatic Old Believers commemorate many of their own members as martyrs and saints, these are not accepted as such by the church under the Moscow Patriarchate.

It is therefore apparent that this traditional requirement, that a true martyr must have died for religious beliefs that are in fact orthodox, was embraced and consistently maintained by the Russian church. Russian martyrs who are formally venerated as saints are all regarded to have practiced the true faith during their lives. But what is less apparent, as should become increasingly obvious in this chapter, is the ultimate motivation for their canonization—for the actual reasons that impelled the hierarchy to undertake the process to declare them to be saints are, more often than not, surprisingly unclear.

B. Process by Which a Martyr Is Recognized as a Saint

1. Spontaneous Recognition by the Local Faithful

We have seen in chapter 1 that in the earliest days of the church, when so many Christians died for the faith during the persecutions, the determination that someone had in fact died as a martyr was largely a spontaneous act by the faithful as a whole. There was no formal, "official" finding after an investigatory process by someone in a position of authority, because there was no formality—no investigation, no process. In general, the Christian community could appreciate intuitively who had suffered true martyrdom, and who had not.

It was only after questionable cases, with gray areas, began to surface that terms were defined, the officials with proper authority to recognize a martyr as such were established, and an actual procedure gradually developed. For as was observed in the preceding chapter, over time cases arose in which popular piety had erroneously led to the veneration of people whom the church subsequently declared were *not* martyrs: some had actively sought death for their beliefs, others were heretics, and the historical facts surrounding the lives and deaths of still others were dubious or even completely unknown. Procedures were implemented in order to correct errors and resolve confusion. Once they were put in place, however, these procedures obviously eliminated the element of popular spontaneity. The Christian faithful were no longer able, on their own, to declare that someone had truly died a martyr's death and should be venerated for it.

Or perhaps it is more accurate to say that while the faithful might believe among themselves that a particular person should be commemorated as a martyr, their private belief had no official weight. They could not, in and of themselves, oblige the church—even just their local church—to accept someone as a martyr/saint. For a process had gradually developed, under the control of the hierarchy, to formally determine just who should be venerated as a true martyr and who should not.

What follows is a reconstruction of the procedural elements that were required for the establishment of a martyr as a saint in the Russian church, beginning roughly within a generation or so of the Christianization of Rus', when we already start to find the first examples of the canonization of Russian saints. It should become evident that while the Russian church intended to follow the practices they had garnered from the Greeks, some of the rules that became established actually appear to have introduced novelties into the procedure that constitute a marked departure from the traditions that they originally were following.

2. But Simultaneously, a More Official Process Exists

a. Liturgical Commemorations—Local Calendars

When Russia became Christian in the tenth century, it adopted the liturgical books and the liturgical calendar of the Greeks. We have already seen in the preceding chapter the manner in which, over the course of the centuries, church calendars evolved from the early diptychs; we have similarly looked at the development of the commemoration of martyrs (and eventually other saints as well) on specific feast-days with special prayers and a reading of the *acta*, describing each saint's life and death. The Russian church thus inherited this "system" of including martyrs and other saints in the liturgical books that was the end-result of nearly a thousand years of theological development.

This logically implies, therefore, that at least in the early years of Russian Christianity, the saints whom the church commemorated were all from places outside Russia and had for the most part lived and died centuries before Russia had embraced the faith. It would naturally take some time before the church in Russia had some saints of its own to add to the calendar.

In the meantime, however, the question arises as to *which* calendar Russia received from the Greeks. After all, as was seen in the first chapter, while many martyrs and other saints were accepted as such by the entire church, and there was likewise a definite trend over time toward local churches accepting saints from other locales into their calendars, there nevertheless remained many local saints whose feast-days were not observed outside of their own local churches. Consequently, it may have been virtually impossible to find multiple locales with liturgical calendars that were completely identical. The number of potential variations was limitless. So when they celebrated the liturgy on a given day, which calendar were the Russians using?

The answer is that we simply do not know. Nor can we even presume that there was a single Greek calendar that the new Russian church began to use; it may very well be that in different parts of Rus', the new church inherited copies of various Greek liturgical books containing different calendars. True, it is possible that the Russians eventually received copies of the *Menologium* of Basil II, a liturgical work commissioned in the late tenth or early eleventh century by the Byzantine emperor and intended to constitute a uniform, general calendar for the entire church in the East;[21] but there is no specific evidence to show that this was in fact the case. What does appear to be clear, however, is that the Greek calendars that were handed on to the Russians did not contain commemorations for every known saint, or even for a majority of them. As an example, Vasiliev notes that an extant calendar from the late eleventh century, not long after the traditional date of the conversion of Rus', contains only 100 to 110 feast-days[22]—obviously omitting many of the martyrs and other saints already accepted either church-wide or at least locally in Greece, and also in the process leaving plenty of "open" dates available for commemorations of future Russian saints.

As was already the case elsewhere, when feasts were added for new saints of the Russian church, the date chosen was generally the day of the saint's death.[23] But with great frequency we also find feast-days established on the day when a particular saint's relics were transferred ceremoniously to a church or chapel dedicated to them—the feast-day of Leontii of Rostov, for example, was established on May 23, the date of the *translatio* of his relics.

To complicate the matter further, one often finds multiple feast-days for the same saint. Thus the feast of Boris and Gleb was established on June 24, the day when Boris was killed; but yet another feast was set for May 2, to commemorate the day in 1072 that the relics of both brothers were subsequently transferred. Yet another feast-day can be found in some calendars on September 5, the date of Gleb's death.[24]

Since Russian saints were, more often than not, canonized locally, it naturally follows that as in the days of the early church, someone could be venerated as a saint in one locale but not in another—and calendars therefore varied accordingly. (This is, incidentally, *the* primary reason why it is essentially impossible to compile a complete, authoritative list of saints who have been canonized as such, in each and every part of the church in Russia and at any time throughout its entire history.)[25] While, as we have seen in the previous chapter, there was a definite trend in the first millennium toward local churches adopting saints from other regions and using calendars that included commemorations of saints from other parts of the Christian world, it is interesting to note that in Russia, the concept of a nationwide, uniform liturgical calendar for the entire church did not become a reality until the twentieth century. Only in 1901 did the Holy Synod (which at that time was the highest governing body in the Russian Orthodox Church) undertake to compile a standardized calendar for the entire church. The *True Calendar of All Russian Saints* was published two years later, but even then it was not embraced by many parishes and monastic communities, which objected to the inclusion of some local saints who were not accepted as such everywhere. At the same time, opponents of the calendar also noted that the faithful traditionally regarded many persons as saints who were never actually canonized and thus were not mentioned in the new calendar.[26] In short, it was felt that this calendar obliged veneration of saints who were largely unknown by the faithful, while it ignored other saints who were in fact widely commemorated—two perceived flaws that hindered its acceptance.

The fact that Russia has not traditionally had a uniform, church-wide calendar is the underlying reason behind the difficulty in determining exactly who has been canonized and who hasn't. For example, a local church may have established a feast-day for a saint who was acknowledged as such solely by this particular church, and by no one else; but if that local church's calendar was lost, or copied incorrectly, this local saint could conceivably disappear from the list of canonized saints entirely. We have already seen above that in the eleventh-century calendars from Greece, the names of many persons who had definitely been acknowledged to be saints in the past were now nowhere to be found. A similar possibility exists in Russia as well, that some persons were in fact canonized in centuries past, but for whatever reason are no longer included on extant calendars.

At the same time, the opposite may also very well be the case: it is possible—perhaps even highly probable—that Russian liturgical calendars contain feast-days of "saints" who were never actually canonized by the competent ecclesiastical authorities. Vasiliev makes a rather startling assertion: since we can see such numerous and significant variations among different liturgical calendars, we may presume (in his opinion) that the copyists who compiled these books were including some "saints" based on their own personal preferences. In this way, Vasiliev states, feast-days were established for deceased persons who, while they may have been informally venerated by the faithful, had never been officially canonized in the strict sense.[27] It is unfortunate that he fails to present concrete examples in support of his claim—which, if true, would imply that some Russians have been "canonized" through the mere fact of their inclusion in the liturgical calendar by copyists.

A possible source of the confusion in this regard is an issue that was seen in the preceding chapter, for it had already arisen in the Christian world centuries before the Christianization of Rus': namely, the blur that occurs between praying *for* a deceased Christian, and praying *to* him. The failure to make a sharp theological distinction between these two concepts, which we already found in the early centuries of the church, continues in many cases in Russia to this day. Writing relatively recently, a member of the Russian hierarchy describes the gradual development of the first type of prayer into the second, in the case of many monastic founders during the medieval period:

> The course of their canonizations, as a rule, was as follows: the brothers at the monastery sincerely revered their deceased founder, offering continuous *panikhidi* [prayers for the repose of his soul], which gradually became imbued with prayers directed toward the servant of God himself. The head of the monastery made a request of church authorities for prayerful veneration of the servant of God with the saints, and received permission and a blessing to do this.[28]

This scenario is altogether consistent with Vasiliev's statement above. Obtaining permission to pray in honor of a deceased person may not necessarily have always been intended to constitute a formal statement that this person is now to be regarded as a saint in heaven; but if that permission resulted in the inclusion of his name in the liturgical calendar, the end result was precisely that.

Golubinskii repeats essentially the same assertion about the wrongful addition of some non-saints to copies of Russian calendars, and presents four cases of saints (all non-martyrs) who were actually canonized *after* their names had already been listed in the liturgical books.[29] These examples would appear, at first glance, to constitute sufficient evidence of this faulty practice; but because so much historical documentation about the Russian church is lacking, it is also possible that these persons were indeed canonized locally before their inclusion in the liturgical books, and that evidence of this has simply been lost. It may be that their subsequent, known canonizations by Moscow were actually instances in which local saints were raised by the metropolitan of Moscow to church-wide veneration (a practice that will be discussed in greater detail below). Regardless, serious questions have been raised as to whether every feast-day included in Russian liturgical calendars is the result of an actual canonization process, by which competent church authorities determined after investigation that a deceased person did in fact merit veneration as a saint.[30] This logically implies that there is a reasonable possibility that some of those venerated in the Russian church as saints are not saints at all, as the process for establishing them as such never took place.

Two martyrs from early Rus' who may fall into this category are described in early Russian historical accounts: the two Variags. Ivan and his father, Theodor the Variag—which latter term, far from being a proper name, simply identifies him as a "Varangian," indicating that he was Scandinavian rather than ethnically Russian—were Christians who entered the territory of early Rus' in the year 980, and were confronted with the still-pagan inhabitants, who wished to sacrifice young Ivan to their idol, and urged his father to acquiesce.[31] Theodor's spirited defense of both his Christian faith and his son led to their violent deaths; the historian who narrated the account did not hesitate to declare them martyrs and hold them up as admirable examples to Russians in later years.[32] One finds the holy Variag martyrs Theodor and Ioann commemorated in the liturgical calendar on July 12, but it is unknown when, where, and by whom the two were canonized, if indeed they were ever canonized at all.[33]

b. Writing the *Zhitie*, Composing a *Sluzhba*

Another element of the process for the canonization of a saint in Russia in centuries past was fundamentally the same as that which developed in other parts of the Christian world in the first millennium, as was described in chapter 1: when a feast-day was established for commemoration of a new saint (martyr or not), there necessarily followed the need for prayers and hymns proper to the liturgy on the new saint's day, as well as a written account of his life that could be read during that day's liturgy. Accordingly, when a new saint was made, the Russian church composed an account of his life (in Russian known as a *zhitie*), as well as a *sluzhba*, or the prayers and hymns proper to the liturgy on the new saint's feast-day.

Frequently, the composition of a *sluzhba* that references a saint on his feast-day is not specifically mentioned in documentation pertaining to a new saint's canonization; but as an example, references to various elements of a feast-day's liturgy can be found in the sixteenth-century decree of Patriarch Iov, who approved the veneration of the martyrs Ioann, Stefan, and Petr. These three new saints had been killed in the same century by the Tatars. The document by which the patriarch approved their new cult indicates the manner in which they are to be commemorated in various aspects of the liturgy, including a remembrance in the *litiia* (part of an all-night liturgical service).[34]

As for the writing of a *zhitie* as a component of canonization, a clear-cut example can be found in our own day, when Patriarch Tikhon of Moscow, who died in 1925 after an extended period of imprisonment and overall persecution by the Soviet government, was canonized by the Moscow Patriarchate in 1989 as one of Russia's "New Martyrs and Confessors."[35] Just a few months after the official canonization, a *zhitie* was published by the Patriarchate, providing an official account of the life and virtues of the new Saint Tikhon.[36] Since the *zhitie* was written only a few decades after his death, and a plethora of biographical documentation was still extant at the time of its composition, there is no particular reason why it should include anything factually dubious or any significant lacunae.

But not all *zhitiia* were composed at the same time as or shortly after a person was officially declared to be a saint. As was the case in the first millennium, so also in Russia it happened in previous centuries that sometimes a *zhitie* was written many years, even centuries, before a person's canonization—and frequently we simply do not know at what point it was written.[37] Sometimes, as with Tikhon, these writings were composed specifically for official use, to be read during the liturgy or at least on the feast-day commemorating the saint in question; but frequently *zhitiia* were written simply for private devotional purposes, and were never intended to constitute definitive accounts of saints' lives. Consequently, just as the historical veracity of many *acta* written about martyrs and other saints in the days of the early church was questionable, so likewise the *zhitiia* of many Russian saints were not necessarily factually accurate. The intention of the author was not always to provide an exact account of the events of the saint's life and death; rather, hagiographers often wrote in a style intended more to provide readers with a memorable legend or a dramatic narrative that may have bordered on fiction.

Assuming that there was no claim or presumption that such quasi-fictitious works were factually accurate, we can without difficulty accept them for what they are. But problems arise when we realize that in a fair number of cases, Russians were canonized as saints centuries after their deaths, based almost entirely on the "facts" contained in their *zhitiia*.

The numerous *zhitiia* written about the martyr-bishop Saint Leontii of Rostov are an excellent case in point. Leontii is said to have died in 1077, after missionary work leading to the conversion of the people of the city of Rostov. But he was not revered as a saint until his tomb was discovered and opened in 1164, after a fire in the church where he was buried. At about that time, the first version of a *zhitie* was composed, but in subsequent years five more, vastly different *zhitiia* were written about Leontii's life and death.

Kliuchevskii analyzes the contents of these six *zhitiia*, noting that each became more detailed and complex than the previous one.[38] Descriptions of Leontii's previous life in Constantinople, his journey to Rostov, and his preaching to the pagan inhabitants were not found at all in the edition written at the time of the finding of his relics; rather, they suddenly appeared in those versions composed years afterward. Why, then, should we accept these subsequent additions as truthful?

As tempting as it may be to instantly dismiss as fictitious these details that were added to Leontii's later *zhitiia*, Kliuchevskii notes that there was a Rostov Chronicle, which has since been lost, that contained information about the region from the period in which Leontii is said to have been converting the inhabitants.[39] It is entirely possible that many of the facts were taken from this source, and thus could be quite accurate.

All the more reason, then, to wonder why the *zhitiia* do not all describe Leontii's death at the hands of pagan residents of Rostov. Mikhail Tolstoi cites an early document written by the bishop of Vladimir, noting that Leontii was "the third Russian martyr for the faith," after the two Variags (the father and son, killed by pagan inhabitants of Rus', whom we met previously).[40] Why would such critical information have been omitted from accounts of Leontii's life? It could of course be that Bishop Simon of Vladimir was in error, confusing Leontii with someone else; or perhaps he was using the term *martyr* in a metaphorical sense—as did John Chrysostom, whom we saw in the previous chapter equating a life filled with penitential sacrifice and the practice of virtue to literal martyrdom. It would seem that at a minimum, the most basic facts written about Bishop Leontii are highly questionable; yet it appears that his canonization as a saint was based on these same questionable facts.[41]

To cite an even more extreme case, the multiple *zhitiia* written about the martyr Saint Merkurii, the patron of Smolensk, appear to have in themselves constituted the justification for declaring him a saint; but their accuracy is so dubious that it is unclear whether a person named Merkurii even lived in Smolensk at the time he was supposedly martyred. Merkurii is said to have been killed in battle against the Tatars in 1238/9, after having triumphantly led the people of Smolensk in the fight against them. A church sacristan, praying in the cathedral of Smolensk before this battle took place, saw a vision of the Blessed Virgin, who ordered him to find Merkurii and tell him that he was to engage the Tatars in battle—which he did.

While a *sluzhba* appears to have existed from an earlier period, the *zhitiia* written about Merkurii date no earlier than the sixteenth century—in other words, a good 250 years or more after the events allegedly transpired. The variations in the versions of the account found in the different *zhitiia* are so dramatic as to immediately call into question virtually every aspect of the story. Kadlubovskii does a brilliant job of analyzing what he finds to be two families of *zhitiia*, presenting fundamentally different life stories of Merkurii and written in markedly different tones.[42] One issue that instantly gives one pause is the fact that November 24, the feast-day of Merkurii of Smolensk, also happens to be the feast-day of a much earlier martyr with the same name, Saint Mercurius of

Caesarea, who died in 250 AD. Coincidentally, Mercurius was also victorious in battle, after seeing a vision of Saint Michael encouraging him to fight. Kadlubovskii notes that some sources assert that the saint of Smolensk was killed on the same day as the earlier Mercurius, a claim that appears highly improbable at best—a more likely explanation being that details from the accounts of the lives of the two military men were at some later point conflated into one.[43]

Or need we even assume that the second Merkurii existed at all? For even the general description of the battle against the Tatars in Smolensk is questionable. As Kadlubovskii points out, none of the chronicles even mentions a battle between the Tatars and the city of Smolensk during the period in which Merkurii is alleged to have fought.[44] And writing about the history of the city of Smolensk, Golubovskii notes that the Tatars do not appear to have approached Smolensk earlier than the mid- or late 1200s, and that Smolensk seems to have been independent from Tatar rule until that time.[45]

At the same time, the variations between the earlier and later versions of *zhitiia* about Merkurii would indicate that the original story was subsequently embellished with details taken from the *acta* of Mercurius of Caesarea. In the later accounts, for example, the Blessed Virgin does not appear to the sacristan and give him a message for Merkurii; rather, the sacristan becomes a purely secondary character as Merkurii has the vision himself—just as the original Mercurius personally saw an apparition of Saint Michael, urging him to fight. A dramatic addition, definitely not mentioned in the earlier versions, is the appearance before the townspeople of Smolensk of the martyred Merkurii, coming to them carrying his own head, which had been cut off by the Tatars.[46]

In short, such problems abound with the *zhitiia* written about Merkurii of Smolensk as to raise the serious possibility that he is an entirely fictional character, whose "biography" was gradually pieced together from various events understood to have taken place in the life of Saint Mercurius of Caesarea. The likelihood that this was the case is strengthened when we see that it was only in the sixteenth or seventeenth century that he appears to have been declared the patron of Smolensk, hundreds of years after his alleged martyrdom.[47] By that point, obviously, eyewitnesses who could have confirmed—or denied—the circumstances surrounding his life and death were long gone, and it would have been a relatively simple matter for even the best-intentioned biographers to have become confused about the historical facts. This may very well be a case in which the Russian church canonized someone as having died a martyr's death, when in fact he might never have even lived. We thus have here an instance in which a saint was apparently canonized, based entirely on the accounts of his life as contained in his *zhitiia*—yet those *zhitiia* clearly raise grave questions of factual accuracy.

c. *Elevatio/Translatio* of Relics, and Two Requirements that Subsequently Develop from It

As we saw in the first chapter, in the first millennium, when the church declared that a deceased Christian was a saint, the body was located (if possible) and moved to a church or chapel where it could be properly venerated. This practice continued unchanged in Russia, where, as in the church elsewhere, the date of a saint's *translatio* often became the saint's feast-day.

Golubinskii notes rightly that in the Russian church in past centuries, sometimes the body was moved before the canonization actually took place; while on other occasions the *translatio* took place at the same time as the person was formally declared a saint, or even afterward.[48] Since the Russian church learned this practice from the Greeks, we may presume that their motivation for moving a saint's body was likewise originally the same: the church intended to honor this saint by moving the remains into a place of worship, where they would be venerated by the faithful.

Rather quickly, however, we find other conditions for canonization established in Russia: the need for miracles, and the requirement that the saint's body be incorrupt. On the surface, these might seem to have little directly to do with the original practice of formally transferring a new saint's physical remains to a church or chapel. But if we examine the circumstances leading to the canonizations of individual Russian saints, it will eventually become clear that these obligatory conditions grew imperceptibly out of the original practice of *translatio*.

For on many occasions, once a body was transferred to a church building, miracles began to take place near the new tomb. As we saw in the preceding chapter, the desire for miracles was not the reason for the *translatio*; the purpose of transferring remains was to pay the person greater honor. But historical documentation from Russia indicates that miracles were often an unintended consequence of it. It appears that very soon in the life of the church in Russia, cause and effect became inverted: bodies of potential saints began to be moved into churches or chapels *in order to see* whether any miracles would take place—and if they did, the miracles became the grounds for declaring such a person a saint. And so miracles, in and of themselves, ultimately became regarded as a requirement for canonization.

i. Requirement 1: The Need for Miracles

Russian historians agree that the Russian church has traditionally considered miracles an absolutely critical component—a sine qua non—of the process of recognizing someone as a saint. If we consider that the church in

Russia was from the very beginning emulating the church in Greece, we might naturally conclude that this emphasis on miracles must have traditionally been a necessary condition for canonization in the Greek church as well. But as can be seen from the established criteria for sainthood discussed in chapter 1, there is no specific historical evidence extant today to indicate that this was ever in fact the case in the first thousand years of Christianity, in Greece or anywhere else. In the case of martyrs in particular, traditional theology suggests that the very fact of martyrdom constitutes sufficient proof that the martyr merits veneration as a saint.

It is, in fact, rather misleading to suggest (as Russian church historians generally tend to do) that the Greek church could have been doing anything substantively different in the first millennium than were the Latins with regard to canonization of saints. As noted previously, external elements of the liturgical ceremonies in the East may certainly have been altogether unlike those celebrated in the West; but this should not be taken to imply that the theological understanding of either sainthood or canonization was significantly different in different areas of the Christian world.

Be that as it may, Golubinskii theorizes (without, however, providing any concrete examples whatsoever) that the need for miracles may have developed in the Greek church at some point in the eleventh century, as the number of patriarchs of Constantinople—non-martyrs, in other words—who were being recognized as saints was on the increase, while simultaneously the incidence of martyrdom was decreasing. Miracles were, after all, a surefire way to establish that a deceased member of the hierarchy was indeed able to intercede with God for the faithful on earth, and so they quickly became a measure of holiness.[49] This was not inconsistent with the notion that a Christian's sanctity was sometimes demonstrated by an ability to work miracles even in life. If miracle-working was an indication of holiness while on earth, it follows logically that miracles after death should be similarly accepted as divine evidence that a person is truly a saint.

True, Golubinskii's unsubstantiated claim that by the eleventh century the church in Greece had come to require miracles before canonization pertains specifically to *non*-martyrs. But even if we accept his unsubstantiated thesis, it still would not explain why Russian historians in general assert that miracles have traditionally been a requirement for canonization, period—regardless of whether the potential saint died a martyr's death.[50] Furthermore, the fact remains, so far as we can conclude from the historical sources still extant from the first thousand years of Christianity, that the praxis on this particular point was the same in both the East and the West. Therefore, if the church in Russia has in fact traditionally required miracles as a precondition for all canonizations, even those of martyrs, it would appear that this constitutes a shift *away* from the established tradition of the preceding thousand years of Christianity. What has been the traditional process of the Russian church with regard to martyrs and miracles, and how did it develop?

Before we can even begin to resolve this issue, a procedural question immediately arises with regard to the acceptance of miracles as evidence of sainthood in the Russian church. Did they constitute subsequent *corroboration* of the church's finding that a now-deceased Christian either had suffered martyrdom, or in some other manner had demonstrated exceptional holiness during life that would warrant canonization? Or did miracles, in and of themselves, lead the church in Russia to declare that someone should be considered a saint, regardless of the circumstances surrounding the person's life and death?

As already noted, there are no official documents in existence that could answer this question by providing an explicit description of the Russian canonization process in centuries past but we ought to be able to establish what it was by examining some concrete historical examples. If perchance we can determine that, historically, Russian martyrs were recognized as saints only after miracles had occurred through their intercession, and that martyrs have never been publicly accepted as such without miracles, then we can reasonably conclude that in Russia, martyrdom per se has, for whatever reason, traditionally been considered an insufficient rationale for canonization. On the other hand, if we can find instances where martyrs have been officially recognized without any known miracles performed through their intercession, it would seem logical to deduce that in Russia, as was the case in the first millennium of Christianity in other parts of the world, veneration as a saint was justified simply by martyrdom itself. Unfortunately, however, we immediately encounter difficulties, because in general, the actual basis for canonizing someone in Russia who had died a violent death (which may or may not have met the standard definition of martyrdom that had, by that time, been well established throughout the Christian world) is historically unclear.

The princes Boris and Gleb, probably the most prominent martyr-saints about whom there is much historical information still extant, are a case in point. As surprising as it may seem, Russian historians cannot agree on the original grounds that led to their canonization in the earliest decades of Russian Christianity.

At first glance, as we have already seen above, the reason they are regarded as saints appears obvious: their patient and meek acceptance of death at the hands of their brother Sviatopolk was the ultimate demonstration of Christian virtue, indicating as it did their willingness to accept suffering and even death for the sake of maintaining peace. Certainly this is the traditionally accepted understanding of the underlying rationale for the official recognition by the Russian church of Boris and Gleb as saints.

But the question arises as to the canonical status of yet another brother who apparently also died under essentially identical circumstances. Sviatoslav was also killed by agents of Sviatopolk, during the same period, and was buried in Hungary near the site of his murder. Yet he never has been regarded as a saint. Why not?

Golubinskii makes what he plainly feels is a safe assumption. He states that the reason for the distinction is that miracles were soon taking place near the tombs of Boris and Gleb in Russia, while God did not choose to glorify Sviatoslav in the same way, for at his place of burial, "somewhere in the Carpathian mountains," there were no miracles being reported. In other words, Boris and Gleb were really declared to be saints *not* because they were *strastoterptsy*, but because they were miracle-workers. Golubinskii admits honestly that they were only canonized because of the miracles, and not because of their virtuous attitude in the face of impending death—although he quickly points out that God only worked the miracles because they had indeed been so patient in their sufferings.[51]

There is, however, no hard historical evidence whatsoever to explicitly justify this interpretation of events, and Suvarov draws a totally different conclusion from the very same facts. Scornfully dismissing Golubinskii's explanation, Suvarov instead presumes that Boris and Gleb were proclaimed to be saints solely because of their patient acceptance of death—and that Sviatoslav, in contrast, was not canonized because his attitude toward his own impending death was substantially different. Sviatoslav is not a saint because he did not demonstrate that he was truly a *strastoterpets*.[52] Neither author, however, is able to provide clear-cut historical documentation to support his interpretation of the known facts; and thus we can see that it is not possible to determine with any certitude the precise reason that originally motivated the Russian church to declare Boris and Gleb, but not Sviatoslav, to be saints.

And this is not an isolated case. Barsukov documents the circumstances leading to the canonization of the monk Adrian of Poshekhonie.[53] In 1550, Adrian was killed by robbers, and his body thrown on the bank of a nearby river.[54] Subsequently he was buried by pious Christians under the floor of a "deserted church." Despite the isolated location, healings began to take place near Adrian's grave, and word of the miracles spread to other cities, leading sick people to flock to the site.

In 1626, these events evidently came to the attention of Patriarch Filaret in Moscow. He ordered the head of Adrian's monastery to celebrate a *panikhida* (or requiem) for Adrian, and then to move his remains into the monastery church—to carry out, in other words, a *translatio*.

Adrian has been described as a *prepodobnomuchenik*, or monk-martyr.[55] If we apply the traditional definition of martyr in this case, this terminology would naturally suggest that the reason for Adrian's violent death was his Christian faith. There is, however, no indication in Russian historical accounts that he was killed specifically for his beliefs; the only passing reference to his death indicates that the killers were robbers.[56] On the contrary, it appears quite clear that the motivation for Adrian's formal *translatio* in 1626 was actually the miracles occurring at his original burial place. Adrian was declared a saint not specifically because of his manner of life or the reasons for his unnatural death, but because of subsequent miracles—indicating that in this case, miracles did not serve to corroborate an already existing cult of a martyr; they were actually the driving factor in this process.

If the circumstances surrounding Adrian's canonization were typical, this would indicate that as a rule, the *translatio* of a new saint, martyr or not, followed reports of miracles at his original burial site. But one can find other examples that suggest that this was not necessarily an invariable pattern. In 1246 Prince Mikhail Chernigovskii, along with a nobleman named Theodor, were martyred for the faith by the Mongols, after refusing to worship the Mongols' pagan idols.[57] Their bodies were then taken back to Chernigov, where miracles began to take place immediately afterward.

One might question whether the transfer from Orda to Chernigov constituted a formal *translatio*, or was simply a return of their remains to their hometown, as might have been done with the body of anyone who had died abroad. Given the public and clear-cut circumstances surrounding their deaths, it appears that they were accepted instantly as martyrs, which might lead us to conclude that their return to Chernigov was carried out with some degree of religious ceremony. If we accept that their transfer constituted a *translatio*, this would indicate that in their case, the miracles did not precipitate their *translatio*; rather, they followed it.[58] Put differently, Mikhail and Theodor appear to have been accepted immediately as saints, without any miracles preceding that recognition. It would thus seem that historically, in Russia it was possible to become a saint without miracles, if one were martyred.

An even clearer example is Avramii of Bulgaria, who was killed in 1229 by pagan Bulgars because of his Christian faith. The chronicles provide a detailed account of the transfer of his remains "with great honor" from Bulgaria to Vladimir in 1230. The description of the formal ceremony, involving members of both the Russian hierarchy and the nobility, indicates that without a doubt this should be understood as a formal *translatio*; yet the narrator does not mention any specific reason that motivated Russian Christians to transfer him to a church in their own territory.[59] One can only wonder whether miracles had taken place at his grave in Bulgaria, perhaps among Russian Christians there, prompting his transfer to Russian territory.[60] If so, it is curious that the chronicler, in his otherwise detailed account, fails to mention them. If not, Avramii would constitute an example of a martyr whose *translatio* took place without any miracles preceding it.

While the *zhitiia* of Russian martyrs frequently make mention of miracles taking place near their burial-place, they are generally silent both about the specific nature of the miracles, and as to whether an attempt was made by ecclesiastical authorities to verify them. Generally, as we have just seen, accounts simply make reference to generic "miracles," without even describing their nature; presumably, however, they usually involved otherwise inexplicable medical cures.

Iakov Chernorizets, the presumed eleventh-century author of the "Tale of the Holy Martyrs Boris and Gleb," recounts several miracles that took place before their official canonization at the tomb of Boris. These included the healing of a crippled man who prayed at the tomb for a cure, and then was visited by the two brothers in a dream, whereupon his leg was healed. A blind man suddenly regained his sight after praying at the tomb as well, and the author suggests that it was this particular miracle, news of which eventually reached the metropolitan, that prompted the establishment of the saints' feast-day on July 24, the day of Boris's murder.[61]

Count Mikhail Tolstoi, in his nineteenth-century account of the history of Rostov, collected some descriptions of miracles that took place at the tomb of Leontii of Rostov. These include forty cases in one month, at the time of the consecration of the new cathedral in 1408, in which the blind, deaf, lame, and other sick were miraculously healed. Another incident termed miraculous concerned a servant of the prince, who by means of a false oath attempted to seize church property. Tolstoi quotes earlier sources as saying that the servant "was miraculously punished" and forced to return the property. The nature of the miraculous punishment was not mentioned.[62]

How were these alleged miracles verified—or was there any attempt to verify them at all? Golubinskii, with his characteristic tendency toward sweeping generalities, asserts that even from the first centuries of Christianity in Russia, a part of the process to declare someone a saint involved interviewing witnesses to these alleged miracles, so as to determine their authenticity.[63] While this certainly seems logical enough, he does not offer a single concrete example in support of this statement.

Kliuchevskii rightly points out that there are in fact extant documents indicating that when Moscow's Metropolitan Makarii convoked his 1549 synod (which will be addressed in greater detail below), canonizing an entire group of Russian saints, the process included among other things compiling accounts of the miracles performed.[64] Since the accounts of the actual process itself have been lost, however, we cannot determine how exactly these reports of miracles were documented.

We can, however, get an inkling of the manner and degree to which miracles were investigated in past centuries from a tiny handful of still extant reports of miracles pertaining to cases subsequent to Makarii's synod. For example, Grand Prince Mikhail Iaroslavich of Tver, killed by the Tatars in 1318, was popularly regarded as a martyr, although his official recognition as a saint did not take place until centuries later.[65] In 1634, the local archbishop ordered Mikhail's tomb to be opened, whereupon the gravedigger declared that his hand had been miraculously healed. The archbishop, together with his synod, then caused the relics to be moved into a church, and the sick began to come to Mikhail's tomb to pray for a cure. True, we do not know what prompted the archbishop's original decision to open Mikhail's grave; but the fact that he and his synod reacted to the grave-digger's healing by moving the body yet again would suggest that, at a minimum, inquiries about the healing were made and the hierarchy found the claim credible.[66]

Numerous miraculous healings were reported at the tomb of the official/unofficial saint Kirill of Vel'sk (whose death and subsequent veneration will be addressed in greater detail below), over a period of several decades in the sixteenth century. These include at least one that, the chronicler specifically notes, was witnessed by "the priest and people" present in the church when a blind old woman was praying beside Kirill's tomb—and suddenly regained her sight.[67]

More recently, we can see that efforts were being made to examine purported miracles before seeking to canonize the person at whose tomb they allegedly occurred. In 1916, when the Holy Governing Synod had already displaced the patriarchate as the chief governing organ of the Russian church for nearly two centuries (about which more presently), it examined the case for canonizing Iosif of Astrakhan, who had been martyred in the seventeenth century. The dossier submitted to the synod included the proceedings of a special eparchial commission established to investigate the accounts of miracles that had taken place near his tomb.[68] Clearly attempts were being made by the church to verify that claims of healings were in fact authentic.

Regardless of the authenticity of the miracles that took place, one fact seems incontrovertible: historically, the mere fact of a person's martyrdom was insufficient, in and of itself, for canonization in Russia. In practice, miracles—real or at least perceived—were a necessary condition for even a martyr to be formally declared a saint by the Russian church.[69] As we have already seen, this requirement represents an added procedural element with no basis in early Christian tradition, and which is at odds with the traditional Christian theological understanding of what martyrdom really means.

ii. REQUIREMENT 2: INCORRUPT RELICS

As with the requirement of miracles, a virtually identical historical uncertainty exists with regard to the incorruptibility of a Russian saint's remains. If we try to find an actual requirement that someone's body had to be found incorrupt before canonization could take place in the church of the first millennium, whether in the East or West, we will search in vain. And this finding is completely consistent with theology from the very beginning of the church, for as we have already seen in chapter 1, theology was always focused on the interior motives of the potential saint—and in the case of martyrs, also on the factual circumstances surrounding their violent death. Additionally, as is obvious with many of the earliest martyrs, some of whom were discussed in the preceding chapter, their bodies could not possibly have been preserved incorrupt if they were burned (as was the case with Polycarp of Smyrna), or even lost entirely (as happened to those martyrs from Nicomedia, whose bodies, according to Eusebius, were cast into the sea). Thus it is undeniable that incorrupt relics were not a necessary precondition of canonization in the first thousand years of the church's existence.

Yet at some point early on in Russian history, incorrupt remains became obligatory for canonization, regardless of whether the person was a martyr or not.[70] The discovery that the mortal remains had been miraculously preserved constituted confirmation by God that the person in question was indeed a saint. It appears, in reality, to be nothing other than a species or subset of those miracles, discussed above, that had soon become a mandatory precondition for canonization in Russia.

And exactly the same procedural question arises with the issue of incorruptibility as we faced with regard to miracles: does the discovery that a potential saint's remains have been preserved incorrupt constitute additional *corroboration* that he merits canonization? Or has the Russian church moved to declare people to be saints, based principally on the finding that their bodies are incorrupt? As we saw before with miracles, there is no historical evidence that explicitly documents the procedure and directly describes the role that incorruptibility placed in saint-making in centuries past; but we can look to concrete examples involving incorruptibility in order to establish how the procedure worked in actual practice.

Bishop Leontii of Rostov, martyred in the eleventh century by pagans, was buried in the cathedral church of Rostov. During construction work there in 1164, his grave was opened and his remains were discovered to be incorrupt.[71] Popular veneration of Leontii appears to have dated not from the time of his death and burial, but rather from the finding of his incorrupt remains.[72] Vasiliev notes that the finding of incorrupt remains was the initial catalyst for the ultimate canonization of a number of martyrs and other saints. The discovery spurred the faithful to revere a person as a saint, ultimately leading the hierarchy to confer official recognition as such.[73]

The case of Kirill of Vel'sk, who drowned in the fifteenth century, seems similar. A local woman was visited by a vision of an "unknown young man" who told her that his body was lying on the bank of the river. Clergy and people found an old tomb that had floated to the river bank, and they carried it into a church. Kirill's tomb was opened and his body was found to be incorrupt, even though "they thought to find only bones" after so many years. Eventually his identity was determined, while a cult to him appears to have begun immediately—based on both the apparition of the young man and Kirill's incorrupt remains.[74]

Golubinskii documents the extreme case of an entirely unknown man whose body was found floating in the river near the village of Borovich at some time in the early sixteenth century. His identity, and the circumstances surrounding his death, were never determined through normal means; but the deceased soon appeared in a dream to an inhabitant of Borovich, stating that his name was Yakov. A local legend gradually developed about Yakov, and his remains were placed in a chapel especially constructed for them, where the residents of Borovich habitually came to pray. When miracles began to take place at Yakov's tomb, the archbishop of Novgorod sent a team of clergy to investigate events—an investigation that involved examining not only the authenticity of the alleged miracles, but also the state of Yakov's physical remains as well. Among their findings, the commission of clerics made a point of describing in macabre detail the discovery that much of Yakov's body was still intact, a fact that seems to have made a significant impression. Apparently satisfied that all was in order, the archbishop obtained from the metropolitan a decree stating that after celebrating a *panikhida* for Yakov, his remains, which at that point were buried underground, were to be moved to a shrine aboveground, inside a church. This was done in 1544.[75]

While this seems rather clearly to have constituted a canonization of the mysterious Yakov, his true identity and the facts pertaining to his life and death remain entirely unknown. The veneration given to him by the local people, and the subsequent actions taken by the archbishop and metropolitan, appear from the evidence to have been entirely motivated by the fact that his body did not completely decay as one would have expected, and by miracles taking place in the vicinity of his tomb. It would seem safe to conclude that we have here a case of a person being declared a saint based not on his life, and/or death, but on miracles and perceived incorruptibility.

When Russian historical accounts claim that a saint's remains were found to be incorrupt, what exactly does the term mean? While they clearly regarded this finding as miraculous, it appears that these "incorrupt" bodies had in fact undergone some degree of mummification.[76] This understandably may have struck believers in centuries past as an event outside of the normal bounds of nature; but of course we know today that the process of mummification need not involve a miracle and was presumably due to entirely natural conditions.[77]

C. Authority: Who Makes the Decision to Canonize a Saint?

Historically, there is no single, consistent answer to the question of exactly who in the Russian church has the authority to determine in an official, formal sense that a deceased person is to be venerated as a saint. Rather, the thousand-year history of the church in Russia has seen a series of shifts in the roles of various levels of church hierarchs with regard to canonization. A look at events in the church at several key points in this history will show that in various periods, different members of the hierarchy had the ultimate say. To fully understand the process, it is therefore necessary to examine several different stages in church history, where ecclesiological issues played a role in determining who exactly had the right to canonize and why. In so doing, we can also understand more fully the reasons that the current process (which will be addressed below) has taken the form it has today.

1. The Earliest Russian Martyrs in the First Centuries in the Life of the Church

We have already established that the originally spontaneous decision of the early Christian faithful to venerate a deceased person as a martyr/saint gradually gave way of necessity to a more consistent and formalized process of official canonization. The authority to make these decisions fell to the church hierarchy, who alone could formally add a new martyr to the ever-increasing calendar of saints (although we have also seen in chapter 1 a number of civil rulers in the East who clearly believed that their position as secular leaders allowed them to make regulations in this regard as well).

Thus, while the earliest liturgical calendars contain the names of martyrs who were never formally canonized by the church hierarchy—since there was as yet no such thing as a process for declaring someone a saint—the names of those saints who were subsequently added to the calendar in later centuries were presumably, at least in theory, put there by someone recognized as having authority to do so. In newly Christianized Russia, as was discussed at the beginning of this chapter, the church received its calendar from the Greeks, and only later were Russian bishops themselves establishing feast-days for new saints, whose names were then added to the calendar. The Russian church, therefore, simply continued the practice already established throughout the Christian world during the first millennium; and within a few generations of the conversion of Rus', new martyrs and other saints were being included in local calendars by individual bishops, with the participation of their local synods.

While the canonization of saints was thus largely at the local level, relatively soon after the Christianization of Rus' several saints were canonized whom the metropolitan decreed were to be venerated by the entire Russian church. The best-known of these were of course Boris and Gleb, the actual date of whose canonization is not known—although it appears that it was not long after their deaths that Metropolitan Ioann I wrote the *sluzhba* for their feast-day, which was established during the reign of their brother Iaroslav.[78] Theirs was not merely a local canonization; rather, they were saints for all of Rus', and their feast-day was to be celebrated throughout the entire church.

Leontii of Rostov, whom we have met previously, was canonized in 1190 by the local bishop Ioann. The chronicles note that this was done "with the blessing of Metropolitan Theodor," but this need not be taken as an indication that the Russian metropolitan necessarily had to approve of the saints who were canonized by local bishops.[79] It may, however, be another example, albeit less clear than in the case of Boris and Gleb, of a new saint who was intended by the Russian hierarchy to be venerated church-wide.

It is important to note that there does not appear to have ever been a requirement imposed on Russia by the patriarchate of Constantinople that new Russian saints be canonized directly by the Ecumenical Patriarch, or at least submitted for his advance approval. History records a single instance of such a submission in 1339, when Metropolitan Theognost of Moscow requested that the patriarch of Constantinople give his approbation to the canonization of his predecessor, Metropolitan Peter of Moscow, who had died in 1326. The reply from Constantinople indicated that while the patriarch did indeed approve, his consent was not in fact necessary, as Russian bishops could themselves establish new saints on their own.[80] This case of Saint Peter, therefore, hardly constituted a precedent—and still less does it illustrate a typical example—for turning to an ecclesiastical authority higher than the local bishop for the canonization of new saints.[81]

On the other hand, however, while the local bishop had the power to establish new saints, who were to be venerated within his territory, the influence of the lay faithful in Russia was not entirely diminished. As can already be seen from some of the historical examples illustrated above, it was generally the Russian laity who first began to venerate someone as a martyr or other saint; official recognition by their bishop subsequently followed. While popular veneration certainly did not constitute an assurance that a deceased Christian would automatically be canonized, it definitely was the typical impetus for Russian bishops eventually to act.[82] As the Bollandist Peeters phrased it so succinctly, the Russian church confirms the cult of a saint; it does not institute it.[83]

This is the reason that in Russia even today, centuries later, there are many persons unofficially revered as "saints" who were never actually canonized as such by the Russian hierarchy. The laity may very well establish among themselves a popular cult to a particular deceased person; they may pray at his tomb for his intercession and hold his relics in high esteem. And it may happen that the clergy are aware of these expressions of popular piety and permit them to continue. But the mere tolerance of such an unofficial cult has not, in and of itself, ever constituted canonization. Rather, such persons may be considered to be saints, among the Christian faithful of a certain locale, but in these cases it is an appellation with no official weight whatsoever.[84]

But while Russian bishops have traditionally tolerated these unofficial cults of persons who are not actually canonized saints, this does not mean that the laity have simply been permitted to venerate every person they wished. The hierarchy have, on occasion, intervened to correct what they perceived to be erroneous cults, and have prevented (or at least tried to prevent) the faithful from continuing to pray for intercession to persons whose veneration the Russian bishops believe is unjustified. A particularly complicated example of this is Kirill Vel'skii of Novgorod, who was drowned in the Vaga River in the fifteenth century while fleeing from his master, a deputy of Novgorod, who was trying to kill him.[85] It is unclear whether the laity of that city regarded him as a martyr (the deputy's reason for wanting to kill Kirill is not known), but there is no other obvious fact about his manner of life that would explain what motivated the people to bury Kirill's body in the cemetery church. It was in that church, as was discussed in a previous section, that many miracles occurred; and when it was destroyed by fire in the seventeenth century, Kirill's remains were moved to an altar inside another, larger church.[86]

It may be, although nothing certain is known, that in the interval a feast-day had been established in Novgorod for Kirill; it is otherwise difficult to understand why his remains would have been moved to a place of honor in a different church if he was not already being venerated in some way. It is possible that he had been formally canonized by the local bishop, although no evidence of it exists today; but it is equally possible that Kirill's cult had always been of an unofficial, informal nature.[87] Barsukov notes that a *sluzhba* had evidently been written in Kirill's honor (which would suggest at a minimum that the hierarchy was somehow involved), but he subsequently ceased to be honored in this manner, at about the time when the region, formerly a part of Novgorod, became the separate city of Vel'sk in 1780.[88] Golubinskii posits that the clergy of Vel'sk discontinued celebration of his feast-day because its original establishment had been "illegal."[89]

The lay faithful, however, objected to this perceived demotion of Kirill, and to placate the populace, an altar was dedicated to Kirill in the cemetery church, which had previously been burned down. His feast-day is listed in the Russian liturgical calendar to this day.

The one fact that is undeniable here is that the history of Kirill's veneration is fraught with uncertainties. His actual status as a saint—still less as a martyr—is simply impossible to determine today. Kirill's problematic situation thus constitutes a good example of the complex levels of veneration in the Russian church and of the relationship (and occasional tension) between the lay faithful and the hierarchy.

Golubinskii acknowledges frankly the historical difficulty in determining whether many persons venerated as saints from centuries past were ever actually canonized.[90] While the lack of evidence for a formal canonization by the local bishop long ago might lead one to conclude that it simply never happened, it is equally possible that a bishop did indeed officially canonize a person as a saint, and that the relevant documentation has since been lost.

2. The Unprecedented Canonization Councils of Metropolitan Makarii, 1547 and 1549

In the sixteenth century, however, a unique pair of events occurred in Moscow, documentation from which is still readily available. Metropolitan Makarii, only five years after becoming the leader of the Russian church in 1542, convened a *sobor*, or council, at which he solemnly canonized all at once a number of Russian saints for the entire church. Two years later, in 1549, Makarii canonized yet another group of saints at a second *sobor* convoked for the same purpose.

By this point, Russia had been officially Christian for over five hundred years. Its hierarchy had already been establishing feasts for new saints for generations, adding them to their local calendars for generations—without the direct involvement of the metropolitan in Kiev, and later in Moscow. What, then, led Makarii to take the action that he did?

Golubinskii is surely not alone in suggesting that the metropolitan's decision to undertake these group canonizations was politically motivated.[91] Because Constantinople had fallen less than a century before and the doctrine of Moscow as the Third Rome had become popular among Russian believers, could very well have been intended simply as a means by which Moscow could manifest its authority before the rest of the Christian world in a very public way.

But we can only speculate about Markarii's reasons for these canonizations, for he simply provided a list of saints whose feasts were now to be celebrated on particular dates, without explaining his motivations. All of the new saints without exception were described as "miracle-workers," which suggests that they were being declared saints not because of their manner of life, but because it had been determined that miracles had been performed at their tombs after death. This is entirely in keeping with the historical evidence surrounding the canonization of Russian saints at various other periods in history, indicating that miracles often seemed to be the primary factor motivating the Russian church to declare someone a saint.

According to the official decree, fourteen of Makarii's feasts were to be observed "everywhere," throughout the entire territory of the Russian church.[92] There were nine others, however, which were only to be observed locally: Bishop Arsenii of Tver, for example, was to be commemorated on March 2 in Tver, and only Ustiug was to commemorate Saints Prokopii and Ioann of Ustiug.[93]

Interestingly, on this list of twenty-three saints, only five names are completely new, including the Saint Ioann just mentioned; all the others were already being commemorated in the liturgy in their local churches.[94] This implies, therefore, that the fourteen now to be commemorated by the entire church were existing saints whose cult was now being extended church-wide—a phenomenon already seen in the earliest calendars of the church in the first centuries of its existence and thus consistent with previous practice in other parts of the Christian world.

But his pronouncement regarding the nine local saints, most of whom were already commemorated locally, raises questions. Since they had previously been canonized by local bishops and were already being venerated in their respective locales, what was the purpose of a declaration by the metropolitan of Moscow that basically repeated what had previously been done by the competent authorities at a lower level? There is nothing in Makarii's declaration that explicitly or even implicitly suggests that the procedure for canonizing saints in Russia was being changed, and that henceforth the approval of the metropolitan was also required even for local canonizations. That no precedent was being set for routine canonization synods in the future is likewise seen in the fact that no *sobor* was ever convened again by the hierarch in Moscow for the express purpose of canonizing saints, as Makarii had done.

Nevertheless, in the opinion of some scholars, subsequent practice indicates that from this point in history, all new saints, including those proposed by local bishops for veneration in only one locale, required approbation from Moscow. As Vasiliev noted (to cite only one example):

> Beginning from the time of these Synods, the right to conduct a canonization passed exclusively to the highest central authority of the Russian church, which until the end of the sixteenth century was comprised of the Metropolitan with his Council, and from the end of that century (1589) was the Patriarch. Until the Synods of Makarii the right of canonizing continued to belong to local bishops not only de jure, but also de facto . . . in the whole period from the second half of the sixteenth century and through the entire seventeenth century, we never meet a single case of a canonization of a saint conducted by a local bishop.[95]

Three cases of martyrs who were canonized not long after Makarii's synods would appear to constitute good examples of this new practice. In 1592, Metropolitan Hermogen of Kazan asked Patriarch Iov of Moscow to recognize three new martyr-saints. Ioann was a Russian from Nizhny Novgorod who was imprisoned and subsequently killed by the Tatars in 1529; Stefan and Petr were converted Tatars who were martyred by their fellow Muslims in 1552. An *ukaz*, or decree, from the patriarch constituted approval of the metropolitan's request.[96]

On a practical level, thanks to a near-total dearth of evidence, what was routinely happening during the post-Makarii period is far from clear. But it seems that while local bishops could investigate potential new saints and conclude that they were worthy of canonization, this could no longer done without approval from Moscow. In other words, to the already existing components of the saint-making process there was now added a new requirement, the approbation of the supreme authority of the Russian church—regardless of whether the new saint was to be venerated throughout the entire church in Russia, or only locally.

If we assume that this was in fact the case, then this practice was presumably consistent with the case of the twelfth-century canonization of Bishop Leontii of Rostov, which we saw previously: while Leontii was declared a saint by the local bishop, the canonization had also received the approbation of the metropolitan in Moscow. Thus both the investigation of the possible saint and the canonization ceremony itself were still actually being handled by the local hierarch; but before the case could proceed to its final stages, the supreme authority of the Russian church had also to give his consent.

One now encounters periodic formal publications by Moscow of new *ustavy*, or officially issued liturgical books, which by definition included a permanent calendar of all saints who were to be commemorated on specific dates. In the *ustav* issued by Moscow in about 1634, for example, one finds instructions stipulating that on February 4, the church was to commemorate the "great martyr" Prince Georgii Vsevolodovich of Vladimir. It appears that Georgii, killed by the Tatars in the year 1238, was considered a martyr much like Mikhail Chernigovskii, who was (as we have already seen above) killed by the Tatars during the same period and under roughly the same conditions. And like Mikhail, Georgii was to be venerated as a saint not merely by one locale, but by the entire Russian church.[97]

But to complicate matters, the undeniable fact is that there are many persons from this post-Makarii period, venerated as saints in various regions of Russia, who yet were apparently never publicly approved by an *ustav* from Moscow. To cite only one of numerous examples, the youths Iakov and Ioann Meniushskie, who died near Novgorod about the year 1570 ("possibly as martyrs," according to Golubinskii), were unearthed in the following century and found to be incorrupt.[98] Their relics were moved into a church built in their honor. There is no evidence of an *ustav* ever having been issued by Moscow to declare their canonization and establish their feast-day.

If such an *ustav* were a requirement for canonization, it would thus appear that Iakov and Ioann were never approved as saints in the manner established by authorities. Yet the church housing their relics under its main altar was renovated in 1895, and an announcement of its consecration was published by the Holy Governing Synod—which in turn would suggest that the supreme authority of the Russian church saw nothing improper about venerating these two youths as saints.[99] Since their names are not found in the *True Calendar of All Russian Saints*, promulgated by the Holy Governing Synod in the early twentieth century (and discussed above), they presumably were established as local saints, only for the region around Novgorod.

If we accept the above assertion by Vasiliev, that the supreme ecclesiastical authority of the Russian church had to approve all new saints, it would appear that Iakov and Ioann are not saints and never have been. Yet there is no question that they have been venerated in Novgorod for centuries as saints.

On the other hand, if we posit that the traditional system of local canonization was still being practiced even after the synods of Makarii, we can conclude that Iakov and Ioann (among countless others) are indeed saints, although not for the entire Russian church. This would then imply, of course, that historians holding the position of Vasiliev are in error.

It is a paradox that, absent any concrete historical documentation that explicitly delineates the criteria for saint-making during this time period in Russia, it is simply impossible to resolve.

3. The Holy Governing Synod as the Supreme Authority in the Russian Church

With the reign of Tsar Peter the Great (1682–1725) came a radical overhaul of the hierarchical structure of the church in Russia. In the early 1700s the patriarchate of Moscow was effectively abolished, to be formally replaced by the Holy Governing Synod in 1721. The supreme authority in the church was now a branch of the imperial government. And it was this government department that now decided who should be canonized a saint throughout the entire Russian church.

Obviously this meant there were no more church-wide canonizations by the patriarch of Moscow—since there was no patriarch. But apart from this very definite shift in competence, the actual substance of the process for the canonization of saints remained essentially unchanged. A local bishop would submit to the synod a dossier containing an account of the proposed saint's life (a *zhitie*, in other words), outlining the candidate's life and virtues. And of course it was still necessary to demonstrate that the deceased Christian's remains were "incorrupt," and that miracles had occurred through the person's intercession.[100]

The synod next simply appointed a commission to examine the submitted documentation, and if they decided in the affirmative, the synod issued a formal proclamation of the new saint's inclusion on the official, universal liturgical calendar.[101] In 1820, for example, the synod canonized as a martyr the six-year-old Gavriil of Belostok. The boy had allegedly been kidnapped and killed in 1690 by a Jew, who then drained his blood as an element of a ritual murder at the time of the Jewish Passover.[102] The child's body was determined to be incorrupt, and miracles were reported at his tomb, particularly cures of sick children.[103] Gavriil's canonization took place during a period in Russia in which accusations against Jews of the ritual killing of Christians in order to use their blood to make the matzoh used in Passover celebrations, were rife; historically they may be seen to have reached their climax with the publication by Vladimir Dal' of a book purporting to document the practice in Russia.[104] Gavriil's murder is included in Dal"s lengthy list, which notes that the documentation pertaining to the court trial of his Jewish killer was subsequently destroyed in a fire.[105]

Some decades later, in 1897, the synod established a feast for the martyr Saint Isidor of Iu'rev and seventy-two others who were martyred with him in 1472.[106] Noting that the *zhitie* for these martyrs was not written until the mid-sixteenth century under Metropolitan Makarii, Russian writers raise serious questions about the accuracy of the biographical account of them, suggesting that there were political motivations underlying its composition.[107]

Apart from questions of politics, in general it seems that, procedurally, little about canonization had changed in the Russian church after the patriarchate was abolished; the requirements for determining someone to be a saint remained fundamentally the same. And the need for the supreme authority in the church to officially approve any saint who was to be venerated throughout the entire church was unchanged as well.

Part 2: From the Bolshevik Revolution in 1917 to Today

A. The Restoration of the Patriarchate and the Beginnings of a Procedural Shift

With the *sobor* of 1917–1918, the authority of the Holy Governing Synod was ended and the Moscow Patriarchate was restored. This momentous event in the life of the church more or less coincided, however, with the Bolshevik Revolution, which ushered in a wave of active persecution of the church in Russia. Semenenko-Basin traces the simultaneous chronologies of events, beginning in October 1917 with the first Russian cleric killed for his faith, the archpriest Ioann Konchurov of Tsarkoe Selo.[108] Metropolitan Vladimir of Kiev was then shot the following February, while the *sobor* was still in progress—prompting the church in Russia several weeks later to establish a new liturgical commemoration on January 25 for all the victims of the ongoing Russian religious persecution, "confessors and martyrs."

On the surface there may appear to have been nothing especially profound about establishing such a feast-day, given the violent situation; but procedurally, this decision actually reflected a radical shift in the way that Russian martyrs were determined to be saints—for establishing a feast-day to commemorate "confessors and martyrs" in the liturgy constituted just that. Obviously it was unique insofar as it essentially prepared in advance for the veneration of martyrs who were presumably going to die in the future—already establishing a day to commemorate saints-to-come, in other words—but there was also at the same time a marked departure from the requirements heretofore considered obligatory for the canonization even of martyrs: miracles and incorrupt remains. We find instead for the first time in the Russian church a document from the hierarchy clearly indicating the presumption that martyrs, *qua* martyrs, merited liturgical commemoration based on the manner of their deaths—and *not* because of wonders worked at their grave sites in subsequent years. At the same time, it should be noted that the need for a clear definition of what really constituted martyrdom was avoided, as the new martyrs were included in the same group with "confessors," and no delineation between the two categories was made.

More concrete, exterior practices were changed as well: in November 1917, a commission was established in Moscow by the *sobor* specifically to investigate the causes of new saints. At that time Patriarch Tikhon also raised the issue of a return to the pre-synodal canonization practices, which had created two categories of saints, those venerated church-wide and those commemorated only locally. Instead of the previous system of canonization by a government bureaucracy, he noted that from ancient times, the right of local canonization belonged to the eparchial bishop, while those saints who were to be venerated throughout the entire church were established as such by the *sobor* in Moscow.[109]

It seems, then, that during this brief period the process of canonizing saints (and martyrs in particular) in Russia was undergoing a significant overhaul, both in terms of the theological understanding of the importance of the act of martyrdom to the overall procedure, and also with regard to jurisdiction. But the traditional requirements were not immediately jettisoned entirely; when the martyr Saint Iosif of Astrakhan was declared a saint in April 1918,[110] the obligatory conditions of miracles and incorrupt remains were formally established to have been met.[111] The Russian church had acknowledged that martyrdom in itself could justify sainthood; but it was not yet ready to eliminate altogether the additional criteria that had been a part of the canonization process for centuries.

Under Soviet rule, the Russian church was of course unable to openly move to commemorate those clerics and lay-persons who were murdered for their faith by the Communist regime. But with the period of glasnost came greater opportunity for the Russian church to discuss more freely those who had died during the twentieth century under Soviet rule, particularly those who had perished during the persecution of Stalin in the first decades of Communist control. Had these persons died as martyrs? Should they be canonized and venerated as saints? The new openness now gave the church some chance to freely deliberate these very questions. In 1988, the Moscow Patriarchate reestablished the Commission for the Canonization of Saints, which had originally been founded under Patriarch Tikhon during the 1917–1918 *sobor*, but had understandably languished during the Soviet period.[112]

Tikhon could hardly have imagined that his statements about martyrdom, canonization praxis, and the authorities competent to canonize would eventually be applied by one of his successors to Tikhon himself. In 1989 Tikhon was canonized as one of an ongoing series of the "new martyrs and confessors" at a meeting of the local *sobor* in Moscow.[113]

The official declaration is a fascinating combination of older practices and newer ideas. For Tikhon was canonized at the same time as Iov, the first patriarch of Moscow, a non-martyr who had died in 1605. The declaration cites the "wonder-working and healings of suffering Christians, which took place near the tomb of *Sviatitel' Iov*"—in complete accord with the centuries-old practice of requiring miracles for canonization.[114] But if we were to conclude from this assertion that miracles were still a necessary criterion for every saint, the same document's discussion of the new Saint Tikhon instantly shows that this was not the case: citing among other things his pure life, service to the church, courageous steadfastness for the faith, and missionary activity, there is no mention whatsoever of any miracles taking place at his tomb after his death (or performed by Tikhon during his life, for that matter).[115] It is therefore odd that the declaration twice makes reference to both patriarchs together as *chudotvortsy*, or miracle-workers; this may simply be a misplaced use of the traditional formulation used heretofore in the canonization of saints, who normally had been found to have worked miracles. The document notes that the bodies of both men are now to be regarded as holy relics; but there is no mention of either of them being incorrupt.[116]

Other traditional components of canonization can still be found, for the Russian hierarchy declared that *zhitiia* were to be written for both new saints, and their names were to be included in the liturgical calendar for annual commemoration. It is evident that the practical effects of declaring someone a saint in the Russian church had not essentially changed; but the criteria used to reach the decision to canonize apparently had—at least in this case.

Or had they? With the collapse of the Soviet Union two years later, the canonization commission now found itself completely free to discuss the concept of martyrdom within the context of the recent Soviet persecution. Suddenly there arose the possibility of canonizing as martyrs significant numbers of Russians who had died just in the past several decades—without fear of government reprisals. For the church in Russia, it was these numerous potential cases of twentieth-century martyrdom that led the hierarchy in Moscow to reexamine both the process of canonization of saints, and also what it means exactly to die as a martyr for the faith.

1. A Sidebar: The Possibility of "Decanonization"

We have already seen earlier in this chapter that historically, if the faithful in Russia have begun to venerate as a saint someone whom the hierarchy believes should not be commemorated as such, the practice can be stopped. This is completely in keeping with those cases found in the early centuries of the church and addressed in chapter 1, in which the local bishop forbade the people from venerating martyrs/saints whose history was insufficiently known, or who in life had not been orthodox in their theological beliefs.

These cases, however, involved unofficial veneration, never formally approved by church authorities. But once the local bishop has formally declared that someone is indeed a saint and is to be commemorated in the liturgy, is it possible for either his successor or a higher-ranking member of the clergy to overrule him? In short, can a canonized saint be "de-canonized" in Russia?

Historically, this has indeed happened, and more than once. Golubinskii recounts the case of Simon of Iurevits, a non-martyr who died in 1584 and was made a saint for local veneration in 1635. His canonization, approved by Patriarch Joachim, was motivated by miracles occurring at his tomb. The matter would seem to have been settled; but in 1722, Bishop Pitirim of Nizhny Novgorod visited the monastery where Simon was buried, forbade the monks from celebrating his *sluzhba* on his established feast-day, and took Simon's *zhitie* with him for further study, indicating that he would eventually make a more definitive statement. Pitirim died in 1741 without ever having done so; but Golubinskii notes that in any case the local feast-day was never reestablished.[117]

The rationale for this action against Simon is unclear, but ecclesiastical politics were undoubtedly the motivating factor for removing Saint Anna Kashinskaia from the Russian liturgical calendar. Anna, the wife of Grand Prince Mikhail Iaroslavich (who was himself, as we have seen above, killed by the Tatars in the early 1300s and canonized as a martyr in the eighteenth century), died in 1337 and was canonized in 1650.

But Patriarch Ioachim removed Anna from the list of saints twenty-seven years later, after an investigation by a special commission had officially determined that her *zhitie* contained discrepancies; that accounts of the miracles attributed to her did not agree; and that her remains, originally declared to be incorrupt, were definitely in a state of decay.[118] In actual fact, however, the patriarchate was during this very period also dealing with the aftermath of the Nikonian reforms and the rise of the Old Believers; because Saint Anna was associated with the pre-reform liturgical practices, it was expedient to explain to the faithful that she was not to be honored.[119]

While these cases do not specifically involve martyrs, they do indicate that for the Russian church the general notion that a saint has been canonized does not necessarily carry with it an aspect of permanence. Peeters reasonably concludes that declaring someone a saint in Russia is merely "an exterior manifestation, that implies no definitive judgment categorizing the saint" as such.[120]

In the 1970s, the late Russian priest Aleksandr Men' advocated the decanonization of the martyred child Gavriil and other Russian saints who, like him, were alleged to have been killed by Jews in ritual murders. In an interview with a Jewish journalist, Men' condemned as anti-Semitic the belief in such ritual killings, noting, "I hope that these saints will be decanonized. Processes of decanonization are known in Russian Orthodoxy."[121] While there has been no move (at least publicly) to remove Gavriil and others like him from the list of Russia's saints, it is obvious that even today, one may find in Russia the understanding that a saint can be decanonized, and thus no longer a saint.

B. From the Collapse of the Soviet Union (1990) until Today

1. Theological Concept of Martyrdom Revisited

Countless Russians were murdered by the Communist regime, but of course not all of them died specifically because of their religious beliefs. Determining who should properly be considered a martyr and who should not first required a thorough discussion and final decision by the Russian church as to what martyrdom actually is. The newly restored canonization commission therefore undertook the task of tracing, for the first time, the historical development of this concept from the days of the early church, through the establishment of Christianity in Russia, and right up to the present—a continuous period of nearly two thousand years.

The resulting report was presented at a meeting of the Most Holy Synod in Moscow on March 25, 1991.[122] While the first sections, recounting the earliest persecutions of the church, summarize the development of the notion of Christian martyrdom in a way that can hardly be construed as controversial from a historical point of view, of greater interest is the commission's interpretation of the definition of a martyr as seen in the Russian church since the conversion of Rus' to Christianity a thousand years before. Consistent with tradition is the necessity of the complete orthodoxy of a martyr's religious beliefs; no heretics or schismatics can rightly be considered martyrs, for "the sin of schism is not washed away by the shedding of one's blood."[123] But the report also notes that the historical examples of Russian martyrs reveal that the church has traditionally placed an emphasis not so much on the external, formal features of martyrdom as on the internal motivation to suffer for the love of Christ. In this way, meeting the definition of martyrdom is not so dependent on external conditions, for dying a martyr's death is a higher expression of faith, hope, and love.[124] Within the parameters of this definition, the commission is able to show, first, that Russian saints who died as the result of persecutions not only by pagans (as in the first centuries of Christianity under Roman rule), but also by heretics, schismatics, and apostates have rightly been regarded traditionally as martyrs. Among others, the report singles out as examples Isidor of Iur'ev, killed by the "uniates"; Boris and Gleb, killed by apostates; and the boy Gavriil, killed by Jews—all of whom have been discussed above—and in so doing provides official confirmation that all of these did indeed die as true martyrs for the faith.

And secondly, applying this definition of martyrdom to those who died during the Soviet persecutions, the commission further asserts that victims of political violence (as opposed to that which is specifically motivated by religion) could ultimately be regarded as saints who are *strastoterptsy*. Canonizing such persons would be akin to the church's canonization of Saints Boris and Gleb, who were, the document notes, likewise victims of political warfare.[125]

In short, the commission's description of the criteria required for acknowledging that a Russian killed during the Communist period is truly a martyr is little changed from the standards applied by the church in Russia to martyrs in centuries past. And the commission has simultaneously indicated that it does not question in any way the designation as martyrs of those saints traditionally regarded by the Russian church as such.

2. The Process by Which a Martyr Is Now to Be Recognized, According to the Canonization Commission

In 1991, the canonization commission issued guidelines for local bishops wishing to canonize new saints, both martyrs and non-martyrs, at the local level.[126] Not only do they enumerate the criteria by which a potential saint is to be evaluated; but they obviously also show us that the Russian church has definitively returned to the traditional system under which some saints were canonized by the metropolitan/patriarch in Moscow for the entire church, while others were canonized by eparchial bishops for local veneration. This also happens to be the first time in the history of the Russian church that an official document has actually delineated the specific elements necessary for the canonization of a new saint (assuming, of course, that there never existed any earlier documents on the subject that have since been completely lost).

The instructions indicate that the local bishop is to gather "materials about the life and actions" of each potential new saint.[127] He is also to collect information about miracles—although the document does not suggest that miracles are a necessary condition for sainthood.

The bishop is also required to determine whether the deceased person has been and is being venerated by the people. This is in complete accord with Russian tradition since, as seen earlier in this chapter, veneration of a person by the faithful has commonly been the impetus for the local bishop to subsequently move to canonize. Evidence that someone is in fact held in reverence by the people of the locale in which he or she lived and/or is buried is therefore a significant factor in the decision to formally declare sainthood.

Additionally, a *zhitie* is to be written about the person's life, and the local bishop is also to arrange for the new saint's image to be portrayed in an official icon.[128] It should be noted that there is no mention whatsoever of the need for the body to be incorrupt, or even for it to be examined by church authorities at all.

Some of the elements contained in this text are hardly new. We have seen that miracles and *zhitiia* have been required components of canonization in the Russian church for centuries. But the repeated references to the importance of the "life and actions" of the potential new saint are anything but traditional. In a church where, on numerous occasions over the centuries, virtually unknown persons have been canonized solely because perceived miracles took place at their tombs, this emphasis on the personal life of the potential saint— mentioned in the text before miracles and other elements—is markedly new. It echoes the statements made by Patriarch Tikhon at the *sobor* taking place at the onset of the Communist persecution of the church, underlining for the first time the procedural importance of the act of martyrdom in itself, and in the process downplaying the need for external, miraculous manifestations of the person's sanctity.

And as we already saw in the case of the canonization of Patriarch Tikhon himself, so it has repeatedly happened since the end of Communism that martyrs have been canonized in Russia without any miracles whatsoever. In 1993, for example, the Moscow patriarch together with the synod formally declared that seven Russians who died during the Bolshevik uprising—including Metropolitan Vladimir of Kiev, who was, as we saw earlier, killed while the 1917– 1918 *sobor* was being held in Moscow—were to be venerated as saints by the entire church in Russia.[129] The decree specified that these new saints were to be considered martyrs. It declares that a *sluzhba* was to be composed and a *zhitie* written for each of them, and also notes the feast-day of each new saint.

The document further mentions that their remains are now to be revered as holy relics, but it makes no mention of them being incorrupt; nor is there any mention of miracles having occurred through the intercession of any of these new martyrs. Their canonization is plainly grounded in "the shedding of their blood for Christ," which appears to have constituted sufficient justification for the *sobor*'s decision.

Similar canonizations of martyrs soon followed. By far the largest mass canonization in the history of the Russian church took place in Moscow in August 2000, when the patriarch of Moscow canonized the "Assembly of Russian New Martyrs and Confessors of the Twentieth Century."[130] Over eight hundred new saints were created, including four metropolitans and 150 lay people; the common thread uniting this group was their persecutions and/or deaths under the Communist regime, mostly during the Stalinist purges in the late 1930s. The patriarch's official decree states:

> They have served the life-giving Spirit, displaying the spiritual strength of the church in the trials of the recent past.... In enduring great afflictions, they have preserved in their heart the peace of Christ, and have been beacons of the faith.... Oppressed by exterior circumstances, they have passed through all trials with strength and resignation.... Glorifying the ascetic act of the new martyrs, the Russian Orthodox Church hopes in their intercession.[131]

Weight is clearly being given here to the spiritual life and motivations of those Russians who died (whether as martyrs or not) during the Communist persecutions of the twentieth century. In contrast, we once again find no mention whatsoever of evidence of miracles having been performed through the intercession of *any* of this large group of new saints; and references to incorrupt remains have disappeared completely.

Of interest is the fact that this immense number of new saints is grouped together collectively as "martyrs and confessors." Individual names are not labeled as either one or the other, the implication clearly being that while these persons died during the period of Communist persecution, the Russian church cannot always determine conclusively whether a person was directly killed out of hatred for holding Christian beliefs. Since it avoids conferring the specific title of martyr on each individual in this group, the church does not need to establish the traditional aspects of martyrdom, some of which might be historically impossible to determine with certainty in these cases: was the person killed for political, rather than religious motives? Was this a death at the hands of someone who intended to kill this person for his or her religion, or was it perhaps due to illness during imprisonment? By canonizing these new saints as a group, the Russian church indicates that the faithful may safely presume that if a given individual did not in fact meet all of the standard criteria for true martyrdom, he or she is in that case a confessor-saint instead—and in this way the canonization is not open to question.

While this mass canonization naturally garnered much public attention, its most interesting aspect, at least in the eyes of the general public, was undoubtedly the inclusion of the imperial family in this group of new saints. The decree notes that Tsar Nikolai, his wife Alexandra, and their five children were *strastoterptsy*, who "sincerely desired to live out in their lives the teachings of the Gospel," and who "endured martyrdom with meekness, patience, and resignation."[132] Once again, the document attributes no miracles to the Romanov family, and there is certainly no assertion that their remains were found to be incorrupt. We have only this simple statement describing their virtues during life and at the time of their violent death—which the document describes as that of martyrs.

The timing of the decision to canonize the Romanov family raised more than a few eyebrows. With the official dissolution of the Soviet Union in 1991, the world saw the rebirth of the nation of Russia; and many traditional aspects of Russian culture that had been either repressed or diluted under the Soviet system began to come to the surface of Russian everyday life. The historical association between the Russian government and the Russian Orthodox Church, which of course had been destroyed during the Communist era, became at least a theoretical possibility once more.

A discussion of the nature of the intellectual and theoretical debates that subsequently took place among both Orthodox and non-Orthodox Russians alike, regarding the ideal nature of the relationship between church and state, is beyond the scope of this work; but suffice it to say that indications of developing cooperation between them simultaneously rankled a large number of Russians, even as they were viewed with approval by many others.[133] In the years following the collapse of the USSR, any public signs of rapport between the Russian Orthodox hierarchy and the Russian government were invariably being watched very closely. Consequently, the suggestion that the last tsar was now going to be canonized a saint—for purely theological reasons, without any hint of political motives—was naturally greeted with skepticism.

Apparently well aware that the canonization of the Romanovs would provoke allegations that they were being made saints simply because of their imperial status, the head of the canonization commission, Metropolitan Iuvenalii, issued a long statement on the matter at the same time as the decree mentioning their canonization. Its purpose was to refute immediately any suggestions that the imperial family was being canonized for purely political motives, and that they otherwise would not merit inclusion on the list of Russia's saints. This is of particular interest to us here because in the process of explaining what was *not* the motivation behind canonizing the Romanovs, Iuvenalii's document naturally describes what that motivation really *was*. We thus have an official, formal document from the Russian hierarchy in Moscow, discussing the exact reasons why all seven members of the tsar's immediate family were declared saints. In the entire thousand-year period of its existence, the Russian church probably has never explained its rationale for canonizing saints so clearly before.

In this report, the head of the canonization commission said openly that it had "tried to free the canonization of the royal martyrs from any sort of political or other type of ideology."[134] Of importance was not the tsar's political successes (or lack thereof), but rather the manner in which he had been able to embody Christian ideals in his life. During the Romanov family's incarceration in Ekaterinburg by the Bolsheviks, clerics who were permitted to visit them could see that they endured for the love of Christ the sufferings inflicted on them. As a result, it was determined that the family were *strastoterptsy* not because of their noble background, but because their virtuous acceptance of suffering had been amply documented.[135] And it was, incidentally, the lack of this very sort of documentation that left the commission unable to determine whether those servants of the imperial family who had remained with the Romanovs and were also executed with them had accepted their sufferings with a degree of virtue sufficient to warrant their canonization as well.[136]

Among other factors supporting the cause of the imperial family, Iuvenalii described in detail the popular devotion to the Romanovs that began almost immediately and has continued among the Russian faithful to this day.[137] We find here an acknowledgment of a traditional feature of the making of saints in Russia, as frequently the display of popular piety among the laity leads eventually to a formal canonization by the Russian hierarchy.

The same document also addresses another traditional component of canonization. Numerous accounts of miraculous events—including medical cures, or myrrh exuding from their icons—have been associated with the Romanov family.[138] Yet while Iuvenalii clearly lists these events as additional evidence supporting their cause, there is (as remarked above) no mention whatsoever of miracles in the formal decree declaring their canonization.

It should be noted that the official decree of canonization is formulated in the same manner as the 1989 decree of canonization for Patriarchs Tikhon and Iov, discussed above, which specifically notes the miracles attributed to Iov as evidence supporting his cause. And although the outline of the 2000 decree is essentially identical, a corresponding paragraph mentioning miracles is nowhere to be found. This suggests that, while the miracles described by Iuvenalii in his other document may certainly have had some weight before the canonization commission, they do not seem to have been a pivotal sine qua non. There is little doubt that evidence pertaining to the internal, spiritual motivations of the members of the Romanov family, rather than external evidence of miraculous events after their deaths, was the primary factor leading to the canonization commission's ultimate decision.

By this point, the criteria for the Romanovs in particular and for Russians in general to be canonized in contemporary Russia seem clear enough. But the definitions and descriptions contained in these August 2000 documents were evidently not taken for granted by the entire hierarchy of the Russian church, or even by the whole canonization commission. Several months before these decrees were issued, another member of the commission, Archpriest Georgii, gave an interview to the secular media on the very issue of the Romanov canonizations. In it he articulated criteria and definitions that were a far cry from the wording of the final documents issued by the commission later in August.

An oral newspaper interview is hardly of the same nature as an official written decree, so the actual import of Georgii's words should not be weighed against the documents discussed above, as if both were of equal significance. Yet at the same time, during the course of his remarks Georgii never suggested that he was merely offering his own personal opinions: he clearly intended to convey to the interviewer some specific, definite factual information about the ongoing process of canonization in the Russian church, and to provide definitions of relevant terms. In a number of instances he did just this, but in ways that were most decidedly not in accord with either the terminology of the decrees emanating from the patriarchate, or with Russian canonization tradition.

With regard to the term *martyr*, Georgii offered a definition that seems unprecedented in its narrowness: "A martyr's death presumes that the person who accepts it has the chance to save his life by renunciation [of his faith]."[139] But if this had been the meaning of the term traditionally in use in the Russian church, one could only question the canonization as a martyr of—to cite only one example—the six-year-old Gavriil, who (as discussed above) allegedly was murdered by a Jewish man as part of a ritual killing. Furthermore, in those questionable cases of martyrdom addressed previously, where Russians were killed by robbers or in largely unknown circumstances yet now bear the title of "martyr," application of this definition would seem to eliminate them conclusively from the ranks of Russian martyr-saints.

Georgii's definition of *strastoterptsy* was no less problematic: he indicated that the term was to be applied only to princes and other royalty, for he claimed that "in the ancient tradition, the glorification of *strastoterptsy* [pertained to] princes, sovereigns, who accepted a death they did not deserve with Christian humility."[140] It was for this reason, he claimed, that the servants who attended the Romanov family could not be canonized as *strastoterptsy* with them. Needless to say, such a narrow definition of the term is not only inconsistent with Russian tradition; it is also difficult, if not impossible, to justify on theological grounds. While it is true that those who have been canonized in past centuries as *strastoterptsy* do tend to be members of royal families, this presumably is due more to the tendency to canonize persons whose circumstances were well known than to any theological supposition that Russian non-royals were unable to endure sufferings with meekness!

And so significant elements of the documents subsequently issued by the canonization commission were in decided conflict with these positions articulated by the Archpriest Georgii, a member of that very commission. It would thus appear that while the commission publicly articulated its decisions in a definitive way, the positions taken by the commission were not necessarily held by all its members. In other words, while much helpful explanation of the canonization process had been provided by Moscow, there still seemed to exist some uncertainty and a lack of clarity about the precise reasons why the Russian church has traditionally canonized its saints.

Some years later, yet another member of the canonization commission weighed in on the issue, with a written explanation titled "Methodology and Practical Difficulties in the Accomplishment of the New Martyrs and Confessors of Russia."[141] Written in 2009, this document by Hegumen Damaskin of Moscow was subsequently posted by the Russian Orthodox Church on its website among its "Official Documents"—thereby indicating, at least indirectly, its importance in the eyes of church officials. While initially approaching the topic from a spiritual standpoint, Damaskin nevertheless addresses the church's current position on the canonization of twentieth-century "New Martyrs" in a decidedly analytical way. In the process, he also gives some concrete examples of individuals who, in the opinion of the Russian church, do *not* merit canonization as martyrs.

Damaskin states up front that dying a violent death does not, in and of itself, constitute martyrdom. As an example, he notes that a military commander might have "won many victories and served the earthly homeland... [but] it is necessary that this person has chosen heaven as the center of his life."[142] It's worth noting that this distinction between civic and spiritual greatness, *if* applied consistently to future Russian Orthodox canonizations, should effectively avoid politicization of the process, at least to a marked extent.

Citing theological grounds for his position, Damaskin hones the definition of martyrdom even further. With regard to those Orthodox believers who died as a direct result of Soviet persecution, he specifies:

> The circumstances of martyrs' deaths are important, because it often happened that shortly before his death in a concentration camp ... a person showed cowardice. Or having courageously withstood interrogation and then ending up in prison, he revealed such a great degree of cowardice and despair that characterizes not merely momentary weakness, but almost a denial of Christ.[143]

For this reason, Damaskin emphasizes repeatedly the need to investigate carefully the details of the life—and the death—of a candidate for canonization, without assuming that a violent death at the hands of Soviet persecutors automatically rendered someone worthy of sainthood. He also stresses that every priest who died during the period of Soviet oppression is not to be considered ipso facto a saint/martyr,[144] citing cases in which an imprisoned cleric abjured his faith or otherwise displayed a less-than-saintly weakness while in prison. Damaskin's conclusion is clear: when canonizing new saints/martyrs, the Russian church must take nothing for granted and thoroughly examine the available facts that reveal the spiritual state of every candidate for canonization.

If such attention to detail in each individual case had already been the norm back in 2000, one can only wonder how many of the new martyrs and confessors could actually have been canonized. The sheer paucity of factual information in many cases might logically have precluded their inclusion in the Russian church's roster of saints.

3. Church Authorities Competent to Canonize: A Return to Prior Praxis

The instructions published by the canonization commission in 1993 indicate that the local bishop has the right to determine whether a deceased member of the faithful within his territory should be declared a saint. The evidence in support of this determination, however, is to be collected by the bishop and first submitted to the Synodal Theological Commission for review; after which it is to be sent for further scrutiny to the canonization commission. If there are no objections, the patriarch then gives the cause his approval, at which point it is returned to the local bishop who had originally submitted it. The actual canonization is then carried out not by Moscow, but by the local bishop within his eparchy.[145]

At the same time, of course, saints who are intended to be venerated as such throughout the entire Russian church are canonized by the patriarch himself.

The system is straightforward, and thoroughly consistent with the tradition established even in the earliest decades of the church in Russia.

Of interest, however, is the requirement that before a local bishop can canonize a new saint, the cause must first be examined and approved by Moscow. We see that while the cause for a potential new Russian saint is initiated at the local level, there is still a significant amount of involvement on the part of the church's supreme authority. Presumably such intervention is intended to prevent abuses—harking back to the repeated problems in the first millennium, that (as we saw in the first chapter) led to increasing restrictions placed on the canonization process. But it also should naturally result in a more *consistent* appraisal and judgment of the causes of new saints throughout all of Russia. This notion of uniformity is an aspect that we will quickly encounter in the following chapter, when we examine the canonization of saints in the Catholic Church, which of course has a much more centralized ecclesiological structure in general.

Just as the patriarch has the authority to canonize a saint for church-wide veneration, so too it is the patriarch who can determine whether a proposed martyr/saint is *not* a suitable candidate for canonization. In the 1990s there arose a movement proposing the canonization as a martyr of Grigorii Rasputin, the mysterious healer-monk who was so famously associated with the imperial family. Rasputin was murdered in 1916 by a group of Russian noblemen, who feared his influence over Tsarina Alexandra.

Since he was as well known in Saint Petersburg for his dissolute moral life as he was for healing the hemophiliac Tsarevich's bouts of bleeding, Rasputin hardly seemed a serious candidate for sainthood. Nevertheless, publications appeared alleging that his reputation had unfairly been tarnished by "Jews and Masons," and calling for his canonization as a martyr.[146]

In vain did the patriarch of Moscow scornfully dismiss the notion with comments that were public, yet informal;[147] and so in 2008 the canonization commission ultimately weighed in with an official document decrying the movement to have Rasputin declared a saint.[148] Noting that the promoters of Raputin's cause were members of extreme right-wing groups that sought to combat "Moscow church bureaucrats" and "pseudo-orthodox ultra-liberal journalists," the document disparages them as "theologically ignorant" and indifferent to the real facts of Rasputin's life.[149] Among these it cites Rasputin's own ignorance of, theology, his false "healings," which he learned to perform under the tutelage of a professional hypnotist, and the "unrestrained drunkenness and lewdness" in his personal life—which the commission asserts are in stark contrast to the traditional criteria required for canonization by the Russian Orthodox Church: "The occurrence of miracles, positively attesting to one's holiness of life; widespread veneration among the faithful; a righteous life and irreproachable orthodox faith."[150] In the opinion of the canonization commission of the Moscow Patriarchate, there was no question that Rasputin had hardly met these criteria; and this judgment was deemed sufficient to close the matter.

Preliminary Conclusions

In its theological teachings and liturgical practices, including its canonization process, the church in Russia emphasizes the importance of following tradition—and there is no question that in many aspects, it has consistently done just that. But it is equally obvious that there are some features of the "traditional" Russian process of making saints in general, and martyrs in particular, that deviated markedly from the practices of the church in the first millennium, which were discussed in chapter 1. It would be understandable if, for theological reasons, elements of the process gradually developed over time, perhaps evolving as the church's perception of the concept of sainthood/martyrdom became richer and more profound. In general, however, it appears clear enough that changes were made not as a result of new theological insights but rather through ignorance or error, by members of the Russian church who were truly unaware that they were creating innovations not found in the process of canonization as they had originally inherited it.

This was the case regarding saints in general, but it holds especially true for martyrs—and the issues begin with the Russian church's definition of martyrdom itself. The liturgical calendar received by Russia from the Greek church (regardless of exactly which calendar it actually was) would doubtless have contained a significant number of martyrs, and one would think that the concept of martyrdom was sufficiently comprehensible; but a distortion of the definition occurred in Russia very quickly, with the church-wide canonizations of Boris and Gleb. With the introduction of the concept of the strastoterpets, which is *not* traditional, we find for the first time a sort of subcategory of saints, somewhat comparable to, but not identical with, the martyrs. At the same time, however, literary references to *strastoterptsy* frequently use the term interchangeably with *mucheniki*, meaning martyrs in the traditional sense. True, this certainly was not done with the deliberate intent to deceive; but the end result was that among Russians, the parameters of the notion of martyrdom appear to have been widened far beyond the limits of the definition that developed in the first millennium, as described in the first chapter: a martyr is killed because of confessing the Christian faith, and knowingly and freely accepts that death out of love for God. Such a description implicitly excludes both political executions and killings that occur in the course of a commission of a crime (during a robbery, for instance); yet we have seen that there are saints in the Russian liturgical calendar who are commonly referred to as martyrs who died in exactly these circumstances.

The precision of the definition of martyrdom that evolved over the course of the first thousand years of Christianity necessarily suggests that if someone is to be formally declared a martyr for the faith, an investigation should first be carried out so as to determine whether that death truly constituted martyrdom or not. And it is just this sort of investigation that appears to have been lacking in the Russian church for so many centuries. In its place, one frequently finds persons being canonized based on a factually questionable story contained in a centuries-old *zhitie*, or because miraculous events purportedly occurred near the individual's tomb—sometimes immediately, but often hundreds of years after burial. As presented in chapter 1, inaccurate, fanciful stories recounting the lives of the saints are hardly unique to Russia. But reliance solely on historically suspect *zhitiia*, which had not even necessarily been written with the intention of providing an accurate factual narrative of events, led the church in Russia to canonize as martyrs persons who, as we have seen, might possibly never even have existed; while accepting claims of miraculous cures as sufficient evidence to canonize has often led the church to create saints of people about whose lives little or even nothing is known. This in turn caused the significance of the potential saint's life (and death, in the case of a potential martyr)—which traditionally had always been not simply one important feature among others, but *the primary motivating factor* in the canonization process—often to be completely neglected altogether.

At the same time, the role of miracles in the process in Russia took on key significance (indeed assumed pride of place), although in the first millennium it is clear that the occurrence of miracles had not traditionally been a requirement for canonization. In the case of martyrs, the church in its earliest years had quickly determined that the act of martyrdom in and of itself justified a Christian's canonization as a saint, and as a rule no further confirmation of the martyr's sanctity was needed. It appears probable that, in Russia, accounts of miraculous events originally spurred the church to formally canonize the person through whose intercession they presumably took place; if the miracles had not occurred, perhaps nobody would have thought to canonize the deceased as a saint. This seems to be the reason why miracles eventually came to be regarded as a sine qua non for all new saints, even for persons already acknowledged to have died a martyr's death.

Similarly, the requirement for canonization in Russia that saints' bodies be incorrupt—which has no basis whatsoever in the first thousand years of Christian tradition—probably developed as a reversal of cause and effect. Discoveries of "incorrupt" (i.e., mummified) remains were viewed as miraculous instances of Divine intervention, undoubtedly intended by God to show the great holiness of the person in question—an acknowledgment that naturally led the church to canonize the person as a saint. Such findings caused the Russian church to canonize many persons who otherwise would never have become saints. Over time, the church in Russia came to view incorrupt remains, like miracles, as a necessary condition for canonization.

In the meantime, the ambiguity about what precisely were the primary, motivating factors in canonizing a saint, and what merely constituted additional evidence in support of his cause led members of the church to become understandably confused about just what the criteria were for declaring someone a saint—martyr or not. The uncertainty was compounded by the dearth of clear, written historical records explaining who had been canonized and when, and describing the motivation for making the given individual a saint.

In the absence of consistent historical rules of evidence for the canonizations of Russian martyrs, it should not be terribly surprising if skeptical minds raise the possibility that at least some of them may have been politically motivated. Certainly there is no overt evidence that any Russian martyrs were canonized simply out of political expediency; some sort of theological justification, however weak and/or incomplete, always seems to have been provided. But the unquestionable inconsistency found in these justifications throughout history leads one to wonder whether the primary motivation for canonization, at least sometimes, was more political in nature. The case of the probably nonexistent Merkurii of Smolensk is a good example of this: as was seen earlier in this chapter, Merkurii was declared patron of the city of Smolensk several centuries after he allegedly fought off a Tatar invasion of that city—even though Russian historians do not recount any such battle during the thirteenth century, when Merkurii allegedly lived there. The evidence for Merkurii's existence (let alone his martyrdom) is so weak, and the motivation for his later canonization so murky, that one can only wonder if his elevation to sainthood may have been carried out in order to promote or strengthen the political position of the leaders of the city of Smolensk, or elevate the status of the city itself in some way.

The murkiness spans the centuries, and the possible political motivations could have varied over time. For example, as Burgess notes, "From the thirteenth to fifteenth centuries, as Russian cities struggled to free themselves from the Tatar-Mongol yoke, the church canonized Russian princes almost exclusively."[151] This does not necessarily mean that the new saints did not merit canonization, of course; but at a minimum, political factors might very well have played a role in determining *when* these canonizations took place.

The uncertainty increases when we look at the liturgical calendars in use in Russia over the years since its conversion to Christianity. Establishing a feast-day to commemorate a saint was, in the early years of the church, the only way in which a new saint was made; only gradually did there develop a specific process for canonizing new saints, of which inclusion on the calendar was the end result. But in Russia, the lack of historical records leaves us with calendars containing many feast-days with names about which we know absolutely nothing. We are unable to determine whether they were placed on the calendar after some sort of canonization process, or were added arbitrarily by copyists, who certainly had no authorization to "canonize" a new saint in this way!

And speaking of authority, it seems quite clear that the church in Russia carefully followed the traditions of the first millennium of Christianity with regard to the persons who were empowered to canonize new saints. For centuries, it was the local bishops in Russia who added new saints to their liturgical calendars, exactly as had been done throughout the Christian world for centuries. Occasional canonizations by the recognized head of the Russian church, who intended to create saints to be commemorated church-wide, may very well have been meant to create a sort of church unity, but the fact remains that they did indeed depart from traditional practice. Presumably it was the precedent set by these individual instances that led in the sixteenth century to a decided shift in competence, away from the local hierarch and toward a single, centralized authority—first the metropolitan/patriarch in Moscow, and later the Holy Governing Synod in St. Petersburg. This might have developed naturally, as a means to ensure consistency and/or to curb perceived abuses by individual local bishops; in reality, however, it appears to have been begun by Makarii primarily as a method of asserting the authority of Moscow, following the fall of Constantinople the century before.

We can see that by the time that the Russian church celebrated its millennial anniversary in 1988, it had indeed established its own traditions regarding the canonization of saints. Russia's traditions, however, in many ways contradicted the traditions set by the Christian world in the millennium before. Such was the situation at the time of the collapse of the Soviet Union, when the church in Russia regained its freedom and had the opportunity to examine the possibility of canonizing as martyrs untold numbers of Russians who perished under Soviet rule. It is no wonder that, far from simply reasserting the procedural praxis in use prior to the Bolshevik Revolution, Moscow instead first undertook a historical review of the canonization of martyrs in Russia from the time of the conversion of Rus', and an evaluation of the process of making new saints.

The conclusions reached by the then newly created canonization commission are evident in the wording of the declarations of the canonization of new martyr-saints who had been killed under Communism, for these decrees clearly indicate the significant factors that caused the commission to support a given person's canonization. They show us that the Moscow Patriarchate began to evaluate martyrs in a markedly different manner from that used in Russia in the past—but at the same time, in a manner that was in accord with the methods historically employed by the Christian world in the centuries before Russia's conversion to the faith. As the Russian church today gradually becomes less insistent about the need for incorrupt remains and miracle-working, it finds itself returning to the praxis of the church in its earliest centuries. That's why Metropolitan Iuvenalii, the former head of Moscow's canonization commission, admitted frankly that as the canonization criteria and the demand for miracles that had been added later by Russia are being weakened, ancient Byzantine rules about the creation of saints are once again becoming manifest.[152]

For the first time in the history of Christianity in Russia, we find clear examples of martyrs who are being canonized primarily because of the circumstances surrounding their deaths. The external, miraculous manifestations that constituted such pivotal evidence in earlier centuries are not even mentioned in more recent canonization decrees—usually because these manifestations presumably did not even take place. Instead, we read of the virtuous lives and heroic deaths for the love of Christ that characterized these new saints. The importance of objective, factual proof is evident from the documents issued by the canonization commission, which obviously has been attempting to investigate thoroughly the backgrounds of potential martyr-saints; when there is insufficient evidence, as in the case of the servants of the Romanov family, the commission has ruled that a determination one way or the other simply cannot be made.

If we assume that it is indeed to be considered the official position of the Russian church, then the more recent discussion of the term *martyrdom* provided by canonization commission-member Damaskin, and his insistence on the need for objective evidence of a potential saint's spiritual dispositions in the face of religious persecution, refine even further the church's official theological understanding of what martyrs really are. Again, Damaskin's statement places emphasis on factual proofs obtained by a thorough investigation of the person's life and the circumstances of his death—without assuming automatically that every person who was killed because of his faith had maintained the correct, internal spiritual outlook to the very end of his life. He also observes that simply because a person killed by Soviet persecutors was a cleric does not mean he remained heroically courageous in his faith until his final moments. In conclusion, Damaskin stresses that in the absence of sufficient evidence that an individual merits the appellation of martyr, he should not be canonized.

It seems safe to say that Damaskin's logical, systematic theological discussion of the elements that make up true martyrdom is the most precise, comprehensive definition of the term that the Russian church has ever provided. Not only does it constitute an explanation of Russian church teaching, but it also provides instruction to anyone in the Russian church wishing to have a person canonized as a martyr in future. The concrete specificity of the points it outlines is noticeably unlike the vague, highly spiritual declarations by Russian clergy about the nature of martyrdom made in the past, as we have seen in this chapter. It provides much needed criteria that were missing in previous centuries.

To a legalistic Westerner, there is still an obvious lacuna here, nonetheless: while the canonization commission asserts in its formal statements that the evidence has been reviewed, or (as in the case just mentioned) evidence is lacking, they have never publicly explained exactly what "sufficient evidence" really is. It is possible that Moscow has privately communicated with Russian bishops and described the type of documentation that must be submitted in order to prove that a proposed saint merits canonization; but since there is no evidence of the existence of such a communication, we cannot be sure that the patriarchate has done even this. In the absence of clear, objective rules and uniform procedures, it is all too easy to conclude that canonizations have in the past been done arbitrarily and inconsistently—and this may very well be the case even today. It is a system that, as we will see in great detail in the next chapter, stands in stark contrast to the almost obsessive concern in the Catholic Church for public, explicit rules and regulations, outlining the requirements for every conceivable aspect of the canonization process, openly and in advance.

At the same time as Moscow is assessing the life, virtues, and (in the case of martyrs) facts surrounding the death of the potential saint, it has also placed weight on the popular veneration enjoyed by persons being considered for canonization. This procedural aspect is not only in accord with Russian tradition, but it is also found in earlier canonization accounts in other parts of the Christian world. The fact that a deceased Christian in Russia is already being venerated among the ordinary faithful is of significance in the decision-making process.

Finally, with regard to the authorities competent to canonize today, the Russian church has now returned to its original practice, so that local bishops once again have the power to canonize new saints for commemoration in their own liturgical calendars, while the patriarch of Moscow retains the right to canonize saints who are to be venerated church-wide, by all. The return of authority to local bishops is fully in keeping with the traditional practices established during the first millennium of Christianity. At the same time, the canonization of church-wide saints only by the patriarch of Moscow himself indicates an aspect of centralization that, as will be seen in the following chapter, seems to resemble the Catholic theological concept of papal authority.

In short, it seems clear that while Moscow has appeared to make some radical changes recently in its method of canonizing saints (and martyrs in particular), in general these changes have actually returned the canonization system of the church in Russia back to the earliest established traditions of the Christian world. Those elements of the process in Russia that in fact deviated from that tradition—the tendencies to rely on perceived supernatural manifestations instead of evidence of the holiness of a person's life—are the very elements Moscow seems now to be jettisoning. Far from being innovations, the recent changes in the process are in fact taking the Russian church back to a more faithful following of canonization tradition.

Such is the situation regarding the process of canonization of martyrs in Russia today, after over a thousand years as a Christian nation. We turn now to the West, to see how the process developed (or not) during the same period within the Catholic Church.

CHAPTER THREE

The Catholic Church, from the Great Schism (ca. 1054) to Today

Introduction

Russia has spent over a thousand years embracing, then developing, and eventually refining its understanding of the traditional Christian concepts of martyrdom and the canonization of saints. Given the great age of the church in Russia, it has obviously been afforded a tremendous amount of time to hone and fine-tune its saint-making process.

Yet in contrast, the church in the West—the Catholic Church—had already existed for a full millennium by the time Christianity first found formal acceptance on Russian soil. One could say that the Catholic Church already had a thousand-year head start on Russia with regard to the practice of canonizing martyrs—for it was in the West, primarily in Rome, that the very notion of martyrdom had first come into being. And during the period in which the Russian church was determining how to canonize its own saints for the first time, the Catholic Church in the West already possessed a very well-established set of ideas and procedures, rooted in nearly ten centuries of tradition. In other words, in the era when creating new martyr-saints was totally new to the church in Russia, it was far from a novel process in the West.

This certainly does not mean that in the West the process of canonization and the concept of martyrdom have remained unchanged over the course of the last millennium. But it does imply that the Catholic Church had what might be considered an advantage, in the sense that it did not need to adopt—and adapt—the practices of other regions of the Christian world when it wished to canonize a saint. Traditional praxis was its own praxis, and the terminology pertaining to martyrdom was the terminology that had first developed in its own territory.

When the procedure for making saints in the Catholic Church evolved over time, therefore, it was not a case of a newly Christianized region of the world tailoring already existing practices to its own cultural understanding—as was arguably the case in Russia. Still, the process of canonization of saints in general, and of martyrs in particular, certainly did develop in the West in a particularly distinct way, as will be seen in this chapter.

One of the many results of the East–West Schism in the eleventh century was that the subsequent evolution of the process of canonization in Rome was not shared by the church in the East—including Russia. With the official ending of church unity, any advances in saint-making procedures in the West would remain there, unless Constantinople (or the hierarchy of another church in the East) either developed its processes coincidentally in the same manner, or freely chose to accept elements of Roman praxis. The opposite was of course also true, and explains why some traditional aspects of the Russian church's concept of martyrdom, and of its canonization procedures, are unique to Russia.

In terms of historical evidence, there is perhaps as much uncertainty about actual canonization praxis during at least part of the medieval period in the West as there is in the East. But there is no doubt that there exists far more Western documentary evidence of procedural requirements than we saw extant in the Russian church. It is still necessary to fill occasional gaps in factual knowledge by looking to concrete examples of canonizations in the Catholic Church, to see how the process was being carried out; but we will nevertheless find many more examples of specific written instructions and other official documents pertaining to the making of saints than we encountered in chapter 2.

Culturally, establishing written laws has been a strong point in the West since the ancient Roman era. Much of Western civil law today is at least conceptually based on Roman law—and the same holds true for Catholic canon law as well. Basic notions like the importance of documentary evidence, the value of eyewitness testimony, and the need for consistent procedural norms were embraced by the Romans long before the advent of Christianity, and they remain significant today. Thus one quickly finds stark differences between descriptions of the Catholic process of canonizing saints and that of the Russian church—but it is noteworthy that they generally tend to be more cultural rather than theological in nature.

Because the Romans had such a strong tradition of establishing their laws in writing, and promulgating them openly, it is not surprising to find a myriad of written documentation published by the Catholic Church to both describe the process and justify it along theological grounds. Once the Catholic canonization procedure became centralized—which, as will be seen shortly, happened relatively soon after the East–West Schism—documents on the subject routinely began to be issued by Rome itself. At the same time, medieval decretalists and scholars in general started to regularly discuss and write about various aspects of the making of saints. Their general inclination to collect and organize ecclesiastical laws and other church documents chronologically ensured that medieval legal rules and theological teachings were accurately copied and preserved. The great Gratian, the twelfth-century "Father of Canon Law" as we know the field today, was one of the key founders of this practice.

With regard to the collation of laws specifically pertaining to canonization itself, a tremendous debt is owed by the Catholic Church to Prospero Lambertini (who in 1740 was elected Pope Benedict XIV), for his monumental work *De servorum Dei beatificatione et beatorum canonizatione*, which compiled both historical sources and concrete examples of virtually every imaginable aspect of the making of saints. While it is not error-free, the work remains an authoritative source for the historical status and development of the canonization process, and as such it is still routinely quoted today.

Thanks to the codification of canon law in the twentieth century, it is of course a relatively simple matter to ascertain canonization praxis in modern times. Although the days of ancient Rome are long gone, the deep-rooted tradition of creating uniform rules and written procedures remains alive and well in the Catholic Church.

As in the previous two chapters, we will first examine the definition of the term *martyrdom* in use in the Catholic Church, noting further development and refinement of the concept in the second millennium. This will then be followed by an analysis of the various elements of the process of canonizing martyrs. Lastly, and perhaps most significantly of all, the chapter will conclude by tracing the evolution of the increasingly complex rules regarding the members of the Catholic hierarchy who are authorized to canonize new saints, both martyrs and non-martyrs.

A. Theological Concepts of Sainthood/Martyrdom: Refining the Definitions

At the time of the schism, the Catholic Church possessed the definition of martyrdom that had developed in the earliest centuries of Christianity, which was discussed at length in chapter 1: martyrdom involved a violent death, willingly accepted, and imposed on the martyr out of hatred for his beliefs. Catholic theologians subsequently discussed and further honed various aspects of the basic theoretical concepts, but without proffering any substantive changes. Perhaps chief among these was Thomas Aquinas, who addressed an entire question in his *Summa Theologiae* to the topic of martyrdom, and whether or not it constitutes a perfect act of virtue.[1]

The question has periodically been raised in Catholic theological circles, usually during time of war, about whether soldiers fighting in battle can be considered to die as martyrs. Applying the centuries-old definition just cited, theologians have routinely decided the question in the negative. Aquinas himself noted that, while a soldier might freely accept death, he dies for his country rather than for his religious faith.[2] And Benedict XIV, in his authoritative eighteenth-century work on canonization, addresses this issue by referencing historical evidence from the first millennium that soldiers were never accorded the status of martyr. In fact, among others he cites the tenth-century emperor Nicephoras II Phocas, who wished to have his deceased soldiers canonized as saints, but was, as discussed in chapter 1, rebuffed in this matter by the patriarch of Constantinople.[3]

The net result of this debate was that the traditional definition of martyrdom remained unchanged. But one aspect of the definition, which was further refined and ultimately articulated in greater detail, was the notion that "dying for the faith" could also involve dying for key moral principles inherent in that faith. Someone who was killed not because he was a Christian per se, but because he advocated or embraced Christianity's moral teachings can, in accord with this definition, be considered a martyr. As Lambertini (later Pope Benedict XIV) noted, martyrdom occurs "on account of one's faith in Christ, or some other act of virtue referring to God."[4] This is consistent with Thomas Aquinas's discussion of martyrdom, which finds that other virtues can be the cause of martyrdom, "because it is written: 'Blessed are they that suffer persecution for justice's sake,' which pertains to martyrdom."[5]

A relatively recent case of martyrdom pertaining to a Christian virtue rather than to the faith itself is that of Maria Goretti, who was killed in 1902 after resisting her assailant's sexual advances. Maria protested because the act was sinful; her murderer then stabbed her to death, not because she was a Christian, but because she objected to the sin of impurity.[6]

This is not unlike the circumstances surrounding the deaths of some martyrs in Russia. For example, we saw in chapter 2 that Metropolitan Philip II of Moscow was killed by Tsar Ivan the Terrible in the sixteenth century, primarily because of Philip's opposition to the Oprichnina and its spate of political killings. Philip is considered a martyr, but he was not killed simply because he was a Christian. Rather, the tsar, who was ostensibly a Christian himself, had Philip II executed because he was upholding the Russian church's moral teachings.

Apart from this added nuance, which is embraced by both churches, the official definition of martyrdom, therefore, has remained essentially unchanged in the Catholic Church since its original development in the fourth century, which was discussed at length in chapter 1. But when it became a question of concrete application of this abstract definition, one can find multiple examples of persons popularly regarded as saints during the medieval era whose designation as martyrs seems dubious at best. Edward the Martyr had been king of England for only three years when he was killed in 978 while still a teenager. Accurate historical accounts from this period are sparse, but it appears that he was murdered in a political power struggle, and not because of his Christian faith; nevertheless, at some unknown point in time he became known among the people as a martyr.[7] To be fair, there is no evidence that he was ever formally canonized by the church; yet he retains the appellation Saint Edward the Martyr even today. One cannot fail to notice that the circumstances surrounding Edward's death seem strikingly similar to those of Boris and Gleb, the Russian nobles who also were apparently murdered in their youth in a dispute over power and succession. The notion that a member of a royal family has been cut down at an early age may have tended to evoke images of innocence and virtue under attack from evil forces—but while this scenario might understandably invoke popular sympathy, it does not, in and of itself, constitute martyrdom according to the traditional definition of the term.[8]

One might argue that since Edward the Martyr was never actually canonized by the Catholic Church, this notion that the innocent victim-king was a martyr may have existed only in the pious minds of the ordinary faithful. But a member of royalty who really was formally canonized as a martyr was King Canute IV of Denmark, who died in 1086. Canute was widely known for his devotion to the church, but it is less than clear whether it was his faith that led rebels to murder him inside a church in Odense or whether their motives were purely political in nature. A contemporary account of Canute's virtuous life and violent death indicates that his assassins principally objected to Danish control of their territory and had decided "that they would kill the tyrant-king, if they did not want their region to be burned or devastated."[9] Regardless, he was officially declared a martyr in 1101.

And the questionable status of King Canute IV as a martyr is not an isolated case. About fifty years later, yet another Danish nobleman with the same name died in comparable circumstances and was also subsequently canonized as a martyr. Canute Lavard was a prince of Denmark who became embroiled in a power struggle with his uncle and cousin, who had him killed in 1131. Once again, there is no specific evidence that Canute was killed for his Christian beliefs; but he was canonized as a martyr in 1170.[10] In both of these cases, the victim is described by contemporary writers as virtuous and holy, while the killers are understandably portrayed as evil—and the authors appear to conclude that this set of circumstances in itself automatically constituted martyrdom.

The canonizations of these two Canutes as martyrs occurred over eight centuries ago. But much more recently, the Catholic Church formally recognized as a martyr the son of King Canute IV, known as Charles the Good, although his death occurred under similar circumstances. As count of Flanders, Charles was killed in 1127 by members of the Erembald family, whom Charles intended to strip of their noble status. Like his father, he was killed in a church; ironically, one of the chief conspirators in his assassination, Bertolf FitzErembald, was a priest of the very church where the murder took place.[11]

We find here yet another case in which it does not appear that the victim was actually killed because of his Christian beliefs. Yet Charles was beatified as a martyr in 1882, long after his death.[12] Thus while the "official"definition of martyrdom has in the Catholic Church remained essentially unchanged since it was established in the earliest centuries of Christianity, the actual application of the abstract definition to a concrete case appears to remain potentially problematic.

As can already be seen from the examples cited here, questions can all too easily arise as to whether a Christian who died a violent death had actually been killed *in odium fidei*, or for motives that were more political than religious. Determining whether the person died a martyr's death or perished as a victim of a political intrigue can often be an impossible task. In this regard, the Catholic Church in the West has for centuries been facing exactly the same issues as the Russian church. For, as we have seen in chapter 2, the Russian church has also been known historically to canonize as martyrs Russians who were killed in military battles and other political struggles, the circumstances of which raise questions about the precise motivations of their killers. The procedural implications of this uncertainty for the Catholic canonization process will become evident later in this chapter.

We have already seen that in the first millennium of Christianity, not only did a true martyr die willingly for his belief in Christ, but his beliefs in life also need to have been theologically orthodox. Thus a heretic could not be venerated as a martyr, regardless of the possibly heroic circumstances surrounding his violent death. As noted in chapter 1, many Donatists in North Africa were killed for their faith in the fourth century, but were not commemorated as martyrs by orthodox Christians, since the beliefs for which they died did not reflect the true teachings of the church.

In subsequent centuries, the orthodoxy of the beliefs of a potential martyr-saint continued to be a key factor in the West, just as it has always been in Russia. The Franciscan tertiary Ramon Llull, who was stoned to death by

Muslims in present-day Algeria in about 1314, is a case in point. Theologians debated the Catholic orthodoxy of the lay mystic's writings for many decades after his death, in the process underscoring the rivalry existing at that time between Franciscans and Dominicans. At one point the Dominican inquisitor Nicholas Eymeric produced a condemnation of Llull's writings, which he claimed had been signed by Pope Gregory XI in 1376; but a subsequent examination of Llull's works by Rome found no heterodox content whatsoever.[13] Regardless, the questions repeatedly raised as to the Catholic orthodoxy of Llull's vast writings have constituted a stumbling block that has hindered his canonization to this day. Even if the church at some point in the future definitively determines that Llull was truly killed out of hatred of his Catholic faith, the question of the Catholicity of his writings still remains, and will have to be resolved definitively before he can ever be canonized.

The need to determine the orthodoxy of a potential saint's beliefs, which existed from the earliest years of Christianity, took on a very concrete procedural form in the Catholic Church. As the Catholic investigative process began to take the basic shape it still has today, reviewing all the written works of a candidate for canonization became a necessary procedural component in a formal sense. The current law, which reiterates centuries of consistent praxis, requires the bishop who introduces the cause of the potential saint to see to it that any writings the candidate may have published are examined by theological censors.[14] At issue, of course, is the theological orthodoxy of Catholic saints' written words, the importance of which for the canonization process harkens back virtually to the very beginnings of the church.

B. Elements of the Process by Which a Martyr Is Recognized

At the time of the Great Schism in the eleventh century, the essential elements of a canonization in the West continued to follow the practices of the church in the first millennium. Regardless of status as a martyr, a new saint's name was included in the liturgical calendar on a date established as his or her feast-day, and an office was composed for the individual for that day; a life account was written if it did not already exist, documenting sanctity during the saint's life (and in the case of a martyr, the manner of death as well); and the remains were moved to a place of honor, generally under an altar in a chapel or church dedicated to the saint.

Gradually, however, some changes began to be introduced into this saint-making process, which were probably so subtle as to be almost imperceptible at first. Exteriorly, the elements listed above still remained; but over time, their implementation no longer actually constituted canonization in and of itself. Of primary importance became the public, written declaration by the church official authorized to canonize (and precisely who possessed that authority will be addressed in greater detail later in this chapter). The concrete actions of inserting the new saint's name in the calendar, translating the body to an honorable location, and writing a life account for reading by the faithful, were still important elements that remained connected to the saint-making process, but eventually they had no official import in and of themselves. Put differently, if all these historical components of canonization were to be carried out on behalf of a potential saint in the Catholic Church, but an official declaration by competent authority were lacking, the person would not be considered canonized. The formal, public pronouncement by the Catholic hierarchy became key, and all other elements became merely ancillary, albeit still relevant, facets of the process.

1. Liturgical Commemorations: Calendars

The development of liturgical calendars in the first millennium, which was detailed in the first chapter, simply continued in the second thousand years in the life of the Catholic Church in the West. As was seen previously, martyrs and other saints were commemorated in the liturgy on a specific feast-day, their names originally being inserted into the local church's liturgical calendar. In the earliest centuries of Christianity, the canonization process, such as it was, generally proceeded simply by including the deceased Christian's name in the calendar, assigning the saint a feast on a particular date.

Certain "big" saints, such as the Mother of God and the apostles, eventually came to be included on every calendar; but many other, lesser-known local saints (whether martyrs or not) were often found only on the liturgical calendar of their particular region. Over time, as was discussed in chapter 1, there was a gradual but decided move toward a universal calendar, as various local churches began to adopt saints from the liturgical calendars of other regions of the Christian world. Nevertheless, there remained countless variations from one locale to the next. To complicate the matter even further, religious orders and other institutes developed their own calendars and venerated many saints whose feast-days were only commemorated by their members, regardless of the region of the world in which they lived.

To the extent that the Catholic Church in the West continued this practice after the East–West Schism, the end result was identical to the practice in Russia: many saints were commemorated in some regions but not in others, and liturgical calendars varied widely from place to place. Thus the great twelfth-century decretalist Gratian provided a list of major feast-days that were to be announced as such to the faithful—but then noted that every bishop could also establish additional feast-days to be celebrated only within the territory of his own diocese, and not by the entire church.[15]

Increasingly, however, one begins to find references to papal authority over the veneration of saints and the establishment of feasts in liturgical calendars. The *Liber Sextus* of Boniface VIII, published first in the late thirteenth century, contains a decree ordering the observance of the feasts of (among others) the twelve apostles, the evangelists, and the four doctors of the church.[16] Clearly here we have an instance in which authority higher than the local bishop was establishing mandatory feasts to be included in local liturgical calendars.

Yet another instance can be found in the fifteenth century, when the papacy asserted that it had the authority to compel local churches to venerate certain persons as saints, in obedience to the supreme authority of the Catholic Church. At the Council of Florence (1431–1445), which attempted unsuccessfully to reunite the church in the East and West under the pope, one of the conditions of reunion between Rome and the church in Armenia was that the Armenians would henceforth be obliged to venerate Pope Leo I as a saint.[17] That the Armenian church ultimately decided against reunion is beside the point; at issue here is the fact that already in the 1400s, we find Rome insisting that it had the power to require the church in other locales to commemorate certain saints who were from other regions and thus unknown to the local church in question. The centralization of the process of recognizing saints thus continued.

With the Council of Trent in the sixteenth century came a new phase in the Western church, as the Council Fathers entrusted the pope with the revision of the liturgical books. The publication of the new *Missale Romanum* by Pope—and later Saint—Pius V in 1570 was primarily intended to eliminate local variants (and even abuses) in the liturgical rites themselves; but as it also contained the liturgical calendar that was to be followed by all Catholics worldwide, as a matter of course it eliminated the observance of many local feast-days of saints who were unknown in other parts of the Catholic world. Instead, Pius V mandated that all Catholic churches and chapels, including those of religious institutes, were to use the same rites (and the same calendar), unless they could show that their use of an alternate rite had been approved by the Holy See and used for at least two hundred years.[18]

Pius V's intention was specifically to reform the liturgical rites, especially regarding the celebration of Mass. His primary goal, therefore, was certainly not to make any definitive pronouncements regarding the commemoration of certain saints—still less to create new ones! Yet by obligating the entire

Catholic Church to use a uniform missal for liturgical celebrations, the pope was, as a result, incidentally requiring all dioceses not only to commemorate the same persons as saints, but even to commemorate them on the same dates. Many variations in local calendars were in this way eliminated entirely—unless, of course, the pope subsequently granted specific permission to a local church to celebrate a feast particular to its own tradition.

Several dozen days of the calendar that formed part of Pius V's new Tridentine Missal had no commemorations of any saints at all. There are unquestionably countless saints, including many early Christian martyrs who had been commemorated in the liturgies of various parts of the world for centuries, whose names are nowhere to be found in the liturgical calendar of the new missal.[19] It is clear that Pius V did not intend these omissions to imply that these omitted persons were no longer to be regarded as saints. Rather, his calendar included only the universally acknowledged saints, like the twelve apostles, as well as those saints whose veneration had already spread to large parts of the Catholic world, like Francis of Assisi. Lesser-known saints who were being venerated in only one region while unknown to the rest of the Catholic population were omitted from the calendar—but simply because it was designed for universal use.

By mandating that local churches and religious institutes use the *Missale Romanum* unless they received explicit permission not to do so from the Holy See, Pius V introduced the notion that *papal approval* was required to add a saint to the liturgical calendar. Since the calendar was an integral part of the missal and since it was forbidden to amend the missal in any way without Rome's approbation, the end result was that the pope now had sole authority to regulate the celebration of feast-days for all saints, even merely local ones. From this point forward, if a particular church or a religious institute wished to add a new saint to its local calendar, permission first had to be obtained from the Holy See.

At the same time, we see that by this point, the inclusion (or not) of a deceased Christian's name in the liturgical calendar was no longer directly connected to his status as a saint. The saints whose names were not mentioned in Pius V's new calendar were not being "de-canonized" thereby; they were still saints, but without a universal feast-day.

The martyred Saint Stanislaw, the bishop of Krakow who was killed in 1079, is a good example of a saint whose feast-day was nowhere to be found on the reformed liturgical calendar accompanying Pius V's new missal. Stanislaw was canonized a martyr in 1253 by Pope Innocent IV, who specifically ordered that his feast day of May 7 henceforth be observed annually by the universal church.[20]

But according to Pius V's new calendar in 1570, May 7 had no commemoration of any saint whatsoever; and mention of Saint Stanislaw was nowhere to be found. The feast was subsequently reinserted into the calendar and in 1969 it was moved to April 11, which is now believed to be the saint's actual *dies natalis*, the date of his martyrdom.[21]

Stanislaw's status in the Catholic Church as a saint and martyr was established at the time of his canonization in the thirteenth century and has never changed. His exclusion from the church's liturgical calendars and his subsequent reinclusion had no effect on the fact that he is a Catholic saint. Pius V presumably did not include the feast of Saint Stanislaw on the 1570 calendar because he was not sufficiently well known throughout the universal church to warrant mandating his commemoration by Catholics worldwide. The celebration of saints' feasts and their status as saints had become two distinct concepts.

The opposite was likewise true, if perhaps less common: from this point forward, names of deceased Christians could be added to or removed from the liturgical calendar without necessarily affecting their status as saints or non-saints. The early Christian martyr Philomena is a particularly confusing case in point. Her remains were discovered in a Roman catacomb in 1802, but since her name is nowhere to be found in historical accounts of the early Christian persecutions or in traditional Christian liturgical texts, there is absolutely nothing factual known about her. In 1837, the prefect of the Congregation of Rites (which at that time had jurisdiction over matters involving the canonization of saints) publicly asserted that Pope Gregory XVI had approved of the Congregation's decision permitting recitation of the Office and celebration of the Mass of a Virgin Martyr in honor of Philomena on August 11.[22] Thus Philomena now had her own feast-day, and her name was subsequently found in Catholic liturgical calendars—although she had never actually been declared a saint.

But in 1961, in the course of a revision of the Catholic liturgical calendar, the prefect of the Congregation of Rites declared that the August 11 feast of Philomena was to be removed from all calendars.[23] There subsequently has been much undeniable confusion among the faithful as to whether "Saint" Philomena was thus "decanonized"; but the fact is that she had never been canonized in the first place. Because the act of including—or removing—a name on the Catholic liturgical calendar had been separated from the act of canonization, the inclusion and subsequent exclusion of Philomena's commemoration on August 11 never affected her status as a non-saint.

Toynbee probably put it best when she stated, "From all this it will be clear that while, of course, the presence of a name in a calendar is no guarantee of canonisation, neither is absence any proof of non-canonisation."²⁴ An act that had, in the first centuries of Christianity, originally constituted a saint's canonization—i.e., the inclusion of his or her name in the liturgical calendar—had now, with the implementation of the universal Tridentine calendar, been effectively and definitively severed from it. Creating a new saint, and commemorating that person's feast-day, had become two separate, although still related actions.

2. Translatio

We saw in the first chapter that the church came to connect a *translatio*, the act of moving a body from its original burial site to a more honorable location (usually into a church or at least a chapel dedicated to the deceased, and often under an altar), with the canonization of the person in question. Eventually the mere act of translating a person's body constituted canonization—along with a commemoration of the feast in the local liturgy. Cited in chapter 1 as an example was the case of Saint Jeron, the martyred Dutch priest who was translated by the local bishop to an honorable place inside a church in the tenth century. No official, written decree announcing his canonization appears to have ever existed; the *translatio* was sufficient to make him a saint.

In Russia, *translationes* largely continued to amount to canonizations for centuries, as was seen in chapter 2. This practice likewise continued in the Catholic Church even after the Great Schism. Thus the martyr Eugenius was translated by the bishop of Tongres in 1083, unaccompanied (to the best of our knowledge, at least) by any formal decree of canonization. Eugenius's canonization as a martyr-saint was effected simply by the *translatio* of his remains.²⁵

The great Gratian's decretal from the 1100s on this subject is entirely consistent. Describing the regulation of various practical elements of both the outfitting of church buildings and the liturgical celebrations that take place in them, he noted that the relics of saints are not to be moved from one place to another without consulting the prince or obtaining permission of the bishop and holy synod.²⁶ The reference to princes—whose participation in this process appears in practice to have simply died out naturally—is presumably a throwback to the enactments of the local councils during the reign of Charlemagne, discussed in chapter 1.²⁷ Involvement of higher authorities, whether secular or ecclesiastical, was at that time intended to curb the abuses that had taken place in the past.

But with the steadily increasing significance of an official declaration made by competent authority—which will be discussed in greater detail below—the action of translating the body of a potential saint, like the insertion of the individual's name in the liturgical calendar, became disconnected from actual canonization. While a new saint was still, as a rule, moved from his original place of burial to a grander site where his remains would be venerated by the faithful, the *translatio* was no longer the act that determined his status as a saint. Thus it came to take place—sometimes before the decree of canonization was promulgated, and sometimes afterward—without directly affecting the canonization itself. As Kuttner put it simply, "The *translatio* was no longer the decisive act."[28]

And once a *translatio* no longer constituted a canonization in the West, we even find occasional instances of both martyrs and non-martyrs whose relics underwent multiple *translationes* over a period of time. Cardinal Hyacinth, the papal legate to Spain under Pope Alexander III, was asked by the local church in 1173 to preside over the group-*translatio* of the early martyrs Claudius, Lupercus, and Victoricus, who were buried in a monastery named in their honor in the city of Leon. It would seem, since the three were entombed beneath the altar in a church that was specifically dedicated to them, that they had been canonized already at some unknown point in the past, at which time the original *translatio* to their own church had taken place. The trio had, however, garnered the recent attention of the local populace in a dramatic way, when the city of Leon had been attacked by Arabs. An account in the *Acta Sanctorum* notes that the leader of the Arab forces was miraculously hurled from his horse when he attempted to forcibly enter the monastery named for the three martyrs. This perceived act of miraculous intervention by the three saints moved the local bishop, John, to decide to transfer their bodies from their burial place in the earth to a more honorable location aboveground, and in a solemn ceremony presided over by the cardinal-legate, the martyrs were removed to a new, grander tomb within the church.[29]

The intended significance of the legate's action is unclear. The inscription in the church commemorating this event indicates not that Cardinal Hyacinth "canonized" the three martyrs, but that he "confirmed" their status.[30] While the initial impetus for this action was undoubtedly the military failure of the Arabs to conquer Leon, and it clearly was designed to honor the three saints in thanksgiving for protecting the Spaniards, it does not appear to have changed in any canonical way the official standing of Claudius, Lupercus, and Victoricus, who presumably were already saints in the eyes of the church. It is, however, of direct interest to us because it shows a formal, solemn *translatio* that was clearly unrelated to an act of canonization. At the same time, it also indicates the well-established connection in Catholic minds between the saints' ability to intercede directly with God on behalf of the faithful on earth, and the need to honor the saints by translating their relics to a place of honor under an altar, in a church dedicated especially to them.

While this second *translatio* of Claudius and his companions was an unusual (though by no means unique) case,[31] it must be noted that it was carried out by the papal legate, who presumably was acting within the parameters of his authority. When the decisive element of the canonization process ultimately came to be not the *translatio* but rather the formal decree of the pope (which will be discussed below), other components such as a *translatio* could be carried out only with papal authorization. This is why, when the bishop of Prague, on his own initiative, translated the body of the martyred—and already canonized—Saint Adalbert to the cathedral in Prague in the eleventh century, he was formally denounced and punished by Pope Benedict IX for acting without authorization.[32] Adalbert had indeed been canonized as a martyr, and thus the placement of his relics in a place of honor in the Prague cathedral was not wholly inappropriate. The pope's objection, however, was not based on any suggestion that Adalbert might fail to deserve his splendid new burial place in Prague; rather, it stemmed from the fact that the bishop of Prague had undertaken the *translatio* without advance papal permission. As we have already seen with regard to including saints on the liturgical calendar, so likewise in the matter of translating their remains, papal authority became key.

And since a *translatio* henceforth could not be carried out without papal approval, it is thus not unreasonable that Thomas Becket, canonized three years after his martyrdom in 1170, was not translated until after his canonization. Two days after the solemn ceremony in Rome, Pope Alexander III sent word to the clergy of Canterbury, ordering them to transfer Becket's relics in a formal procession to a more honorable place in a chapel, either enclosed in an altar or raised on high.[33] The pope made clear that Thomas Becket had already been canonized; the solemn *translatio* he ordered did not, in itself, affect Becket's status as a martyr-saint.[34]

3. Writing a *Vita*, and the Evolution of an Investigatory Process

It has already been seen in the first chapter that one element of the canonization process that developed in the first thousand years of Christianity was the writing of a *vita*, or *acta*, recounting the life and death of the new saint. These *acta* not only reminded the Christian faithful of the meritorious actions of the saint while on earth; they also constituted a justification for the veneration of the new saint as such. From virtually the very start, the accuracy of these accounts has all too often proved questionable at best—often because they were originally written not with the aim of providing an accurate historical narrative of the saint's life and death, but rather to edify the faithful by nurturing their devotion. Consequently, many of the *acta* for the earliest Christian saints should be read with caution (if not rejected as spurious altogether).

Russian zhitiia continued in the same vein. As was discussed in chapter 2, the accounts of Russian saints' lives are at times soND fanciful, and so factually unreliable in general, as to sometimes raise real questions as to whether the saint even existed. Written, as they often were, centuries after the fact, in many cases even the most honest attempts to compile historically accurate, factual narratives would in any event have been unsuccessful. All too often, concrete facts about a Christian's life and death generations ago were by this point in time completely lost.

Catholic *acta* written in the medieval period suffer from the same problems. And yet another issue affecting the historical accuracy of some Catholic saints' *acta* developed indirectly, as the practice of the *translatio* of a newly declared saint eventually came to have financial consequences that were, at least originally, probably unforeseen and unintended. Pious pilgrims flocking to the burial places of saints generally gave donations that resulted in significant monetary gains for monasteries or churches where popular saints were now entombed. Ultimately, less scrupulous Catholic clerics and religious eagerly sought to transfer the relics of saints to their own churches for primarily financial reasons. We have seen in the first chapter that Emperor Charlemagne had already made efforts in the early ninth century to regulate the transfer of saints' remains from one locale to another, in an apparent attempt to curb precisely this sort of abuse.

How did this affect the accuracy of the *acta*? The desire for monetary gain all too often caused church officials to accept questionable "relics," of "saints" whose lives were either little known, or had not been authenticated at all. This in turn led to the hasty rewriting, and sometimes even creation ex nihilo, of *acta* that were in the end little more than fiction, or at best a compilation of facts purloined from the lives of various genuine saints. Kemp documents just such a case in Ghent in the mid-eleventh century, regarding Saint Livinius, martyred by pagans in the seventh century, whose remains had been transferred to the monastery in 1007:

> Between 1025 and 1058 a forged life of St. Livinius was constructed and attributed to St. Boniface of Mainz. It seems that as no bishop had authenticated the relics in 1007 it was decided to produce older authority by making Livinius one of those who were baptized by the apostle of the English [St. Augustine of Canterbury], and saying that his life was written by the apostle of the Germans.[35]

In other words, financial motivations at times impelled church authorities to promote spurious *acta*, written long after the fact, to justify the *translatio* of someone whose life—and occasionally even identity—were questionable at best.

Consequently, it seems fair to say that in the Catholic calendar there may very well be "saints" whose bodies were translated during the medieval period, who were not really saints at all, or at least were not the saints whose alleged lives are recounted in their official *acta*. Because they never underwent a proper system of authentication at the time of their *translationes*, the lives and deaths of these saints may (at least in some cases) be complete figments of imagination—not because the canonization process at the time was necessarily flawed, but because it was not always followed. Unlike some of the Russian saints seen in chapter 2, they were not made saints based on faulty *acta*, written in some cases centuries before their canonization. Rather, it appears that the reverse is true, and fictitious *acta* were written after the fact to explain and justify their *translationes*.

Yet even when the *acta* were not actually fictitious, their dubious historical accuracy continued to pose problems. A later case of questionable *acta* written after the fact involved the fourteenth-century martyr Saint John Nepomucene. Confessor to the queen at the royal court in Prague, he refused to tell her husband, King Wenceslaus of Bohemia, what she had revealed in confession. As the king, suspecting that his wife had been unfaithful to him, was seeking evidence against her, he was enraged at John's refusal to violate the confessional seal. In retribution, Wenceslaus ordered his henchmen to throw John into the Vltava River, where he drowned in 1383.

This is, in any case, the commonly accepted narrative today. But there is much uncertainty about the actual facts surrounding the case, as it appears historically undeniable that there were in reality two different clerics from Nepomuk named John, both of whom were apparently drowned in Prague in the late fourteenth century. The first, a canonist and the vicar-general of the diocese of Prague, was killed in the course of a power struggle concerning clerical appointments, when he opposed the appointment to an ecclesiastical office of a candidate who was favored by King Wenceslaus. It appears from the historical annals of the period, however, that a different John from Nepomuk was the queen's confessor and was indeed killed on the king's orders, possibly in 1393.[36] One of these two Johns was evidently revered locally as a saint almost immediately after his death (although he was not formally canonized until centuries later); the problem is that it is now impossible to determine which it was—because adequate documentation of the case has either been lost, or was perhaps never compiled in the first place. Had clear, factually reliable *acta* been written and officially accepted and disseminated by church authorities as soon as the veneration of John Nepomucene as a saint had begun, this problem would have been obviated entirely.

It was the repeated occurrence of this and similar types of problems with inaccurate *acta* that led Pope Urban VIII to strictly regulate their dissemination. In 1634, the pope issued his decree *Caelestis Hierusalem cives*, which complained openly about the abuses regarding (among other things) the dissemination of factually unreliable *acta*, attributing miracles and describing revelations allegedly given to the potential saints in question. In order to counter these abuses, Urban VIII asserted that henceforth, written works were not to be published about purported saints and their supposedly miraculous lives and actions without the approval of the Holy See.[37] For it was within the purview of the Holy See alone to determine whether any allegedly supernatural events took place during the life (or after the death) of a possible saint.

From this point forward, when the process was properly followed, *acta* were generally written during or after an investigation conducted into the life (and in the case of martyrs, also the death) of a potential saint. Factual accuracy came to be of critical importance, as the Catholic Church strove, ideally, to avoid canonizing as saints any persons whose history was less than certain—regardless of the possible financial benefits that might accrue to those churches where the tombs of these possible saints were located. Thus the writing of *acta*, which had already come to constitute a part of canonization procedure in the first millennium, developed further into an element of an increasingly complex investigative process. The facts needed to be documented objectively, so that the church could demonstrate that a new saint was being canonized based on either martyrdom or a virtuous life. There could be no reasonable doubt that the person being canonized fully merited this new status as a saint. And as Urban VIII asserted openly, without the Holy See's involvement and control over the process in the past, abuses in this regard had definitely taken place.

As Hertling points out, the modern evidentiary process has its origins in the fact that in centuries past, before the *translatio* of a new saint, someone trustworthy (ideally) was charged with writing a *vita* with an attached list of miracles. The completed work was then examined by the Catholic hierarch with authority to canonize (previously the bishop or his synod), and after it was approved, the *translatio* could take place, thus effecting a canonization.[38] In this way, the simple act of writing the life story of a future saint eventually evolved into the investigative process that we have today. And as will be seen shortly, the centralization of the process under papal authority is what led to the requirement that an account of the potential saint's life be submitted to the Holy See, as a key element of the process.

This is certainly a far cry from the instant, popular recognition of martyrs qua martyrs in the first centuries of Christianity. As was already discussed in chapter 1, the mere nature of a martyr's death was sufficient; no other investigation into his manner of life was necessary. But when the church began also to acknowledge that non-martyrs could be included in the liturgical calendar as confessor-saints, some level of investigation became unavoidable. For any determination that a Christian who had died a natural death was so virtuous in life that he merited canonization by the church was, by its very nature, a subjective one. The black-and-white, factually undeniable nature of martyrdom during the early Christian persecutions had been relatively easy to establish; but this alternate standard, that of a life of virtue, required further assessment to determine whether or not it had been met.

The inevitable end result was that already in the period preceding the Great Schism, a system to gather evidence gradually began to develop throughout the entire church, to enable church authorities to make an informed decision on those cases of potential saints who had not died as martyrs. Those candidates for canonization who were determined to have indeed led lives of great virtue were ultimately declared to be saints; and they were, among other things, included in the calendars alongside the martyr-saints.

While those elements of the process that pertained specifically to non-martyrs do not, in and of themselves, concern us here, one quickly finds that many aspects of the procedure for canonizing confessors began soon enough to be applied to the cases of known martyrs as well. Thus it can be seen that, in the evolution of the process for the canonization of martyrs, new procedural elements appear that in fact have no basis whatsoever in early Christian tradition. As a rule, their development would be inexplicable were it not for the fact that they had already become standard elements in the process for canonizing confessors—and their inclusion in the process for canonizing martyrs then followed, as a sort of procedural paralleling. In this way the process for declaring a martyr to be a saint became more complex, including some features that are consistent with the process for confessors, but inconsistent with traditional practice—and theologically difficult to justify.

a. Development of a Detailed Evidentiary Process

In spite of some of the examples cited above, reliance on dubious *acta* as the chief evidence of a virtuous life or a martyr's death was never accepted as the general norm in the West. Rather, some sort of investigation, no matter how rudimentary, into the life of the potential saint appears to have taken place since the earliest centuries of Christianity. In the case of confirmed martyrs, we saw in chapter 1 that the establishment of martyrdom was considered to be sufficient evidence in itself to justify regarding the martyr as a saint. In those cases where the killer's hatred of the faith was undeniable—during the various Roman imperial persecutions, for example—the attestations of eyewitnesses to the martyr's arrest and subsequent death appear to have sufficed. But in less clear-cut cases—when the killer's motivation was possibly clouded by political considerations, or the attitude of the potential saint toward his impending death was either not known or perhaps raised questions about his acceptance of martyrdom for the love of Christ—further investigation into the situation was inevitably required.

In the early centuries of the church, there was no set formula for determining what constituted sufficient evidence in these cases. As a rule, the final decision rested with the local bishop, who had the authority to declare that a deceased Christian had indeed died a martyr's death and was henceforth to be commemorated as a saint. Over time, as was seen in the first chapter, a series of precedents were gradually set with regard to the true definition of martyrdom; but generally a bishop's decision that adequate evidence existed for him to make an official determination was still, at least to some extent, unavoidably subjective. Thus in theory it is entirely possible that the bishop of one local church might have concluded that existing evidence established definitively that a certain Christian had died a martyr, and should be venerated as a saint—while the bishop of a different local church might have reviewed the very same evidence and concluded that he was unable to make a decision without more information.

In the West, with the increasing centralization of the process under the papacy (which will be addressed shortly), it was only natural that a single, consistent measure of precisely what constituted sufficient evidence gradually began to be established. This is a development one finds conspicuously absent in the church in Russia, but not because of any deep-rooted theological differences. Culturally, this tendency in the West toward an orderly systematization of procedure was entirely consistent with Roman legal praxis, which had, long before the Roman Empire became Christian, been known for the methodical ordering of its legal norms—and in writing.

Writing lots of rules, in other words, is a characteristic that comes naturally to Rome. It is a strength historically lacking in Russia, where (as was seen in chapter 2) one struggles all too frequently to ascertain the most basic facts about Russian society in previous centuries—because they were not clearly documented. Given this Western tendency, it is hardly surprising that over the past thousand years, one can trace a dizzying array of frequently changing rules and regulations established by the Catholic Church regarding the nature and quantity of evidence that must be submitted to ecclesiastical officials on behalf of a potential saint. In 1588, Sixtus V established the Sacred Congregation of Rites, which was tasked with (among other things) the canonization of saints; it continued to define, and regularly refine, the evidentiary requirements and overall procedures.[39] This Congregation was, in turn, succeeded by the Congregation for Causes of Saints in 1969, which is now dedicated exclusively to the saint-making process.

Documenting and detailing all the myriad procedural regulations that have emanated from Rome regarding the canonization of saints over the past several centuries would require volumes in itself and is beyond the scope of this work. But it would also be beside the point, which is simply that the Catholic Church has firmly established the practice of writing pages of rules explaining exactly what sort of documentation is necessary to establish that a deceased Catholic died a martyr's death (or in the case of non-martyrs, lived a life of heroic virtue) and should henceforth be venerated as a saint. Although the early church appears to have had little difficulty canonizing saints without such explicit and numerous directives, the Catholic Church clearly believed it necessary to ultimately create a uniform set of regulations, which was made available to all those throughout the Catholic world who wished to promote someone's canonization. And at the origin of them all is simply the need for competent church officials to have sufficient, reliable evidence of a candidate's sanctity, in order to make an informed and accurate decision regarding his or her canonization.

To cite just one aspect of the evidentiary process as an example, *witnesses* have naturally always been a key source of information regarding the life and virtues of a potential saint. The testimony of witnesses became not merely beneficial, but a necessary component of the evidentiary process. Already in the thirteenth century, in the documentary process for John Sordi Cacciafronte, the martyred bishop of Vicenza, one can see the importance not only of eyewitness testimony in itself, but also of the actual number of witnesses available and willing to testify. The process for Cacciafronte, who was killed in Cremona in 1183, took place forty years after his death. While many of his contemporaries presumably had already passed away as well, there were still sixteen witnesses who testified at an inquest in Cremona, and another twenty-three who provided evidence at a separate session in Vicenza; some witnessed to his life and the circumstances surrounding his death, while others testified regarding miracles that had occurred through his intercession after death.[40]

Thirty-nine witnesses is an impressive number; but the quantity does not suffice if quality is lacking. In order to create as uniform a process as is humanly possible, the Catholic Church gradually established specific laws governing the testimony of witnesses in general. In the section of the 1917 Code of Canon Law pertaining to the canonization of saints, nine separate canons addressed the testimony of witnesses, identifying which persons must testify first (c. 2024), those who are inadmissible as witnesses because of the nature of their relationship to the potential saint or for other reasons (c. 2027), and the type of testimony they should give (c. 2029). Some subjectivity in the assessment of the value of various witnesses' testimony remained inevitable, but a detailed framework nevertheless was provided and applied to all.

Today, the directives regarding witnesses are contained in the 2007 Instruction *Sanctorum Mater*, issued by the Congregation for the Causes of Saints.[41] It provides even greater detail regarding the collection of evidence from witnesses than was found in the 1917 Code: the Instruction describes (among many other things) who is to take the witnesses' testimony, how it is to be printed, and who is to be present at their deposition. There is a discussion of the value of eyewitness testimony and of the methods to be used in transmitting it orally or in writing.

As with witnesses, other required elements of the process have been rearticulated many times over since the days of Cacciafronte's process in the 1200s. Documents have to be notarized, written testimony must be signed; it became necessary even to ensure that there were witnesses to the testimony of witnesses. Over subsequent centuries the Catholic Church has established and reestablished the criteria to be evaluated when determining whether or not a deceased Catholic merits canonization. But one may safely say in general that historically, it has always been necessary that claims be documented, and evidence be submitted—and Catholic authorities will ultimately decide whether or not the evidence is convincing enough to warrant canonization.

It is noteworthy that this complex aspect of the Catholic canonization process may be its most obvious external feature, and yet it is one that is wholly unseen in the canonization process for the Russian church. As was discussed in the preceding chapter, while there is unquestionably an investigation into the lives and deaths of prospective Russian martyr-saints, no explicit instructions have ever been published that could help us to ascertain exactly what evidence needs to be submitted, or how it is assessed by those with authority to make the final decision. Ironically, the contrast between the two procedural systems on this one point could not be more different: the Catholic process might be criticized for its complexity and excessive detail, while the Russian process can be faulted for failing to provide any detailed directives at all.

b. Proofs of Sanctity: Do Martyrs Need Miracles?

The need to establish that a potential saint had indeed lived a life (or in the case of a martyr, died a death) that merited canonization appears to have led to the gradual development of the acceptance of miracles as evidence.[42] A miracle that could be attributed to a deceased Christian's intercession constituted incontrovertible proof that the deceased in question was truly a saint, in heaven with God.

In this the Catholic Church in the West appears to have been developing its ideas along the same fundamental lines as the church in Russia. But while we saw in chapter 2 cases of Russian saints who have been canonized solely on the basis of miracles allegedly occurring through their intercession, Western praxis has steadily been the opposite: during the process for potential Catholic saints, whose lives and purported virtues were already known, miracles were sought as additional, corroborating evidence of their sanctity. In other words, in Russia, the canonization process was sometimes initiated because miracles were taking place; while in the West, miracles were sought because a canonization process was already underway.

The Russian church can argue (and has) that miracles have traditionally been a component of its canonization process. In Russia, as was seen in chapter 2, what constitutes tradition has been, determined by internal praxis since the conversion of Russia to Christianity in the tenth century. But the Catholic Church cannot make the same claim, as the practice of requiring miracles to establish that a potential saint is able to intercede with God is not grounded in early Christian tradition—which is the "tradition" upon which the praxis of the Catholic Church purports to be based. As can easily be seen from the discussion in chapter 1, there simply is no indication that in the first centuries of Christianity, miracles ever constituted a formal prerequisite for declaring someone a saint. Theologically speaking, either martyrdom or a virtuous life was the ultimately determining factor in any decision to declare a deceased Christian a saint in the first centuries of the life of the church. There is absolutely no evidence whatsoever that early Christians began to venerate their martyred fellows only after their ability to intercede with God was demonstrated by the working of miracles here on earth—in fact, for many centuries there is no mention at all of miracles associated with the decision to establish a deceased Christian as a martyr.[43] If the candidate's death met all the criteria for true martyrdom that had evolved in the first several centuries of Christianity, that was enough.

In the case of non-martyrs, however, the church eventually found it necessary to develop a method to ascertain that the potential saint really had lived a life of true virtue. The average Christian did not live through dramatic, external events during life that would clearly demonstrate to all that he was genuinely holy, and so his virtues were generally lived interiorly, thus rendering their authenticity extremely difficult to prove in a concrete way. The church came to accept (at an unknown yet early date, well before the Great Schism) that miracles worked after death constituted sufficient evidence that the potential saint had indeed lived a holy life, for they showed that this soul was now in heaven, and able to intercede with God for the faithful still on earth. Thus miracles ultimately came to be a standard element in the canonization processes of non-martyrs, as part of the documentation collected to establish the virtues they practiced during their lives.

But since the church had, from the beginning, accepted that the very act of martyrdom was (as Aquinas would later phrase it) the ultimate act of virtue, any requirement that miracles be performed by a person who had definitely died a martyr's death would have been theologically superfluous. After all, for Christians who had voluntarily given their lives for Christ, who had courageously undergone violent death for the love of God, why should it be considered reasonable to demand even further proofs of their holiness?

Nevertheless, as was seen in the preceding chapter, miracles did indeed become a required element of the canonization process for martyrs in Russia—presumably by making a parallel with the process for non-martyrs. In the West, the question of whether miracles actually constituted a sine qua non requirement for canonizing martyrs appears for at least several centuries to have been less than clear. But in a number of well-known historical cases involving the canonization of martyrs, official documents specifically mention that miracles had indeed been recorded and were believed to be the direct result of the martyr's intercession with God.

In 926, Saint Wiborada was martyred in Swabia (modern-day Switzerland) by invading Magyars, who destroyed her monastery and killed her while she was kneeling in prayer. The Bollandists note that she was canonized by Pope Clement II in 1047, after he had heard an account of her life and of the miracles that had been attributed to her intercession.[44] But while the miracles might have been a key factor in the pope's decision, the rather general wording of the text does not indicate that the pope would necessarily have refused to canonize Wiborada without them. The account in the *acta* notes simply that miracles had indeed occurred after the faithful had prayed to Wiborada, and this obviously constituted corroboration of the veracity of her reputation for leading a virtuous life before her martyrdom—but the account does not specifically indicate that the miracles were a necessary condition for her canonization. It is possible that, like the unofficial documentation describing the cause for canonization of the Romanov family in Russia (discussed in the preceding chapter), miracles attributed to Wiborada's intercession with God were mentioned merely as further justification for the pope's determination of her sainthood. We will of course never know whether Clement II would have canonized Wiborada solely on the basis of her martyr's death if no known miracles had taken place. The account of her canonization suggests that miracles were certainly relevant, but it does not show that they were a sine qua non for declaring her a martyr-saint.

The uncertainty continued into the following centuries. In 1198, Pope Innocent III canonized Saint Homobonus, a layman who had died only the previous year. Homobonus was not a martyr, and thus it was natural that the church, before declaring him a saint, first needed to establish that he had truly lived a life of genuine virtue. In the course of his decree canonizing Homobonus, Innocent III made a statement about the elements needed for canonizations in general: "Two things are required, so that somebody may be considered a saint in the Church Militant, namely works of piety during his life, and miracles after death."[45]

Less than two years later, the same pope expanded on this statement when he canonized the non-martyr Empress Cunegunda of Luxemburg, who had died in 1040. Repeating his earlier assertion that both "merits and miracles" were required for the canonization of a saint, he added, "for neither merits without miracles, nor miracles without merits fully suffice to present evidence of sanctity . . . for an angel of Satan can transform himself into an angel of light, and certain persons may do their works in order that they may be seen by men."[46]

Did Innocent III intend these statements to apply to martyrs as well as to confessors? He did not specifically say. While the pope did not provide any historical justification for his assertions—in the context of a bull of canonization, such a citation would have been inappropriate in any case—the fact remains that requiring miracles before the canonization of someone who has been acknowledged to have died a martyr's death constitutes a definite shift away from traditional praxis.

Regardless, the subsequent case of the martyred Pierre de Castelnau clarified any possible ambiguity in Innocent III's statement. The Cistercian was sent as papal legate to France in 1199, to reconcile Albigensian heretics to the church; but in 1208 he was cut down by those with whom he had been trying to negotiate. The same Pope Innocent III publicly acknowledged that his death constituted martyrdom, as he had been killed for his orthodox beliefs by supporters of the Albigensian cause—but he then lamented the incredulity of the local people, which he blamed for the lack of miracles at de Castelnau's tomb.[47] To this day, Pierre de Castelnau has never been canonized.

If miracles were not already by this point a necessary requirement for the canonization even of martyrs, Innocent's failure to declare de Castelnau a saint would be inexplicable. The pope asserted openly that de Castelnau had died a martyr's death—which in the earliest centuries of the church would have been sufficient in itself to warrant his enrollment in the liturgical calendar as a martyr-saint. But Pope Innocent's statement indicates that now, despite de Castelnau's martyrdom, miracles were also required, and because they were lacking in this case, the canonization process did not move forward.

The issue was revisited, however, in the seventeenth century, soon after the martyrdom of Bishop Jozafat Kuncewicz of Polotsk (today in Belarus) at the hands of Orthodox attackers in 1623. As Pope Urban VIII wished to expedite Jozafat's canonization,[48] a question was raised within the Sacred Congregation of Rites, which at that time had jurisdiction over the process for canonization of saints: does an established martyr for the faith need to have documented miracles as well?[49]

The opinion of the Congregation's members, pronounced in 1642, was far from unanimous. While miracles were at that point being required for the canonizations of martyrs and non-martyrs alike, it was acknowledged that there were innumerable martyrs already being venerated in the church, whose intercession with God had never been established by miracles—and yet the church found no fault with this fact. Eventually the members of the Congregation concluded that in cases of clear-cut, undeniable martyrdom, miracles are not necessary for canonization; but in those cases where the person's death as a martyr is more open to question, the occurrence of miracles actually constitutes verification that the potential saint did indeed die a genuine martyr.[50]

Thus the Catholic Church rationalized the answer in both ways: in theory, a true martyr can be canonized without miracles, because his martyrdom is sufficient to establish his sanctity and ability to intercede with God for us. Nevertheless, in most cases of martyrdom the circumstances include a real possibility that the potential saint did not die a martyr after all—because the motives of the killer, or because the candidate's own internal dispositions are less than completely clear. Requiring miracles for the majority of most martyrs, therefore, effectively constitutes a sort of insurance policy guaranteeing that even a candidate for canonization who did not in fact die as a martyr is still able to intercede for the faithful on earth in miraculous ways. This stance thus acknowledges historical tradition, which originally never required that martyrs demonstrate their sanctity with miracles; but at the same time it protects the church from the possibility of canonizing as a martyr someone who may in reality have died for political reasons, or whose spiritual state at the time of death was in actuality not in accord with the heroic acceptance of martyrdom for the love of Christ that is required of a true martyr.

If miracles are therefore necessary for the canonization of most martyrs, how many are sufficient? Back in the early thirteenth century, Pope Innocent III gave the church an estimate, in a rescript concerning the evidentiary process: he ordered Catholic officials investigating a potential saint at the local level to submit two, three, or four miracles, indicating that the lesser number would suffice if they were more obvious.[51] At this point, the question was evidently one of quality rather than sheer quantity.

And the quantity/quality dichotomy was probably likewise at issue in 1244, when Innocent IV ordered the process for (non-martyr) Edmond of Canterbury to be redone, this time "omitting the multitude of miracles."[52] Presumably there were also other procedural defects in the presentation that prompted the pope to take this action; it is difficult to imagine that an overabundance of sound, well-documented evidence would have provoked such a critical response.

For centuries, it does not appear that there was any official numerical formula that actually quantified, in a concrete way, either the absolute minimum acceptable number of miracles or the types that were most convincing. In this aspect, the Catholic Church's canonization procedure was essentially following the same largely subjective lines as did that of the Russian church. The hierarch who was authorized to decide whether or not to canonize had the power to assess the overall mass of evidence and reach his own conclusions. The loose structure of this system logically implies, of course, that one man might determine that the evidence submitted about miracles in a given case was sufficient, but in another might not be.

One thing is quite clear, however: for centuries, there was no particular distinction in the Catholic Church between the amount of evidence of miracles required for a martyr and that required for a non-martyr. Even if it could be established that a potential saint had died a martyr's death, this in no way lessened the need to demonstrate that miracles had taken place through that candidate's intercession.

The procedure laid out in the 1917 Code of Canon Law was typical in this regard. With respect to the requirement of miracles, no distinction whatsoever was made between martyrs and non-martyrs. For beatification (which will be discussed shortly), the law required two, three, or four different miracles, depending on their verifiability—those attested to by eyewitnesses held more weight than those authenticated from hearsay.[53] After beatification, at least two more miracles were required for canonization.[54]

The law did provide, however, for an exception in the case of a martyr whose death for the faith had been firmly established: canon 2116.2 specifically noted that if miracles were lacking, the Congregation could decide to request that the pope dispense from the requirement of miracles in such a case. And starting in the 1970s, it became commonplace for both martyrs and non-martyrs to dispense from the second miracle needed for beatification, as well as from the second miracle required for canonization.[55] But as Piacentini noted, the idea nevertheless remained entrenched at the Vatican that while miracles, in the case of martyrs, were not strictly necessary, they helped to confirm the authenticity of the martyrdom. For this reason, it was standard practice to formally oppose the granting of a dispensation from the requirement of miracles, even in the causes of martyrs.[56]

Regardless of the formal opposition within the Vatican Congregation, the commonplace praxis became the norm. One proven miracle is now required for beatification, and one for canonization. But the rules currently in force contain a new twist: in the case of a martyr, it is no longer necessary to establish that a miracle has been performed in order to obtain beatification. Once martyrdom has been proven, a candidate for Catholic sainthood can be beatified without any miracles at all—simply by virtue of being a martyr.[57] We see here the beginnings of both a return to historical tradition and a greater emphasis on a right understanding of the intrinsic theological implications of martyrdom. For the first time in hundreds of years, the established fact that a potential Catholic saint has suffered a martyr's death carries with it enough weight to override the need for established miracles—at least for this stage of the canonization process.

i. Miracles and Incorrupt Remains

As was seen in chapter 2, a requirement developed in Russia that the bodies of potential saints, whether martyred or not, had to be found incorrupt if they were to be canonized. This represented, of course, a marked departure from the praxis of the first millennium, in which no such prerequisite existed.

In the West, the process throughout the second millennium has in this regard been exactly as in the first: there has never been any need to demonstrate that the body of a candidate for sainthood is miraculously incorrupt. At the same time, it has definitely been established scientifically that the remains of a number of Catholics saints have inexplicably defied normal corruption—a finding that is popularly regarded as miraculous.

Since there is no need to demonstrate that the remains are incorrupt if a potential saint is to be canonized by the Catholic Church, the discovery of a normally corrupted body would in itself have no negative bearing on his canonization. But if the remains were found to be incorrupt, and the incorruption were determined to be medically inexplicable, could this fact be considered as one of the miracles required by the process?

Historically, there is absolutely no evidence to indicate that this was ever a standard practice. The martyred Pierre de Castelnau, discussed above, has never been canonized, and Pope Innocent III indicated obliquely that the lack of miracles was to blame. Yet when his tomb was opened in 1208 so that his remains could be translated to a grander place, it was found that they were incorrupt and emitted a sweet fragrance. The account in the *Acta Sanctorum* suggests that this discovery did indeed constitute a miracle; but since Pierre was not canonized, it is clear that either the incorruption was not regarded as a miracle for the purposes of canonization or that it was insufficient.[58]

Several centuries later we find the martyred Saint Jozafat, whose cause (mentioned above) prompted an extensive debate among Catholic officials in the time of Urban VIII as to whether miracles should be required for the canonization of martyrs. Jozafat's body had been found incorrupt—a fact apparently not accepted as a miracle for purposes of his canonization. If it had been standard practice to accept as miraculous the fact that a person's remains had not decayed, there would have been no need even to raise the issue of requiring miracles for martyrs; the pope could simply have acknowledged the miracle of incorruption, and the whole discussion would have been moot. As it was, numerous medical cures were presented, and evidently accepted, as proof of the miraculous intercession of the martyred Jozafat.[59]

But the case of the incorrupt relics of the martyred Jesuit Andrew Bobola is perhaps the most extraordinary. Bobola was tortured extensively and partially flayed before finally being killed by Cossacks in 1657. Despite its severely mutilated state, which if anything should have hastened its decomposition, his body was discovered to be completely incorrupt when it was exhumed in the early 1700s. Nevertheless, the evidence submitted for Bobola's beatification—a procedural aspect that will be addressed later in this chapter—included descriptions of twenty different medical cures asserted to have been miraculous, and no mention whatsoever is made of the martyr's incorrupt remains.[60] During the process for his canonization, which was conducted in the 1930s, extensive evidence of two additional medical miracles was submitted and accepted.[61]

It thus seems quite clear that a determination that a potential saint's remains have been preserved incorrupt does not constitute, and traditionally has not been accepted as, one of the miracles necessary for proof of sanctity. While it may be biologically impossible to explain why the body of a candidate for sainthood did not decay, the fact of incorruption does not constitute evidence in support of canonization in the Catholic Church. Therefore it should not be surprising that incorrupt relics are not a requirement of the canonization process, as they are in Russia. Incorruption might perhaps be viewed unofficially as corroboration of a person's sanctity, but it has no direct bearing on the decision to canonize a Catholic saint, which is dependent on other, unrelated evidence.

C. Authority: Who Makes the Decision to Canonize a Saint?

Without a doubt, the most significant—as well as the most complex—developments in the Catholic canonization process concern those who are authorized to create new saints, whether martyrs or non-martyrs. Initially, and in complete accord with the tradition established in the first millennium, a canonization was carried out by a diocesan bishop, and the new saint was then venerated only in that particular diocese. However, the preexisting practice of one locale accepting saints from another continued, causing numerous saints to be venerated as such throughout wider regions of the Christian world.

There had been, it is true, occasional canonizations solemnly performed not by the local bishop but by the pope himself. The first known papal canonization was that of the non-martyr Saint Ulric, bishop of Augsburg, who died in 973 and was declared a saint in 993 by Pope John XV.[62] There is absolutely no evidence, however, of any suggestion at this time that the pope alone had authority to canonize in the Catholic Church; local Catholic bishops still continued to create new saints as they had been doing for centuries. Thus while the case of Saint Ulric does provide a sort of historical precedent for papal canonization, it did not, in and of itself, represent any shift in procedure. As we are about to see, however, subsequent events led to exactly that: a radical procedural shift that permanently altered the system for canonizing all new Catholic saints.

1. Centralization of Authority, Originally as a Response to Local Abuses

The original impetus for the changes in the second millennium had already been seen in the first: abuses of the existing process, resulting in the veneration of persons who most decidedly were not saints, had caused the church to tighten the restrictions on who was, and who was not, permitted to canonize. As was already discussed in chapter 1, in the ninth century Charlemagne himself was involved in convoking local church councils that placed strict limitations on the creation of new saints, insisting that this could only be done by the local bishops. Bishops alone had the authorization to determine who was to be venerated as a saint; for it had been amply demonstrated, at least in the Frankish kingdom over which Charlemagne ruled, that when this decision was left to those of lesser ecclesiastical rank, persons quite undeserving of sainthood were wrongly being canonized.

A particularly important example of such abuse occurred in the twelfth century, when Pope Alexander III wrote to King Kol of Sweden, castigating the Swedish people's veneration as a saint of a man who had been killed while he was drunk.⁶³ The pope noted that even though miracles may indeed have occurred near the tomb of this man, it was not permitted to venerate anyone as a saint without the authorization of the Roman pontiff.⁶⁴ While canonizations had occasionally been performed by the pope himself in the past, this is the first time we find papal approval described as an actual requirement. This did not entirely preclude bishops from creating new saints in their dioceses, of course, but it now became necessary for them first to obtain consent from Rome before carrying out the local canonization.

Alexander III's intention in making this statement—commonly referred to henceforth as *Audivimus*, from the first word of the relevant paragraph—is not entirely clear. It would be strange for a pope to use the occasion of a private letter to a secular ruler to promulgate a new law, which the rule about papal approval does appear to be. He may have simply made this statement in order to assert his authority over the church in Sweden and to correct what he perceived to be a clear-cut case of abuse. It is thus entirely possible that the pope did not originally intend this general assertion about papal involvement in the canonization of saints to acquire the force of general law.

But regardless of Alexander's actual intent, *Audivimus* soon became accepted as universal law when it was included in the *Decretals* of Gregory IX (compiled by Raymond of Pennafort, who would eventually be canonized as a saint himself) in the early thirteenth century. "Without papal approval, it is not permitted for anyone to be venerated as a saint," according to Gregory's decretal on relics and the veneration of saints.⁶⁵ Thus, a paragraph from a twelfth-century papal letter to the king of Sweden regarding a single instance of abuse quickly came to be enshrined in canon law binding the entire Catholic Church. As Kuttner notes frankly, one could argue that it was the decretalists, rather than the pope, who actually created this new universal law.⁶⁶

Abuses with regard to saints were not confined to Sweden, for just a few years before Gregory's *Decretals*, the Fourth Lateran Council had addressed the general veneration and sale of the relics of saints. Already at that time it was the effort to curb abuses occurring at the diocesan level that had led the highest level of authority in the Catholic Church to regulate the veneration of the relics of saints:

> The Christian religion is rather often disparaged, since certain persons put the relics of saints on sale and display them everywhere; in order that it might not be disparaged in future, we declare with this decree that from now on, ancient relics are not to be displayed outside of a reliquary, nor are they to be put up for sale.⁶⁷

It may be safely assumed that if the council fathers felt it was necessary to establish a law on this matter, there must already have been sufficiently widespread abuse of the relics of saints (authentic or otherwise). If relics were not being sold, displayed, and generally treated in an unbecoming manner, there would have been no need for this canon. This ruling of the Fourth Lateran Council must therefore have been a response to objectionable practices at the local level. Promulgating a uniform universal law for the entire Catholic Church was a means of combating abuse—and this would henceforth be the Catholic hierarchy's method of curtailing what it perceived as bad practices, and ensuring that sound ones would be implemented instead.

A concrete and well-known example of a "martyr" whose public veneration as such was blocked by the papacy is Simone of Trent, who died in 1475 at the age of about two. The toddler disappeared on Holy Thursday, and his mangled body was found on Easter Sunday floating in a pool of water near the home of one of Trent's Jewish families. The local bishop ordered the city's Jews to be interrogated under torture, whereupon they confessed to the ritual killing of the child on Good Friday.[68] Soon the bishop was fostering a cult to the martyred Simoncino; as civil ruler, the bishop had ordered the execution of fifteen local Jews purportedly involved in the boy's martyrdom, and he was now propagating the notion that other ritual murders of Catholics by Jews were also taking place. In the meantime, miracles allegedly were already taking place through Simone's intercession.[69]

Thus far, the case seems remarkably similar to that of the six-year-old Russian martyr Saint Gavriil of Belostok, discussed in chapter 2. But before Simoncino could be formally declared a martyr, Pope Sixtus IV quickly intervened from Rome. Issuing a letter to authorities throughout what is now Italy, he objected to the veneration of Simone of Trent as a martyr without papal approbation, and demanded further information about the case.[70] The pope took account of the anti-Semitic atmosphere of the time, and indicated that the facts about the manner of Simoncino's death had not been satisfactorily proven.

It may very well have been the threat of indiscriminate, retaliatory violence against all Jews that actually prompted Sixtus IV's intervention in the interest of public order; but of chief interest to us here are the procedural limitations the pope consequently imposed on the cult of Simone of Trent. It was not permitted to publicly declare that Simone was a martyr, or even to describe him as "blessed"; to disseminate either images of him with a halo, or *acta* recounting the alleged manner of his death; or to declare that miraculous cures had been performed through Simoncino's intercession. All of these aspects of the cult of a true martyr, said the pope, were subject to his approval—and he did not give it.

In 1588, however, Pope Sixtus V permitted the diocese of Trent to celebrate Simone's feast-day with a proper Mass and Office in his honor, but this concession did not carry with it approval of the stories of his martyrdom. Historians subsequently cast sufficient doubt on the truthfulness of the account of Simone's death,[71] and in 1965 his feast-day was removed from the liturgical calendar of Trent, with the approval of the Holy See.[72]

Simoncino of Trent was never declared a martyr-saint. While the local bishop appears to have enthusiastically embraced the idea of canonizing the child, the pope refused to do so on the grounds that factual information about his case was lacking.[73] A very limited cult was eventually permitted, but it appears to have eventually died out by mutual consent of both Rome and the local church. If the papacy had not, by the time of Simone's death, reserved to itself the power to canonize new saints, it seems safe to assume that the child would wrongly have been declared a martyr-saint. An error thus appears to have been averted by the combined caution of several popes who were involved in this case.

Presumably it was precisely cases like this that gave added justification to the insistence of numerous popes since Alexander III that the decision to canonize belongs to the papacy alone.[74] Eventually every essential aspect of the investigatory process was made subject to papal approval. It was the pope who ultimately determined whether the evidence of martyrdom (or of heroic virtue, in the case of non-martyrs) was sufficient; he decided whether enough evidence of alleged miracles had been submitted, and whether they were to be accepted as genuine; and he alone could decide whether the testimony of witnesses was credible or not. It was the pope who established the details of the process, and who made the final decision about canonization. One might easily object to the strict centralization and bureaucratization of the process, but historically it is clear that the process evolved in this way because of the abuses that various popes encountered, and checked, at the local level.

It should be pointed out that in the twentieth century, with the promulgation of the 1917 Code of Canon Law, significant involvement of the local bishops once again in the process was enshrined in written, universal law. It was the ordinary who collected documentation for the evidentiary process, examined any writings of potential saints in order to establish their theological orthodoxy, and determined that no unauthorized veneration of the candidate was taking place.[75] More recently, with his 1983 apostolic constitution *Divinus perfectionis Magister*,[76] Pope John Paul II divided the canonization process into the "diocesan phase" and the "Roman phase," the first of which is entirely the responsibility of the local bishop.[77] On the surface, it may initially appear that the pope at least partially returned power over canonization to those members of the hierarchy who had been creating new saints throughout the first millennium.

But closer inspection will show that this is not in fact the case. While the local hierarch has the power—and the responsibility—to compile the documentary evidence in support of a potential saint's cause, the fact remains that it continues to be the pope who makes the ultimate decision as to whether or not the canonization will take place. The mere fact that a bishop submits what he believes to be a well-documented case to Rome does not in any way guarantee that it will eventually be approved. While the diocesan bishop is without a doubt obliged to be very involved in the process under the current law, the fact remains that only the pope can issue a decree of canonization.[78] Thus the original assertion by Alexander III more than eight hundred years ago, that the pope alone has the authority to canonize saints, still holds today.

a. Decretalists and the Evolution of a Canonical/Theological Justification for Papal Canonization

From this time forward, Catholic decretalists not only continually repeated the assertion that the pope alone could regulate the canonization and veneration of saints; they also included in their writings additional theological and legal arguments in support of this position. The need for Catholicism's supreme authority to control the process for the entire church was constantly reiterated and defended.

The writings of Henry of Segusio, the great thirteenth-century canonist and cardinal of Ostia, are a good example. In his famous commentary, he quotes the letter of Alexander III mentioned above, but explains and justifies it further, noting that canonization should be reserved to the Holy See because it concerns matters of faith. Since it is the pope's prerogative and responsibility to resolve (for example) doubtful passages of sacred scripture, Henry points out that it is only logical that the pope should also be the one to determine doubtful instances of sanctity among potential saints. Similarly, if miracles are to be a key factor in the canonization process—which, as we have seen, definitely came to be so—Henry argues that it is appropriately within the purview of papal authority to determine whether these miracles are authentic or not.[79] Henry's commentary was quoted in numerous subsequent collections of decretals, thus cementing this position even further into the developing corpus of Catholic canon law.

With the advent of the Protestant Reformation in the sixteenth century in the West came attacks on papal authority in general, and Catholic legal scholars responded defensively with strong affirmations of the pope's supreme power over the church. Insofar as the criticisms touched on the issue of the canonization of saints, one finds Catholic jurists in turn reasserting the pope's jurisdiction over the process, as one aspect of a multifaceted defense of the papacy. In the early fifteenth century, for example, the English Carmelite, Thomas Netter of Walden, responded to attacks on the papacy by John Wycliffe (who had already been condemned as a heretic by the Council of Constance, twenty-one years after his death in 1384). "If every bishop has the right [to create new saints]," Netter argued, "then how much more does the Pope, the Bishop of Bishops?"[80] Thus the suggestion that the pope did *not* have authority over the canonization process came to constitute an assault on fundamental Catholic ecclesiology, and assertions of papal primacy logically included the recognition that it was the pope who had control over the creation and veneration of new saints.

As theologians continued to discuss the nature of papal authority in general, and in particular the power exercised by the pope when he canonizes a new saint, it soon became accepted that, in some sense, a canonization should be regarded by the Catholic faithful as infallible. The complex theological issues inherent in this question are beyond the scope of this work; but in short, it is generally accepted that a declaration of canonization is an exercise of papal infallibility, while a beatification is not.[81] That this understanding raises other theological questions is beyond a doubt; but what is certain is that a formal act of canonization by the pope is a final, definitive act that cannot be undone.

b. Can a Catholic Saint Be "Decanonized"? The Case of Philomena

As was discussed in chapter 2, there have historically been cases of Russian saints who had been canonized by competent hierarchs being removed from the calendar years after their cult had been established. But given the different ecclesiology of the Catholic Church and the concept of papal infallibility, has it ever been possible to "decanonize" a Catholic saint? The case of "Saint" Philomena, mentioned above in the context of her inclusion on and subsequent exclusion from the Catholic liturgical calendar, is often cited as an example of an erstwhile saint who is no longer a saint. In actuality, an examination of the facts surrounding her cult reveal instead the increasing emphasis in the Catholic Church on historical accuracy. Philomena's remains were discovered in the Roman catacombs only in the early 1800s, along with a vial of what was believed to be her blood, an indication that she had died a martyr's death.[82] The name on her tomb, "Filumena," is unknown in extant historical accounts of early Christian martyrs; and it may actually not be her name at all, for the Greco-Latin roots of the word simply mean "lover of the light," and thus it may have been intended as a description of the deceased person rather than her personal name.

Since nothing at all was known about this deceased person, the Catholic Church understandably could not, and therefore did not, canonize her. Indeed, no canonization process was ever initiated on her behalf—for the documentary evidence required to support such a cause simply does not exist. But some years after the discovery of the remains, a religious in Naples claimed to have had a vision of Philomena, who explained that she had been a Greek princess who was martyred during the Roman persecution under the Emperor Diocletian in the early fourth century. She purportedly described in detail the torments to which she had been subjected, which scholars subsequently argued perfectly match the carvings on her tomb of an arrow, an anchor, and apparently a rod of flagellation.[83] Devotion to the martyr Philomena subsequently intensified, although to this day, no contemporary historical evidence about her has ever been found; and numerous miracles were alleged to have been performed through her intercession.[84]

As noted earlier in this chapter, in 1837 the Congregation for Sacred Rites issued a decree permitting the celebration of the Mass and Office in honor of Saint Philomena on August 11. The decree was signed by the prefect of the Congregation, who noted that Pope Gregory XVI gave his approval.

Events regarding Philomena up to this point clearly mirror the circumstances leading to the canonization of many unknown deceased persons in Russia, based on dreams or visions purporting to identify the individual in question and describe his or her life and/or death. The extreme case of Yakov of Borovich, discussed in chapter 2, is an example of this phenomenon: the inhabitants of the region had no information whatsoever that could identify the body they had discovered, until a local resident had a vision in which Yakov identified himself.

Unlike the Russian Yakov, however, Philomena was never declared a saint, on the grounds that apart from the account revealed in the dream of one local religious, nothing factual was known about her—including even her name. It is true that in the nineteenth century she was permitted a feast-day, which the universal church was not required to observe; but as we have already seen above, the act of establishing a liturgical commemoration had been separated from the act of canonization centuries before. This action, therefore, can in no way be construed to have constituted her canonization.

Consequently, it is hardly surprising that with the revision of the calendar under Pope John XXIII in 1961, the name of Philomena was removed completely. It is indeed difficult to understand why it had been inserted there in the first place! This action can and should be viewed as a proper example of a calendar correction—and not as the "decanonization" of a previously canonized saint. Philomena (if that is even her name) is not, and never has been a saint in the Catholic Church. "Decanonization" has definitely occurred in the church in Russia; but there is neither historical precedent nor theological justification for such a possibility in the Catholic Church.

2. Canonizations with Territorial Limitations: The Development of Beatification

In the earliest days of Christianity, martyrs originally began to be commemorated in the liturgy only in their local churches. Over time, as we saw in the first chapter, it became common for some locales to adopt the martyr-saints of other local churches, thus spreading the veneration of many early saints far beyond the regions where they had lived and died. At the same time, however, there were still many saints whose commemoration in the liturgy remained within the confines of their locale, resulting in many variations in the liturgical calendars of different geographical regions of the church.

In the West, however, as we have already seen in this chapter, the canonization of new saints was reserved to the pope relatively soon after the Great Schism. Were all Catholic canonizations henceforth intended for the universal Catholic Church? Did papal canonization put an end to the whole phenomenon of local saints?

The answer, perhaps illogically, is no. While the pope, possessing supreme authority over the Catholic Church throughout the world, thus has the power to declare that a new saint is to be venerated by Catholics everywhere, historically it is clear that popes have not always chosen to canonize saints for the entire church. Even after it had become well established that canonization of Catholic saints was the prerogative of the pope alone, one finds cases of new saints who were created by the pope, but only for a particular region or group.

Thus in 1481 Pope Sixtus IV canonized the five Franciscan martyrs of Morocco who had been killed in 1220, but limited their veneration only to the Franciscan order. In his bull of canonization, the pope specified that the Order of Friars Minor could publicly and solemnly celebrate Mass and pray the Office of these holy martyrs on their new feast-day of January 16.[85] While Sixtus IV clearly indicated in his decree that the five Franciscans had endured many torments at the hands of the king of Morocco on behalf of Christ, thus meriting a martyr's palm, he did not permit them to be venerated as saints by the entire Catholic Church.[86] We have here, in essence, a later example of a local canonization. It basically followed the same lines as canonizations during the first millennium, but with one notable difference: the ultimate decision here rested not with the local bishop, but rather with the supreme pontiff.

Similarly, in 1625, the limited veneration of twenty-six Japanese missionaries and converts who had been martyred in 1597 was permitted by Pope Urban VIII. Since three had been Jesuits and the rest Franciscans, the pope conceded that each order could celebrate the Mass and Office commemorating those who had been its members.[87] Interestingly, we find at this point a new insistence on the correct use of precise terminology: when Rome learned that the Jesuit proper for the feast-day used the term *saints* to describe its three martyrs, it objected, noting that this was not permitted because they had not been solemnly canonized.[88]

But if the pope had not canonized them, what had he done? And if they were not saints, what were they? At this stage in history, Catholic theological concepts and procedural praxis regarding the making of saints were undeniably inconsistent. It had been established for several centuries already that the pope, as the supreme authority in the church, had the power to create saints for the Catholic Church throughout the world. Since the time of the Council of Trent and the establishment of the new Roman missal, it was likewise accepted that the pope had the power to insist that these new saints were to be venerated by *all* Catholics. He alone made the final determination as to whether the evidence submitted in support of a potential saint was sufficient for canonization. The notion, therefore, that the pope would occasionally approve of the veneration of a deceased Christian but limit it to a particular locale or religious institute, and refuse to permit the title of saint, naturally gives one pause.

At this point one can see that the historical tradition—local bishops establishing saints for their own local churches—was coming into conflict with the ever-developing Catholic ecclesiological position that the pope has full and supreme power over the church throughout the world. Although one can argue that the dichotomy has never been fully resolved in the purely theological sense, subsequent events would result in a sort of procedural compromise in the canonization and veneration of new saints, whether martyrs or non-martyrs: the development of beatification before canonization, as part of a new, multi-step process.

a. Urban VIII's *Caelestis Hierusalem Cives* as Another Response to Local Abuse

Interestingly, the original impetus for the marked shift in process was yet another instance of a papal reaction to perceived abuse. Mention has already been made above of Urban VIII's 1634 decree *Caelestis Hierusalem cives*, which objected to the veneration as saints of persons whose cause had not been investigated by the Holy See. Citing the need to prevent "fraud or error" in such a serious matter, Urban outlined the need for Rome to examine the documentary proofs supporting every potential canonization.[89] He declared that from this time forward nobody—martyr or not—could be venerated as a saint, portrayed in images with a halo, or described as the worker of miracles unless Rome had first examined the evidence, determined it to be both accurate and adequate, and canonized him.

For potential saints whose causes arose after 1634, the procedure was made entirely clear. Henceforth, for every candidate for canonization whose cause was sent to Rome, the absence of unauthorized cult first had to be established. Unless and until the pope canonized such candidates, the local faithful were prohibited from speaking about them as saints, celebrating feast-days in their honor, and publishing accounts of their lives asserting definitively that their intercession was responsible for miraculous cures. If it was found that local Catholics were indeed already venerating such persons as saints on their own initiative, this veneration had to be stopped.

But Urban VIII also recognized that there were already countless persons who had been popularly venerated as saints for centuries—yet had never been properly canonized. Perhaps devotion to them developed spontaneously among the local faithful after their deaths, and simply remained at that level, without Catholic authorities ever taking any action to canonize them formally. Or it may have been that a proper canonization process had been initiated, but for whatever reason it had stalled and subsequently been abandoned. Regardless of the circumstances, many persons were already informally being venerated as saints without their cause ever having been examined and approved by Rome—and Urban VIII concluded that this was unacceptable.

Was the pope forbidding Catholics to venerate these "unofficial saints" any longer? That is certainly the conclusion to be drawn from his decree. But the Vatican soon published an addendum to *Caelestis Hierusalem cives*, which allowed for the possibility of an exemption: for those "saints" venerated as such from time immemorial, or recognized as saints in the writings of the Fathers, or whose cults otherwise had long been tolerated by the Apostolic See or the Ordinary, an indult *super casu excepto* could be granted.[90] Without it, any unauthorized popular cult had to be suppressed.

When an indult was given, the veneration could continue at the local level, although the person in question still was not to be considered a saint. The indult simply recognized that the reverence accorded to the deceased Christian did indeed have historical merit, as in some way it had been approved by knowledgeable Catholic authorities (albeit not by the pope himself, as required).

Originally, the declaration *super casu excepto* was certainly not intended to constitute what is now known as beatification. For example, the nineteen martyrs of Gorkum, Holland, who were killed in 1572, received a declaration *super casu excepto* in 1649—and they were also formally beatified by Pope Alexander VII twenty-six years later.[91] But as Lambertini, the future Pope Benedict XIV, noted in his seminal work on the history of beatification and canonization in the Catholic Church, this declaration *super casu excepto* soon came to be regarded as *equipollent* (i.e., equivalent to) *beatification*: "For since beatification is nothing other than permission to worship in some determined location, one cannot doubt this permission to worship whenever *casus exceptus* is approved by the decrees of Urban VIII; and therefore one cannot in any way doubt the equipollent beatification."[92]

How did this new process of permitting the continuance of centuries-old cults develop into the system of beatification, which quickly became an obligatory stage in the canonization process? For it seems quite clear that when he promulgated *Caelestis Hierusalem cives* Urban VIII did not have in mind the two-step process of beatification and canonization that later became the norm.

This procedural shift may have been completely unplanned, but there was nevertheless a definite logic in the way that the new process developed. The granting of a decree *super casus excepto* was never intended, nor construed, as a "final step" in officially recognizing someone as a saint—far from it. Since canonization of new Catholic saints was now firmly under the control of the papacy, the indult was designed to constitute permission in the interim to continue the veneration of someone local Catholics believed *should* be a saint. If the local church was in fact commemorating a deceased Catholic who had never been properly canonized, it either had to obtain the indult from Rome or the commemoration had to stop.

Veraja rightly notes that the end result of this new requirement was, in effect, that all causes from this time forward fell into one of only two categories: either the person had never been venerated as a saint by the local faithful, and the Vatican was able to grant a decree *super non cultu*, verifying that no improper veneration had ever taken place; or the person had indeed been venerated as a saint without Rome's approval, either for a lengthy period of time or with the approbation of lesser Catholic authorities, and thus could receive an indult *super casu excepto*, which permitted the veneration to continue, at least in that region. In practice, no third option existed.[93]

The fact that in the second group of cases permission was being given by Rome for a local cult, led to the unintended practice of conducting a preliminary investigation into those cases in the first group as well, so that they too might be permitted at least local veneration while the regular canonization process was underway. Almost without anyone realizing it, the added step of beatification was thus established.

There is no indication that this result was foreseen either by Urban VIII or his Sacred Congregation for Rites, which had by this point been given jurisdiction over the causes of saints. Rather, it simply appears to have been a reasoned response to the situation that had developed after *Caelestis Hierusalem cives*, in which one category of potential saints was being accorded the right to limited cult while the other category was not. Beatification served, in the end, as a method of equalizing them all.[94]

In his massive work on the history of beatification and canonization, Benedict XIV asserted that establishing the practice of beatification, permitting a localized cult, constituted a return to earlier tradition.[95] But on the contrary, it is obvious that the new system directly conflicted with historical tradition, and in a number of different ways. From the earliest days of Christianity, the veneration of martyrs (and later non-martyrs) arose spontaneously among the local faithful—and was subsequently confirmed by the hierarchy in a more official way. Church officials thus were not actually *creating* a new saint; they were rather *recognizing* a cult that had already taken root among the "ordinary" Christian faithful, often without any impetus or influence whatsoever from the hierarchy.

This is still, as was seen in the second chapter, the underlying format of canonization in Russia today: a cult develops among the local people, and is ultimately confirmed by Russian hierarchical authorities, who recognize its origin at the popular level. Even the documentation pertaining to the relatively recent canonization of the Romanov family, by the patriarch of Moscow, referenced a recognition by the church's hierarchy that the Romanovs had been venerated privately by a significant number of the Russian faithful already before their canonization. This acknowledgment was intended as additional justification for the patriarch's decision to declare them saints, and is in keeping with Christian tradition in this regard.

In contrast, the Catholic canonization process since the time of Pope Urban VIII has actually banned the original practice that eventually led to the making of saints. In order to ensure that errors and abuses were avoided, the Catholic faithful were henceforth forbidden to venerate as saints anyone who had not already been approved as such by Catholic authorities. As Piacentini noted, what had initially been regarded as a positive factor now became an obstacle; what had begun as the *only* way to start a cult to a new saint was now explicitly outlawed.[96]

3. Bypassing the Bureaucracy: The Recent Trend of Pope Francis

Catholic or not, any reader may be forgiven if at this point the Vatican's current rules and regulations seem dizzying. The complexity of the system that has developed apparently has not escaped the notice of the reigning bishop of Rome, Pope Francis. Within a few months of his election to the papacy in March 2013, Francis had already used his authority as the supreme head of the Catholic Church—and thus of the Congregation for Causes of Saints—to "fast-track" the causes of several candidates for sainthood by bypassing various aspects of the canonization process entirely. To date, Francis has never directly criticized the current system of saint-making as it has developed over the centuries; and he certainly gives no indication of finding fault with its centralization in the Vatican. But he has increasingly displayed a penchant for evading the bureaucratic morass simply by declaring it unnecessary in individual cases.

The most prominent case occurred on July 5, 2013, when Francis declared that Blessed John XXIII would be canonized a saint, even though the second miracle required by official procedure for this non-martyr was still lacking. The Vatican's press spokesman told journalists that "despite the absence of a second miracle it was the Pope's will that the Sainthood of the great Pope of the Second Vatican Council be recognized."[97] Dispensing from the requirement of a miracle was not completely unprecedented, of course: as was seen earlier in this chapter, the Vatican routinely dispensed the causes of martyrs from the miracle required for beatification in the mid-twentieth century. What is of greater interest in the case of John XXIII is the official reference to "the Pope's will" as the sole, sufficient justification for this decision.

Only a few months later, Francis surprised again with a decree "extending the liturgical cult to the Universal Church" of Blessed Peter Faber, a French Jesuit who died in 1546.[98] Faber had been beatified in 1872, but the process for his canonization lay dormant for decades. The behind-the-scenes activity on this cause is not public knowledge; but it is generally known that Francis had a particular personal interest in the preaching ministry of his fellow Jesuit, and that this decree—an extremely rare case of "equipollent canonization"— came about not through the ordinary workings of the Vatican Congregation for Causes of Saints, but through Francis's own intervention. At the time of the pope's decision, the Jesuits were not even actively promoting Faber's canonization; thus it appears clear that the regular, required bureaucratic procedures were sidestepped altogether by papal fiat.

Are these isolated incidents, or the beginnings of a new Catholic praxis? It's too early to tell. They may simply be a few individual cases of saints who Pope Francis felt should be canonized; if indeed his extraordinary actions are the result of no more than that, then his bypassing of the established procedure should soon come to an end, once he has canonized those he feels ought to be included in the roster of Catholic saints. But the possibility also exists that the pope is obliquely sending a message to the Congregation for Causes of Saints, that the excessively legalistic and complicated Catholic canonization procedure has to end—and if that is Francis's intention, we may very well be witnessing the beginnings of a dramatic sea change.

Preliminary Conclusions

The process of canonization of saints in the Catholic Church today is a far cry from the spontaneous, popular veneration of martyrs during the first few centuries of Christianity. Compared to the system of saint-making that gradually began to develop in the church after the Christian persecutions had ended, the current Catholic canonization process, with its complex system of intricate regulations, is virtually unrecognizable.

At the same time, however, the modern Catholic process was clearly not created ex nihilo. As can be seen throughout this chapter, there is, as a rule, a historical continuity that can be traced in the development of every key procedural element. For example, the requirement that any public writings that the potential saint (martyr or not) may have written must be examined by ecclesiastical authorities for their doctrinal orthodoxy, is certainly a rule that is nowhere to be found in the early centuries of the church. Yet it finds its roots in the concern expressed by Christians already during the time of the Roman persecutions, that no one is to be venerated as a martyr who did not hold orthodox religious beliefs in life. The *form* that this aspect of the process has now taken is obviously different, but its raison d'être is almost as old as Christian martyrdom itself.

Along similar lines, the often bewildering mass of regulations that developed in the Catholic Church over the course of the past thousand years bears no outward resemblance whatsoever to the simple, generally unstructured recognition of martyrs in the early church. Historically, there is no intrinsic need for specific types of witnesses, certain quantities of particular documents, or a set number of miracles, in order to reach a reasonable conclusion that a person was indeed a martyr and a saint. The rules evolved, however, in a typically Roman fashion, as a method of ensuring that this conclusion could in fact be reached, reasonably and consistently.

For we can see in the contemporary Catholic process a tendency that is not so much theological as cultural: the desire to design a uniform set of norms that will enable church authorities to make their decisions in a manner that is consistent and not arbitrary, explainable and not amorphous. The Western mentality, already visible in the sophisticated political and legal system of the pagan Roman Empire, is clearly alive and well in the Catholic Church, which has not hesitated to amass an array of rules and regulations pertaining to virtually every conceivable aspect of the canonization of saints. In this we see a marked difference between the Catholic and the Russian churches, for this insistence on writing a rule for every foreseeable situation—almost bordering at times on an obsession—is altogether absent from Russian culture, even as it constitutes a key component of the Western way of life.

The question could be asked: when canonizing new saints, is it possible to be as correct as humanly possible, and at the same time to be consistent (i.e., to avoid arbitrary decision-making), without devising a system like the one the Catholic Church currently has? It is a question without an easy answer.

But it does tie into another key issue regarding the Catholic canonization process: along with this desire for consistency, one repeatedly encounters evidence of a constant attention paid by the hierarchy to *accuracy*. No one may be venerated as a saint unless there is no doubt that the candidate merits this status; no one is to be regarded as a martyr for the faith whose martyrdom has not been fully established. Because the Catholic Church is plainly anxious that no mistakes be made, we have seen that it has reacted decisively whenever a perceived error was found. Regardless of popular opinion, it wants to *get it right*.

This is undeniably the reason behind the move toward strict centralization of the Catholic canonization process. Just as in the first millennium, we found bishops asserting their authority over the making of saints, and insisting that the faithful could not venerate as martyrs and saints anyone who had not been established as such by episcopal authority, so in the second millennium the popes increasingly came in turn to appropriate that right to themselves alone. And consistently, we can see that the cause of this insistence on approval of new saints by competent authority was the discovery of individual cases in which clear errors were being made by those at a lower level. In each case, the stated concern was to get it right, to ensure that no one was venerated as a martyr/saint unless he or she truly was precisely that.

Thus it seems unfair to suggest (no matter how tempting it may be) that the increasing centralization of the process of canonization was due to nothing other than an increasing desire of the popes for greater power. There is no evidence that their objections to abuses—which they always identify and document—are spurious or even exaggerated. If no errors in the establishment of new martyrs and other saints had ever been noted at the local level, and the popes of the second millennium had been unable to point to concrete cases as justification for reserving the authority to canonize to themselves, would they still have insisted on centralizing the entire process as they did? We will never know, of course; but it seems safe to say that the many intricacies of the process as it is known today would probably have evolved in a different manner were it not for the perceived need to guard against error, based on concrete experience.

Since so many fundamental aspects of the Catholic process can in fact be traced back to the first thousand years of Christianity, the decidedly nontraditional rise of the process of beatification should give even more pause. There is no historical precedent whatsoever for creating a multi-step process, in which a potential saint is first accorded a local veneration that is intended as a temporary measure, and only later is commemorated universally.

Not only do the external aspects of beatification have no basis in tradition; they also do not seem to accord with the Catholic theological understanding of canonization in general. For as has been seen in this chapter, the development of a centralized process progressed hand-in-hand with a theological justification for reserving decisions about the making of saints to the pope alone. A papal determination that a person did, in fact, die a martyr's death, and is now in heaven and able to intercede with God for us on earth, came to carry with it a moral certitude that had not been fully articulated in the first millennium of Christianity. Contemporary theologians might argue as to whether canonization carries with it the assurance of papal infallibility or not; but at a minimum, we can say that if the pope canonizes a new saint, it means that he is absolutely sure of all that this implies.

It then follows logically that if the head of the Catholic Church is certain of his decision, it must be accepted as true for all Catholics throughout the world. The concept of universal veneration of a saint, therefore, makes perfect sense. But how then can one explain, much less justify, the practice of beatification? The notion that a deceased Catholic is worthy of veneration in one locale, but not another, is utterly inconsistent with the fact that it is the pope, the supreme head of the universal Catholic Church, who determines who is to be beatified.[99] It is thus not surprising to find that calls have been made to reexamine the multi-step process of beatification-canonization, perhaps eliminating beatification altogether.[100] If this were to happen, the result would probably be a process even more centralized than before (if that were possible); but at the same time it would, presumably, be more theologically consistent.

And the more recent and very surprising actions taken by Pope Francis, who canonized several saints without following the "correct" process, might perhaps be an attempt on his part to be more theological about saint-making by becoming less legalistic about it. Clearly, Francis has no problem whatsoever with centralization, since he has not hesitated to take matters personally into his own hands, at least in the cases discussed above; but it is equally clear that he has not been willing to let cases languish because of bureaucratic red tape—especially those cases in which, in his view, the potential saint very obviously merits canonization. A non-Catholic might reasonably wonder whether such an "expedited" process might lead to the very errors that the current complex system was specifically designed to avert; but since Catholics believe that the pope, as vicar of Christ, is being guided by God Himself, it seems only logical that they would refrain from second-guessing (much less criticizing) a papal canonization decision, if only for ecclesiological reasons relating to the nature of the papacy itself.

Exteriorly, the complexity of the contemporary Catholic system of creating new martyrs/saints looks little like that of the Russian church. At the same time, however, it seems clear that the substance of many, if not all, of the key procedural elements is exactly the same. It remains to examine each church's canonization process in light of the other. When both churches canonize new martyrs, are they really doing the same thing, or not?

Chapter Four

Comparisons and Conclusions

We have now traced the development of the process employed for canonizing martyrs over a period of nearly two thousand years, and we've taken the investigation in two geographical directions—eastward, to Russia, and westward, to the Catholic Church. It's quite obvious that while there are many evident similarities and parallels between the two sets of procedures, there are numerous points of divergence as well. Both churches are still using much of the same terminology, and the fundamental elements of their theology pertaining to this subject are also essentially in sync.

But as was mentioned at the very beginning of this work, the mere fact that they are using the same words does not necessarily imply that they understand them in the same way. And they might be doing what exteriorly appears to be the same thing, but for markedly different reasons. The question that now has to be addressed is, can the Catholic and Russian Orthodox Churches each acknowledge that the other is canonizing martyrs in the same way and for the same reasons, and reach the logical conclusion that they can and should accept each other's martyr-saints as their own?

A. Can Saints Canonized in the Russian Orthodox Church Be Accepted as Saints by the Catholic Church?

One thousand years of schism has provided both the Catholic and the, Russian Orthodox Churches with plenty of time to develop radically different ideas about martyrdom and the canonization of martyrs as saints. Yet there is no question that with regard to many aspects of this concept, both theological and procedural, the two churches today are operating in essentially the same way.

If canonizing a martyr means basically the same thing in both churches, what implications would this have if, at some point in the future, the Catholic and Russian Orthodox Churches were reunited once again? One might presume that, at that time, they would simply need to merge their liturgical calendars and the issue would be resolved.

But such a position is not merely over-simplistic; it is completely untenable. From the Catholic standpoint, a number of significant substantive differences still exist, that would first need to be surmounted before Russian martyrs could be accepted as Catholic ones. The problematic issues begin as did all three of the preceding chapters, with terminology and accepted definitions.

Even if we accept that both churches hold the same notion of sainthood—which may not be the case, as will be discussed later—the concept of martyr held by the Catholic Church is far narrower than that of the church in Russia. The Catholic definition, which requires a martyr to have died a violent death, accepted freely and willingly, inflicted upon him out of hatred for the faith, is completely in keeping with the definition developed by the early church. In contrast, the uniquely Russian notion of a strastoterpets, as seen in chapter 2, cannot be construed as synonymous with the definition of martyr that developed in the first few centuries of Christianity. If Russian *strastoterptsy* and Russian martyrs were consistently distinguished as two separate categories of saints, this would not be an issue; but we've seen that all too often the two words are used interchangeably to describe saints canonized by the Russian church. If the Catholic Church wished to accept a Russian martyr as a Catholic saint, it would therefore be necessary to investigate ab initio the circumstances surrounding a candidate's death, to determine whether the person did indeed die as a martyr as the Catholic Church defines the term. If not, the next logical step would be to examine whether the potential saint's life, and the process that led to canonization after death, met the Catholic criteria for canonization as a confessor, or non-martyr. In general, we can say that those Russian saints who are termed *strastoterptsy* cannot be considered martyrs in the Catholic sense.

But even a Russian saint who did indeed die a martyr's death, in the traditional sense of the term, still could not automatically be accepted as a martyr by the Catholic Church—because the question of the *orthodoxy of his or her beliefs* would have to be addressed. As we have seen, already in the first centuries of the existence of the church, heretics and schismatics were not accepted as true martyrs, even when the circumstances of their deaths otherwise met the definition of martyrdom. This is still a requirement in the Catholic Church today, and is the reason why a thorough review of a potential saint's writings is necessary before any decision about canonization can be made.

Theological orthodoxy is still required for canonization in the Russian church as well. A Russian Orthodox martyr, therefore, must have accepted all the tenets of Russian Orthodoxy, which means that the Catholic Church regards any saint canonized in Russia after the East–West Schism in the eleventh century as, ipso facto, a schismatic. Juridically, in accord with the process as it is followed today, it would be impossible for the Catholic Church to accept *any* Russian martyrs as Catholic saints for this single reason, unless they were in fact martyred before the Russian church had definitively separated from Rome.

Would it be possible somehow to "override" this requirement, and accept as Catholic martyrs persons who, in their lifetimes, sincerely believed that the Catholic Church was in error, and that only Russian Orthodoxy represented the true faith? This is a question for Catholic theologians to answer. Suffice it to say that significant changes would need to be made to the legal process as it now stands, if the Catholic Church wished to acknowledge Russian martyrs as its own—and the Catholic theological understanding of martyrdom (and/or of the term *orthodoxy*) would need additional nuancing as well.

At this point, we have only examined the terminology involved in canonizing martyrs, and it is already clear that significant problems exist. But when we turn to the procedural elements that traditionally constitute canonization in the Russian church, we quickly encounter even more difficulties.

Including a martyr's name on the liturgical calendar was originally the decisive action that effectively canonized him, long before the term *canonization* even came into use. Consequently, today we know little or nothing about many of the first Christian martyrs, apart from the fact that they have been commemorated on set feast-days from time immemorial. In the absence of any hard evidence to the contrary, the Catholic Church simply accepts that each person whose name is listed on the earliest church calendars as a martyr did indeed die a martyr's death, and merits commemoration as a saint. Russia, in its turn, does essentially the same.

One might argue that, at least in the cases of those Russian saints whose names were added to the liturgical calendars *before* the East–West Schism, the Catholic Church might reasonably accept them as legitimate Catholic saints as well. If they were canonized by local bishops, during a period when those local bishops were de facto in communion with Rome, it seems entirely logical to regard them as saints for both the Russian and the Catholic Churches.

But as was addressed in the first chapter, valid questions about the significance of the inclusion of a given person's name on a liturgical calendar exist. Particularly with regard to the inclusion of names of local bishops, there is a strong possibility that many were originally listed on a diptych intended to contain the names of those who were to be prayed *for*—a type of necrology, in other words—but were later merged with different diptychs listing the names of martyrs and other saints, who were to be prayed *to*. The end result was that liturgical calendars abruptly included names of persons who had never been established to be saints—yet the mere fact of their inclusion on the calendars led to their automatic veneration as saints.

Nobody knows which, if any, early Christian "saints" accidentally achieved sainthood in this way. If, at this late date, it were somehow possible to identify these names, and to demonstrate conclusively that they were originally not regarded as martyrs/saints at all, the Catholic Church would probably be most interested in removing them from the martyrology. This would not be a case of the decanonization of a saint; rather, such an action would constitute a correction of a calendar error, akin to the removal of Philomena's name from the Catholic liturgical calendar discussed in chapter 3. They would not be decanonized, because they had never been canonized in the first place.

In the West, to our knowledge, these questions arise only with regard to names listed already in the earliest centuries of Christianity, before the establishment of clear, written liturgical calendars for local churches. It seems reasonable to assume that if genuine errors like this really do exist in the Catholic liturgical calendar, some of the same erroneous names of "saints" may appear in Russian calendars as well, and therefore the Russian church calendars have the same problems and for the same reasons. But in Russia, as was seen in chapter 2, even more problems may have been occurring centuries later thanks to calendar copyists, who in some cases may have arbitrarily included some names of persons who had never been declared to be saints, but whom the individual copyists nevertheless held in esteem.

By Catholic standards, therefore, it seems safe to say that some of the most ancient saints' names still in the Catholic martyrology may be erroneous; but in the Russian liturgical calendars, the probability of false entries seems even higher. Under the circumstances, given the continuous papal demands for factual accuracy made over the past several centuries, it would be imprudent for the Catholic Church simply to accept en masse all Russian saints whose names are found on the liturgical calendars. Logic would suggest instead that they first be examined individually, so as to ensure that they are being commemorated by the Russian Orthodox Church as saints because church authorities actually declared them to be saints—and not because someone copied a liturgical calendar and randomly added the name of a person whom the copyist personally felt should be commemorated.

If historical evidence existed to show that a saint on one of the Russian liturgical calendars truly died a martyr's death and was canonized by an authorized church official during the period before the church in Russia separated from Rome, it would seem entirely reasonable for Catholic authorities to accept this person as a martyr and a saint of the Catholic Church as well. But this brings us to the next problem, because in the cases of many of the Russian martyrs, there are significant doubts about the accuracy of the accounts of their lives and deaths. Some saints, as was discussed in chapter 2, probably did not even exist! The zhitiia, upon which their canonizations were often completely based, were frequently written centuries after the fact, and sometimes contain discrepancies that lead reasonable readers to doubt their accuracy. The case of Saint Mercurius, who allegedly was martyred as he defended Smolensk from Tatar invaders during a period when there was no known Tatar attack on the city, is a good example.

If the Catholic Church, rather than the Russian, had investigated the causes of these Russian martyr-saints, would they have been canonized? At this point, so long after the fact, it is impossible to be sure. There is little doubt that centuries ago, the Catholic Church's requirements for canonization were less stringent than they are today. Many Catholic martyrs canonized in the medieval era would presumably fail to meet the standards for martyrdom that are now in place. The two King Canutes of Denmark, discussed in chapter 3, are good examples of this: while it is entirely possible that they could be canonized in the twenty-first century as confessors (i.e., non-martyrs) based on their virtuous Christian lives, the likelihood that they would be found to have actually suffered martyrdom seems slim.

Nevertheless, as relaxed as the Catholic criteria may have been in centuries past, overall it seems quite clear that the standards remained markedly higher than those required in the Russian church. All too often one encounters Russian saints about whom virtually nothing is known—although they lived in an era about which written historical evidence is certainly extant. In some cases, the very accounts of their canonization indicate that they were declared saints despite the absence of concrete factual evidence about their lives. A claim that a miracle had occurred near someone's tomb was, often enough, sufficient to lead a local Russian bishop to canonize. Saint Kirill of Vel'sk (addressed in chapter 2), who drowned during the 1400s, is a case in point. Descriptions of his canonization reveal that even at the time he was declared a saint, next to nothing was known about him.

Would an unknown person be canonized in this way in the Catholic Church, even hundreds of years ago? Given the repeated insistences of the popes on factual accuracy, and the need to avoid abuses, it appears improbable. In general, Catholicism's evidentiary standards, which mirror the analytical legal methods of the West, have consistently been at a significantly higher level compared to those of the church in Russia. We can never be completely sure, but one would suspect that, given the constant papal demands for objective documentation, cases like Kirill's would quickly be rejected for lack of evidence.

In more recent cases, like that of the Romanov family canonized in 2000, the Russian canonization commission clearly appears to have applied a more objective standard than that used in the medieval period. The commission's report on the Romanovs indicates that they were concerned with factual accuracy and evaluated objective information. Nevertheless, we cannot be sure that even today the Russian documentary process meets the standards of the Catholic Church—because, in short, the Russian church has never publicly made clear exactly what the process is. There is still no public, written description of the types of documents that are to be submitted to the patriarchate on behalf of a potential saint. Their quantity and nature has never been explained. In the absence of any clear, objective instructions, it is simply impossible for the Catholic Church to evaluate the cause of a Russian saint, to see whether it also meets the criteria for a Catholic canonization—and this holds true regardless of whether the Russian saint was a martyr or not.

The same objection is valid with regard to miracles. Many Russian martyrs in centuries past were canonized after miracles had been confirmed to have taken place through their intercession. But in most cases there is no evidence extant today that even indicates what those miracles were. In the small number of cases where we do have documented accounts of miracles, it is usually unclear whether they were verified, and if so, by whom.

Again, the measure for evaluating and approving miracles in the West was doubtless much lower in past centuries, since medical science was hardly at the level that it is today. But in general, it seems safe to say that the standard for evaluating the veracity of alleged miracles in cases of potential Catholic saints has been higher than that historically employed by the Russian church. In accord with the Western tendency toward explicit, written regulations, the Catholic process has consistently required hard evidence to establish that a medically inexplicable cure did indeed take place. In contrast, judging from the relatively small number of Russian accounts of miraculous cures, it appears that in a fair number of cases, a miracle was announced to have taken place by the Russian faithful themselves, whereupon it was simply accepted as such by the laity as a whole. It is thus difficult to attach any weight whatsoever to such alleged miracles by Catholicism's more legalistic standards.

With regard to the more recent canonizations of martyrs by the Moscow Patriarchate, the case against accepting them as Catholic martyr-saints is even more clear-cut because there are no claims of miracles performed through their intercession at all. As was discussed in chapter 3, the Catholic canonization process requires evidence of miracles even for martyrs, as a sort of added assurance that the person did indeed die a true martyr's death. In theory this requirement can be waived if the evidence of martyrdom is undeniable; yet in practice, the number of miracles required may be reduced, but at least one miracle has been necessary. Therefore, unless the Catholic Church were able to establish that the circumstances of the deaths of the most recent Russian martyrs—i.e., those who died under the Soviet regime—did indeed constitute martyrdom beyond a doubt, it would be unable to accept them as Catholic martyr-saints already, on this one ground alone: that no miracles were verified to have occurred through their intercession.

With regard to incorrupt remains, which has traditionally been such a weighty factor in Russian canonizations, the Catholic Church attaches no official importance to incorruption whatsoever. Consequently, this key factor in most Russian canonizations, even if well documented, holds no weight at all in the Catholic process and can be dismissed as essentially irrelevant.

Overall, the level of scrutiny that has traditionally been given to potential saints by the church in Russia is unquestionably inadequate when viewed through a Catholic lens. The notion that the Catholic Church could accept Russian martyrs and other saints as its own, simply because they are held to be saints in Russia, cannot be entertained from a juridical point of view. Every case would have to be reevaluated individually—and on the surface, it is highly unlikely that the evidence supporting many Russian saints would meet Catholic evidentiary standards. If the Catholic Church wishes to continue to place an emphasis on accuracy, it logically cannot accept as valid any canonizations that were done using such significantly different criteria.

And the Catholic Church would be hard-pressed to jettison its concerns about the accuracy of its canonizations, for reasons that are not only juridical but also ecclesiological. Over time, as was seen in the third chapter, decretalists (and eventually theologians as well) argued that only the pope should canonize, because only the pope possessed the authority to ascertain definitively that a deceased person was now in Heaven and able to intercede with God for us. A decree of canonization, as was seen in chapter 3, essentially came to constitute a virtually dogmatic statement, of the sort that all Catholics are required to accept on faith. Catholic theologians began to assert that a decree of canonization amounted to an exercise of papal infallibility; and while this argument unquestionably poses some theological problems, the fact remains that, at a minimum, the formality of the papal pronouncement carries with it a certitude that leaves no room for error. This is the primary reason why a Catholic canonization is considered permanent, and throughout history none has ever been retracted—because such a retraction would amount to a theological impossibility.

These concerns, about the need for the pope to be completely certain before issuing a decree of canonization, present us with yet another objection to the Catholic Church accepting Russian saints as its own. The fact that a hierarch other than the pope made the final determination as to a person's sainthood is enough to give Catholics pause once again. It makes no difference whether the church official making the final decision was Russian or not, or even whether he was Catholic or not, for the effect is the same: the Catholic Church has required since the twelfth century that canonizations be carried out by the pope himself, and thus it cannot accept as valid any canonizations that were done after that point by someone other than the pope. Consequently, if the Catholic Church wanted to accept Russian saints canonized after the twelfth century, the pope would have to assess all the evidence de novo and make a determination himself on the merits of each individual case.

But what about those Russian saints who had been declared saints by local bishops before the pope arrogated the authority to canonize to himself? Catholic bishops had quite rightly been canonizing new saints until the reign of Alexander III, who (as we saw in the third chapter) effectively put a stop to local canonizations in 1171. In the meantime, Russian canonizations were all being carried out at the local level, at least until the advent of Moscow's Metropolitan Makarii and his canonization councils in the sixteenth century. It would thus appear that ecclesiologically, bishops in Russia, and Catholic bishops in the West, were exercising their power in the same way, at least during the pre-Alexandrine period. So could we entertain the possibility that Russian saints, canonized locally before the time of Alexander III, can be considered saints also in the Catholic Church?

Ecclesiologically, this question leads us right back to discussion of the Great Schism, but this time specifically to the Russian bishops and their communion (or lack thereof) with Rome in the first part of the second millennium. It would be difficult, to put it mildly, for the Catholic Church to justify accepting decrees issued by bishops who were not in communion with the pope. If a Russian bishop who made the decision to canonize a given saint was known to have rejected papal primacy, Catholic theologians would have a hard time justifying the automatic acceptance of his decision by the Catholic Church.

This logically implies that a determination would need to be made as to *when* exactly the Russian church ceased to be in communion with Rome. Traditionally, of course, the date given for the East–West Schism is 1054, the year of the mutual excommunications exchanged between Rome and Constantinople. In reality, however, it would be simplistic to conclude that all Eastern bishops were in fact in communion with Rome just before that date, and completely out of communion the year after. The historical situation was far more complicated and much more fluid than a single date would suggest.

On top of that, it is definitely unreasonable to assume that simply because Constantinople rejected Rome's authority, the Russian hierarchy all instantly followed suit. Jesuit Joseph Schweigl does a masterful job of compiling the radically different historical theories regarding the date(s) when Russian bishops actually broke with Rome: they vary from the early twelfth century until after the Council of Florence in the fifteenth century.[1] To complicate matters further, most historians would agree that for varying periods of time, the Russian hierarchy's position toward Rome was far from uniform, with each individual bishop taking his own view (assuming that he had a view at all) of the Russian church's relationship with Rome, at least until the Council of Florence in the mid-1400s led to a definitive break.

In short, today it is virtually impossible to determine which Russian bishop was in communion with Rome and when. Thus with regard to the canonization of martyrs as saints by local Russian bishops, we cannot know with certainty whether the canonizations performed around and after the time of the Great Schism can be accepted by the Catholic Church. Once again, it seems inevitable that, before accepting a Russian saint canonized during this period, the Catholic Church would want a complete review of the evidence, and a final decision by the pope on each saint's case would first be necessary.

There is yet another objection that has to be raised to the idea that Russian saints could be accepted as such in the Catholic Church, and it goes to the heart of the very notion of canonization. As was just mentioned, and was addressed in greater detail in the preceding chapter, the Catholic understanding of the canonization of saints involves the highest possible level of certitude. Regardless of whether one wishes to hold that a papal canonization constitutes an infallible act, the fact remains that undoing a canonization is unthinkable in the Catholic Church. Once the pope has declared that someone is henceforth to be regarded as a saint, this individual will forever be regarded as a saint. The permanence involved is not, strictly speaking, an element of the juridic process. Rather, it is the end result of centuries of development of a theological understanding of what is actually happening when the pope canonizes a new saint.

In great contrast, the concept of canonizing a saint in the Russian church carries with it neither the notion of full certitude nor that of permanence. As was seen in chapter 2, the decanonization of formerly canonized saints in Russia is a historical fact that, while uncommon, is known to have happened on more than one occasion. This historical precedent has been cited in support of the more recent argument in favor of removing those saints who were canonized—wrongly, in the minds of some Russians—because they allegedly had been martyred by Jews.

And decanonizing saints is not inconsistent with the traditional Russian understanding of what precisely occurs when a new saint is canonized. In essence, as was discussed in the second chapter, the standard Russian approach has historically been bottom-up: the local faithful begin to venerate a deceased member of the church, and eventually this popular cult is recognized by the hierarchy in an official, public way by canonization. Insofar as the impetus to canonize is held by the lay faithful, there can obviously be no theological claim to any degree of moral certitude—and there is none.

When viewed in this light, the Catholic canonization process could not be more different, for in the second millennium it became a process with what might be described as a largely top-down approach. While the laity may privately hold a deceased Catholic in great esteem, only the supreme authority in the church can sanction this individual's veneration. And with the revamping of the process under Urban VIII in the seventeenth century, any external signs of cult among the faithful are absolutely forbidden until a pronouncement upon the cause of the deceased Catholic is made by Rome. This markedly different interpretation by each church of what is actually happening when a saint is canonized may, in itself, be sufficient to lead the Catholic Church to conclude that a canonization in Russia can in no way be regarded ipso facto by Catholics as valid.

B. Can Saints Canonized in the Catholic Church Be Accepted as Saints by the Russian Orthodox Church?

It would be presumptuous for a Catholic to try to make decisions on behalf of the Russian Orthodox Church. Nevertheless, it certainly seems possible for even an outsider to draw reasonable conclusions based on what is publicly known about the canonization process of the church in Russia. Given what we know about the Russian Orthodox procedure for creating new saints, does it appear that Catholic saints, canonized during the second millennium, could be accepted by the Russian church as their own?

If we begin to examine the issue once again by focusing on definitions, we might conclude that not only is the Catholic definition of the term *martyr* much narrower than that of the Russian church but it also fits entirely within the broader Russian definition. In other words, the Russian Orthodox definition of martyrdom is different from that of the Catholic Church, but only because it is more encompassing—not because it excludes any of the elements contained in the Catholic definition. Consequently, those who died a violent death, willingly and freely accepted, inflicted on them out of hatred for their faith—thereby meeting the Catholic definition of martyrdom—certainly meet the definition of martyr employed by the church in Russia as well.

But the related issue of theological orthodoxy raises the same problems for the Russian Orthodox that it does for the Catholic Church. Throughout history, the church in Russia has consistently ensured that anyone canonized as a martyr has held the Orthodox faith. This is why, as discussed in chapter 2, those Old Believers killed because of their beliefs will never be considered martyrs among the Orthodox; it is also the reason Moscow cannot canonize some of the servants of the Romanovs who were murdered with them—for regardless of the circumstances of their death and their own internal spiritual state when it occurred, they were not members of the Russian Orthodox Church. Thus the idea that the church in Russia would now add to its liturgical calendar Catholics who died as martyrs after the Great Schism is difficult to imagine on theological grounds. Russian Orthodox theology is essentially the same in this regard as that of the Catholic Church, so this alone would presumably be sufficient to prevent the Russian church from accepting Catholic martyr-saints.[2]

If we next turn to the procedural elements constitutive of Catholic canonizations, could the church in Russia conclude that the process has historically been basically the same as its own? Generally, the different aspects of the process appear to be present in both churches' procedures: the new saint is included in the liturgical calendar; the saint's remains, if possible, are moved to an honorable location, usually under an altar; and his or her life story is written for the edification of the faithful, if this has not been done already.

In the church in Russia, these elements are still present in canonizations today. The same may be said of the Catholic Church, but as was discussed in chapter 3, these elements no longer in themselves effect a canonization—for now the only truly constitutive element is the formal decree of canonization issued by the pope. Nevertheless, if the Russian church wants to find these elements present in Catholic canonizations, generally they are there. Nothing is missing; but the different components have taken on a different significance in the Catholic Church than in Russia.

As for the evidentiary process, which is employed to determine whether a candidate for sainthood did indeed die a true martyr's death and merits canonization, the Russian Orthodox Church should find no significant fault with the process used by Rome. As was discussed above, the Catholic process requires, without a doubt, a level of documentation that has generally been more thorough than that of Russia. The Catholic process is different from the Russian Orthodox process; but only because it is, if anything, more demanding. Therefore it is difficult to envision the church in Russia objecting to accepting Catholic martyr-saints as its own on this particular ground.

There could, however, be one objection: until only recently, the Russian church required a saint's remains to be incorrupt, whether he was a martyr or not. As we have seen in the previous chapter, the bodies of Catholic saints have occasionally been determined to be incorrupt, but this has not been a deciding factor in their canonization. If the Russian Orthodox hierarchy wished to examine the centuries-old cases of Catholic saints, applying to them the standards of its own process back in that same period, it could easily conclude that the criteria for canonizing saints in the Catholic Church has traditionally been insufficient in this regard.

But as we have seen in chapter 2, the canonizations carried out in the Russian Orthodox Church in the post-Soviet period have not required incorrupt relics. It appears—although we cannot be sure, since the current specific, official Russian requirements for canonization have never been published—that this requirement no longer holds. If, therefore, the Russian church were to apply its modern standards to Catholic cases, the lack of incorrupt relics for most Catholic martyr-saints would presumably not be a problem.

The final aspect of Catholic saint-making that the Russian Orthodox Church would have to peruse is the question of the ecclesiastical authority who carried out the canonizations. Before 1171, as we have seen, this was normally the local Catholic bishop, while after that date the only one authorized to canonize was the pope. We find here exactly the same problem that was addressed above from the standpoint of the Catholic Church, but now in reverse: the church in Russia would have to try to determine whether individual Catholic bishops before 1171, or popes after that date, were in fact Orthodox or not.

Since the Orthodox Church as a whole is far from being in agreement on the question of whether the Catholic Church is in heresy or merely in schism, not to mention the date and the precise theological reasons for which it fell out of communion with Orthodoxy, it is impossible to know for sure how the church in Russia would view the Catholic ecclesiastical authorities who canonized Catholic saints down through the centuries. One might reasonably presume that Russian Orthodox hierarchs would balk at the notion that the leaders of the Catholic Church have genuine authority to create new saints; but it is also possible that a more generous interpretation could lead to precisely the opposite conclusion. The arguments pro and con would no doubt hinge entirely on the question of whether the Catholic hierarchy was in communion with Orthodoxy at the time of the canonizations, or was in schism/heresy. If the latter position were accepted—which, judging historically, seems to be the most likely outcome—the Russian church would logically be able to conclude that *no* Catholic saints can be regarded as genuinely canonized in any case. It follows that an investigation of each individual saint would have to be done, and the patriarch would then have to take the active step of formally canonizing him or her in accord with Russian Orthodox procedures. This precisely mirrors the situation already discussed above, of Russian saints who have been canonized by Orthodox hierarchs being accepted as saints in the Catholic Church.

We can see that, in short, the idea that the Russian Orthodox Church might simply accept en masse all canonizations of Catholic martyrs as valid is simplistic and highly improbable. Even if at some point in the future it was motivated by strong ecumenical considerations, there are concrete, objective problems (generally theological in nature) that would have to be overcome before such a move could be made.

C. Theological Differences, or Cultural/Political Ones?

We have just addressed the theological issues inherent in Catholics and Russian Orthodox accepting each other's saints, and analyzed the procedural difficulties that (at least for now) make such acceptance seem unlikely. By this point it should be clear that the issues also go beyond theology, for many of them are rooted in culture itself. The comment by Castelli cited in the introduction is directly relevant here: when a person is publicly declared to be a martyr, that theological statement carries with it a much broader social message. It tells the faithful that the martyr's behavior deserves respect and is worth imitating, while that of the executioner merits condemnation. With the formal canonization of a martyr, believers are being taught what is important in life—and in death. They learn what constitutes heroic virtue in the eyes of the church, and how they themselves ideally ought to behave in dire situations where their own faith may be threatened. In short, a martyr is meant to be an example for everyone.

The very first systematic Christian persecutions under the Roman emperor Nero in the 60s AD pitted the faithful against a government opposed to that faith. Courageously standing up to political officials for what you believed could cost you your life—and yet the first martyrs did precisely that. Early Christianity found itself with a long list of followers who had been killed for defying a pagan government that had, as an institution, assumed a position diametrically opposed to it. Following one's conscience in obeying the teachings of Jesus was more important to Christians than following the emperor's dictates as to what constituted proper behavior for a good Roman citizen.

But with the legalization of Christianity by the Roman emperor Constantine in the early fourth century, the relationship between Christians and the state shifted dramatically. To the extent that Constantine and subsequent rulers made efforts both to preserve the faith from error and to promulgate Christianity among newly conquered peoples, the government no longer represented a direct threat to Christian believers. On the contrary, for the inhabitants of the Roman Empire, "being a Christian" and "being a good citizen" were no longer automatically presumed to be mutually exclusive. Insofar as the government now sought to promote laws in accordance with Christian values, both church and state were now oriented in the same general direction. Culturally, Christians found themselves living in a radically different society, where they no longer needed to view the leadership of the country in which they lived as an enemy of the faith.

With the Christianization of the state, martyrdoms by civil authorities ceased; but some Christians still lost their lives in missionary areas, martyred as they sought to convert pagan peoples living outside their borders. One could say that with the canonization of such missionary-martyrs, the faithful living in officially Christian lands were getting a new sort of lesson from the church: no longer was it likely that they would be faced with a threat to their faith from their own government, but there were certainly threats to Christianity (and to individual Christians) in foreign lands that had yet to formally accept—or at least tolerate—Christ and the church.

In such an equation it can be hard to separate religion from politics. When a state embraces an official religion, and is threatened by (or itself threatens) another nation that collectively holds a different faith, distinguishing between political issues and theological ones can become downright impossible. The cases of Russian martyrs killed by Tatars, discussed in chapter 2, are excellent examples of this inseparable intermingling of church and state. Were the battles really being fought between Russians and Tatars, or between Christians and pagans? The blur between the two makes it all the more difficult to determine whether the victims were indeed martyrs for their religious faith, or "merely" casualties of war.

And conversely, canonizing someone who died in such a war can send the faithful a potentially ambiguous message: a believer may learn that it is laudable to stand up for your faith in the face of infidels—and/or that it is morally laudable for a citizen of a particular nation (Russia, in this example) to fight against its political enemies (the Tatars). The choice once faced by the very first persecuted Christians—to be either a good Christian, as defined by Christian leaders, or a good Roman, as defined by the emperor—had disappeared. In its place, inhabitants of an officially Christian state were receiving a double lesson when political heros were canonized as martyrs: being a good Christian meant *also* being a good citizen.

Inasmuch as the state's interests genuinely dovetail with those of the church, this might not always constitute an inherent problem. But since church and state obviously have different reasons for existing and different goals that determine their policies and actions, it should surprise no one when their motivations perhaps overlap but are not identical. It's also no surprise when one of the two institutions seeks the assistance of the other, in broadcasting a moral message to the people at large. The case of Danish Prince Canute Lavard, discussed in chapter 3, is undoubtedly an example of this: killed by rival family members in a power dispute, he was canonized as a Catholic martyr by a church that apparently agreed (at least in this case) with the prince's own political faction. With the official, theological declaration of Lavard's martyrdom, the Danish populace simultaneously got the message that the political rivals who had killed him stood on the wrong side of the moral equation.

It might be that this type of blur between the messages of church and state will invariably plague any country with an official religion. But when the religion identifies itself as belonging exclusively to the members of a particular nation, the church–state relationship becomes blurrier still. By definition, the Russian Orthodox Church is intended to be the religion of the Russian people, who at least initially resided within the political boundaries of Rus', later known as Russia. The overlap between the Russian state's concern for social order among its citizens, and the Russian church's concern for the moral well-being of its faithful, can naturally become indistinguishable. What is considered good for the nation may very well be good for the soul, too.

The centralization of the Catholic canonization process in Rome may inadvertently prevent this sort of politicization of saint-making, at least to some degree. Since the final decision rests in the hands of the pope, who generally is an "outsider" (at least in the cases of potential martyrs who were not from his native land), a verdict that a person's death did indeed constitute true martyrdom is being made by someone who presumably is weighing the evidence without the understandable emotion and potential impulsiveness of those directly on the scene. The refusal to canonize Simone of Trent in the fifteenth century, after he was ostensibly murdered by Jews on Good Friday, may be a good example of the sort of calm objectivity possessed by a leader who is not directly caught up in the moment—and who can stand back and see clearly from a distance the potential dangers involved in impetuous decision-making. As was discussed in chapter 3, Pope Sixtus IV objected that hard evidence of the circumstances surrounding the boy's death was lacking, even though the local bishop enthusiastically insisted that Simone was indeed a martyr and should be venerated as such. Sixtus's refusal to canonize Simone was based on the need for accurate, factual proof of martyrdom, not on emotions; and it appears that this is a case where cooler heads prevailed.[3]

It follows that if one church were to consider accepting the martyr-saints of the other, the political context in which the martyr had originally been canonized would have to be taken into account. Did politics influence the church's decision to declare someone a martyr and a saint? Or was the declaration based on solid theological grounds, irrespective of political factors? If there was an evident political interest in canonizing someone as a martyr in generations past, is it nevertheless possible to conclude today that the person merits sainthood for purely religious reasons anyway?

Final Thoughts

Nobody today can predict with any certainty what a Catholic–Orthodox reunification would look like, if indeed it ever takes place. Consequently, there is an element of futility that is necessarily involved in any theoretical surmising about recognizing each other's saints. God's grace could lead such a reconciliation in any conceivable direction—as well as in many directions that are completely inconceivable to us today. But it seems clear that the concerns about definitions expressed in the introduction to this work do indeed have some basis. We have seen that while each church uses many of the same terms, a closer look reveals that they are far from meaning the same things.

Therefore, while it would probably sound reasonable on a superficial level—particularly in the immediate euphoria that would no doubt surround a unification of the two churches—that each would accept the other's martyr-saints as its own, such an acceptance would be far from workable in practice. Ironically, it might very well be the lay faithful themselves who would be the first to recognize, intuitively, that their traditional understanding of the significance of veneration of their own beloved saints was being challenged by the sudden addition of other saints from another church with a very different cultural tradition. In short, average believers (whether Catholic or Orthodox) may not understand the technicalities, but they know a martyr when they see one. They know because they have been raised in a church that established centuries ago what the word *martyr* really means, and in canonizing them, has acted accordingly.

To abruptly import a whole host of new martyr-saints who were declared to be such by those employing different definitions and a different theological understanding of the meaning of canonization would create greater problems than mere cultural discomfiture. The end result would be to dilute the definitions to the point where they defined nothing at all. For when key words like *saint*, *martyr*, and *canonize* acquire meanings that are too broad, they ultimately become meaningless. When a word means everything, it means nothing. Just melding the Catholic and Russian Orthodox liturgical calendars into one, with a single body of saints, might create some initial ecumenical goodwill, but over time it would create far greater problems. The faithful, with their keen instinct, would in many cases transition from suspicion of the new additions to rejection of the whole concept altogether. For if "those people" are to be considered martyrs now too, what does the word mean, anyway? As has (I hope) been shown in this work, such a seemingly simple, ecumenically sensitive solution would not be so simple after all.

Abbreviations

AAS	*Acta Apostolicae Sedis: Commentarium Officiale*. Vatican City: Libreria Editrice Vaticana, 1909–.
ASs	*Acta Sanctorum*. Antwerp/Brussels, 1643–1940.
BSs	*Bibliotheca Sanctorum*. Rome: Città Nuova, 1990–2000.
CCSL	*Corpus Christianorum: Series Latina*. Turnhout: Brepols Publishers, 1953–.
CSEL	*Corpus Scriptorum Ecclesiasticorum Latinorum*. Vindobonae: C. Gerold, 1866–.
MGHS	*Monumenta Germaniae Historica Scriptorum*. Hannover: Hahn, 1826–.
PG	*Patrologia Graeca*, ed. Jacques-Paul Migne. Paris: Migne, 1857–1866.
PL	*Patrologia Cursus Completus: Series Latina*, ed. Jacques-Paul Migne. Paris: Migne 1841–.

Notes

Notes to Introduction

1. Elizabeth Castelli, *Martyrdom and Memory: Early Christian Culture Making* (New York: Columbia University Press, 2007), 198–199.

2. For multiple assessments of the religious, cultural, and political implications of the Union of Brest by a variety of scholars, see B. Groen and William P. van den Bercken, eds., *Four Hundred Years, Union of Brest (1596–1996): A Critical Re-evaluation* (Leuven, Belgium: Peeters, 1998).

3. See, for example, J. Ratzinger, *The Spirit of the Liturgy* (San Francisco: Ignatius Press, 2000), for repeated use of the term "organic" and discussion of the concept of "organic development," in the inter-related contexts of liturgical music, vestments, prayers, etc.

4. Such historical research has already been done by others: see, e.g., Peter Brown, *The Cult of Saints: Its Rise and Function in Latin Christianity* (Chicago: University of Chicago Press, 1981).

Notes to Chapter One

1. For example, Pargoire cites the specific case of Sergius I of Constantinople, whose Monothelite beliefs were eventually condemned in the seventh century. J. Pargoire, *L'église byzantine* (Paris: V. Lecoffre, 1923), 242.

It might be objected that the documents destroyed in this case presumably pertained to Sergius's heretical beliefs, and not to the naming or veneration of martyrs. But in response, it must be noted that many pieces of the evidence that still remains to us are found in letters and other writings that did not have saint-making as their main topic; rather, they are often merely incidental statements made only in passing. Among the writings that were destroyed, therefore, there may very well have been pieces of information that would have enabled us to garner a more complete picture of what the church in the East was doing to venerate the martyrs.

2. *Eumenides* 664. Unless specifically noted, all translations from Greek and Latin are my own. Throughout the book, if no direct translation is given, the presumption should always be that the text contains a close paraphrase of the passage in question.

3. *Gorgias*, 471e.

4. As Delehaye points out, "They are called *martyrs of God*, because they saw the Risen One and they can give testimony." Hippolyte Delehaye, *Sanctus: Essai sur le culte des saints dans l'antiquité* (Brussels, 1927), 102.

5. See Boudewijn Dehandschutter, "The Meaning of Witness in the Apocalypse," in *Polycarpiana: Studies on Martyrdom and Persecution in Early Christianity*, ed. J. Leemans (Leuven: Leuven University Press, 2007), esp. 181 and 185.

6. *Martyrium Polycarpi*, I, 1. D. Rudolf Knopf, *Ausgewählte Märtyrerakten* (Tubingen 1929), 1.

7. Origen, *Commentarium in S. Johannem* 2:88; PG 14:176.

8. Eusebius, *Historia Ecclesiae* 3:32; PG 20:216.

9. Eusebius, *Historia Ecclesiae* 4:26; PG 20:393.

10. See Augustine, *Breviculus collationis cum Donatistis* 13:25; CSEL 26:73ff.

11. Optatus, liber 7, book 3:1, 4, and 8. CSEL 26:68, 83, and 90. CCSL 149:4.

12. CCSL 149:4. To be fair, Athanasius noted that it was, at least in theory, possible to admit an exception to the rule, and to revere someone as a martyr who had voluntarily turned himself over to the authorities. Writing at more or less the same time as this Council of Carthage, he acknowledged that there were some who had handed themselves over to their persecutors; but he noted that they could be considered martyrs, *if* it was clear that this had been done under the inspiration of the Holy

Spirit (*Apol. De fuga sua*, 22–23; *PG* 25:671–673). Delehaye provides several historical examples of early saints who apparently had done exactly that, in *Sanctus*, 168–169.

13. Augustine, *Enarrationes in Ps. 34, PL* 36:340.

14. Canon 9, "The members of the Church must not meet in the cemeteries, nor attend the so-called martyries of any heretics, for prayer or veneration." Mansi, 2:565.

15. Canon 34, "Christians are not to forsake the martyrs of Christ and turn to false martyrs, that is, to the martyrs of the heretics.... For they are alienated from God." Mansi, 2:580.

16. Sermo 223:1; *PL* 39:2158.

17. Epistola 2, *PL* 20:179–180.

18. *AS*s for January 16, vol. 2:9.

19. *Oratio 21, In laudem Athanasii*, 37, *PG* 35:1128.

20. *In Epist. Ad Hebraeos*, chap. 6, homily 11, *PG* 63:93.

21. Εἰς τὸν ἅγιον ἱερομάρτυρα Βαβύλαν 10, *Sources chrétiennes* 362, 312.

22. *Martyrium Polycarpi*, I, XVIII. D. Rudolf Knopf, *Ausgewählte Märtyrerakten*, 6. A paraphrase of the original text is also found in Eusebius, *Historia Ecclesiae* 4:15, *PG* 20:340ff.

23. Epistle XII 12:2; *CSEL* 3, 2:503–504.

24. L. Duchesne, ed., *Liber Pontificalis: Texte, Introduction et Commentaire*, vol. 1 *In Clem.* (Paris: Boccard, 1955), 123.

25. Sozomen, *Ecclesiastica Historia* 4:3, *PG* vol. 67.

26. Eusebius, *Historia Ecclesiae* 4:15, *PG* 20:361.

27. Eric W. Kemp, *Canonization and Authority in the Western Church* (Oxford: Oxford Univ. Press, 1948), 7–8.

28. Canon 20, Périclès-Pierre Joannou, ed., *Discipline générale antique (IVe.–IXe. S.)*, (Grottaferrata: S. Nilo, 1962), 97.

29. Du Cange describes different categories of names included in the diptychs somewhat differently, asserting that there were diptychs of (1) deceased bishops, (2) the living, and (3) other deceased persons. Charles du Fresne du Cange, "Diptycha," in *Glossarium ad scriptores mediae et infimae latinitatis*, vol. 2 (Paris: Ormont, 1733), 1512. Despite his assertion that this three-part division of the types of names was commonly accepted by scholars, different methods of categorization can be found.

30. Robert F. Taft, "Praying to or for the Saints? A Note on the Sanctoral Intercessions/Commemorations in the Anaphora," in *Ab Oriente et Occidente (Matt. 8:11): Kirche Ost und West: Gedenkschrift für Wilhelm Nyssen*, ed. Michael Schneider (St. Ottilien, 1996), 441–442 (emphasis in original). For disagreements and discussions in the early centuries of the church on the issue of the final judgment of the martyrs, see Michael Perham, *The Communion of Saints* (London: Alcuin Club, 1980), 8–11.

31. Joseph-Alexandre Martigny, "Diptyques," in *Dictionnaire des Antiquités Chrétiennes*, ed. J.-A. Martigny (Paris: Librairie Hachette, 1877), 249.

32. *PG* 33:1116.

33. du Cange, "Diptycha," in du Cange, *Glossarium* 2:1513 (emphasis in original).

34. Cited in Taft, "Praying to or for the Saints?" 443 (emphasis added).

35. Christian A. Salig, *De Diptychis veterum, tam profanis quam sacris, liber singularis* (Magdeburg: Renger, 1731), 3, as quoted in Martigny, "Diptyques," *Dictionnaire*, 250.

36. Johannes Cassianus, *Conlationes* 19, vol. 1:1, *CSEL* 13:534.

37. Martigny, "Diptiques," *Dictionnaire*, 251–252. Vasiliev, approaching this issue from the Eastern perspective, reaches identical conclusions. Vasilii Vasiliev, *История канонизации русских святых* (Moscow, 1893), 37–38.

38. The complete text of the Chronology of 354, including both the *Depositio Martyrum* and the *Depositio Episcoporum*, is included in *Le Liber Pontificalis*, ed. L. Duchesne, 1:1–12.

39. L. Duchesne, "De Orientali Martyrologio," in *Martyrologium Hieronymianum ad fidem codicum adiectis prolegomenis*, ed. I. B. de Rossi and L. Duchesne (Brussels [undated]), 50ff.

40. Martigny ("Calendrier Ecclésiastique," in *Dictionnaire*, ed. Joseph-Alexandre Martigny, 105) asserts that this calendar goes back to the fifth century, but this seems impossible since it includes

a feast-day for the local Bishop Eugenius (481–505). Jean Mabillon (*Vetera Analecta, sive collectio veterum aliquot operum* [Farnborough: Gregg 1967], 163) cautiously estimates that it cannot be earlier than the seventh century, but he bases this conclusion on the style of calligraphy on the particular manuscript that he published. It seems reasonable to assume that the calendar was in use in Carthage even before Eugenius was on the episcopal throne, and that additional names, including his, were included over time.

41. Mabillon, ed., *Vetera Analecta*, 163–167.

42. "[Sistus] seems to have been a bishop: but it not been determined at all what place he was the bishop of; he must be distinguished from Pope Sistus, who came a little later." Mabillon, ed., *Vetera Analecta*, 164.

43. "I think that the Januarius here is an African martyr, who in the year 302 received the martyr's crown together with Paulus, Gerontius, and six others. Or else Januarius may be the bishop of Beneventum who suffered [martyrdom] under Maximian in Naples, in Campania, on September 19 with Sosius." Mabillon, ed., *Vetera Analecta*, 165–166. But if the first possibility were correct, it would seem strange that the others who were martyred with him are not mentioned. Since Sosius is commemorated in this calendar on the very next feast-day, the second possibility would be more likely—although then it is unclear why this Januarius is not identified as a bishop (as are many others in the text). In any case, the fact remains that the identity of this Januarius cannot be determined with certainty.

44. Mabillon, ed., *Vetera Analecta*, 163.

45. Mabillon supposes that his name may have been included because of confusion with a martyr of the same name. *Vetera Analecta*, 166–167.

46. See note 29.

47. "For it is clear that not all the Patriarchs of Constantinople have been included in the calendar as they were in the necrology; . . . nevertheless, the diptychs contained [the names of] many deceased Patriarchs, of whom no mention was made in the calendar." Stefano Morcelli, *Menologion ton Euangelion heorstastikon, sive Kalendarum Ecclesiae Constantinopolitanae*, vol. 1 (Rome: Monaldini e Giunchi, 1778), 123; see also Vasiliev, *История канонизации русских святых*, 41–42.

48. Arthur Haddan and William Stubbs, eds., *Councils and Ecclesiastical Documents Relating to Great Britain and Ireland* (Oxford: Clarendon Press, 1871), 391.

49. *CCSL* 149:43.

50. *De gloria Martyrum* 86, *PL* 71:781.

51. See Hippolyte Delehaye, *Les Passions des martyres et les genres littéraires* (Brussels: Bureaux de la Société des Bollandistes, 1921), esp. chap. 1.4, 150ff.

52. Pontius, *Vita e martirio di san Cipriano: Introduzione, testo critico, versione e note*, ed. Michele Pellegrino (Alba: Paoline, 1955).

53. In *The Myth of Persecution: How Early Christians Invented a Story of Martyrdom* (New York: HarperCollins, 2014), Candida Moss takes an extreme approach, arguing that the early Roman religious persecutions (or at least the alleged magnitude of them) were inventions, created by followers of Christianity with their own motives. But while it may very well be true that individual accounts of martyrdom were exaggerated and the overall numbers of martyrs inflated, it seems that fully accepting the author's basic premise leads us perilously close to concluding that Christianity as a whole is fictitious as well, and its teachings concocted for ulterior, political reasons.

54. Morcelli asserts that "Their Acts had been obliterated through the passage of time or negligence, and the collection of sacred books had everywhere been burned by the fury of enemies." But since he does not cite any specific historical evidence, it appears that he is drawing a logical conclusion rather than relying on known examples. Morcelli, *Menologion ton Euangelion heorstastikon*, 6.

55. Augustine, Sermo 315, *PL* 28:1426.

56. *Concilia Africae A. 345–A. 525* (*Corpus Christianorum: Series Latina* 149), 204–205. The extent to which the part of this canon pertaining to dreams was subsequently disregarded, at least by other local churches, will become all too evident in the following pages, for countless persons throughout the entire Christian world were declared in later centuries to have been martyrs based entirely on revelations received in dreams.

57. Albert Dufourcq, *Étude sur les Gesta Martyrum romains* (Paris: Fontemoing 1900), 32.

58. Delehaye also provides detailed examples, *Les Passions*, 157ff.

59. *PL* 59:171–173. Is this rejection of *acta* at least a part of the reason why Pope Gregory I (540–604), writing to the bishop of Alexandria, asserts that in Rome they had a one-volume collection of the names of nearly all the martyrs but had no accounts providing the details of their martyrdom? It seems that Alexandria had a collection of *acta* that, at least in the eyes of the pope, rivaled Rome's. Epistola 29, *PL* 77 t. 3;916–917. Morcelli erroneously cites this as Epistola 28, *Menologion ton Euangelion heorstastikon, sive Kalendarum Ecclesiae Constantinopolitanae* (Roma: Monaldini e Giunchi 1788), 7.

60. Greek text in George Nedungatt and Michael Featherstone, eds., *The Council in Trullo Revisited* (Rome: Pontificio Istituto Orientale, 1995).

61. *Epistola Adriani Papae ad Beatum Carolum Regem "de Imaginibus," PL* 98:1284. This declaration is all the more interesting since the 794 Council of Frankfurt, held during the same period and convoked by the same Charlemagne, acknowledged in its Canon 42 that any official determination that a particular Christian should be venerated as a true martyr had to be based on accurate *passiones*—the tacit implication being that inaccurate ones were in circulation. *Monumenta Germaniae Historica, Concilia* 2, *Concilia Aevi Karolini* pt. 1 (Hannover: Hahn, 1906), 170. See also sec. C, *infra*, for further discussion of legislation on this subject during Charlemagne's reign.

62. "Two testimonials, that of Saint George and the one of Quiricus and Julitta ... should not be accepted; they are worthless and not acceptable." *Iuris ecclesiastici graecorum historia et monumenta* 2:332, ed. J. Pitra (Rome: Typis Collegii Urbani 1868).

63. See Delehaye, *Sanctus*, 124–125.

64. The writings of Bishop Gregory of Nyssa (c. 335–c. 395), who would later be regarded as a saint himself, show the immense respect he held for the physical remains of his deceased sister, St. Macrina, who passed away only a few decades after Emperor Constantine had formally legalized Christianity. See Caroline Bynum, *The Resurrection of the Body in Western Christianity 200–1336* (New York: Columbia University Press, 1995), 83–86.

65. The terms *inventio*, *elevatio*, and *translatio* eventually become blurred and are thus often used interchangeably. But strictly speaking, *inventio* refers specifically to the discovery of a tomb, the location of which was heretofore unknown (as with Gervase and Protase, whose case will be seen shortly); *elevatio* means the removal of the relics from the original, generally underground burial site, bringing them aboveground; and *translatio* to the act of moving them from one tomb to another in a different place. Not every martyr's relics were discovered at an unknown site, of course, and so the term *inventio* does not apply to all. At the same time, a translatio normally implied an elevatio first, although the opposite was not necessarily true. The overlapping nature of the definitions ultimately led to imprecision and so the terms wrongly, though understandably, became largely synonymous.

66. Eusebius, *De Martyribus Palaestinae*, *PG* 20, 1509.

67. I. B. de Rossi and L. Duchesne, eds., *Martyrologium Hieronymianum*, 84.

68. Ambrose, Epistula 77, *CSEL* 82, part 3, 126ff.

69. *ASs* for April 12, vol. 2:90.

70. Kemp, *Canonization and Authority*, 29.

71. *ASs* for August 17, vol. 3:475ff.

72. Delehaye, *Sanctus*, 141.

73. Eusebius, *Historia Ecclesiae* 8, 6, *PG* 20:754.

74. Optatus, liber 7, book 1, 16, *CSEL* 26:18–19.

75. Amore was one scholar who was not convinced that this reference is particularly significant, because "in reality, in all of ancient Christian literature one does not find any trace of '*vindicatio*.'" Agostino Amore, "Vindicatio" in *Dizionario Storico Religioso*, ed. Pietro Chiocchetta (Rome: Studium, 1966), 1139. It is quite possible, however, that at least in Optatus's own diocese some system—even an informal one—could have been established in order to emphasize to the faithful the difference between true martyrs and the schismatic victims of persecution. But Amore is absolutely correct that there is no additional evidence extant today that would support this theory, even for the city of Milevis during Optatus's time.

76. The canon continues with the caution against relying on dreams and visions to establish the existence of a martyr, discussed in the preceeding section. *CCSL* 149:204.

77. Sulpicius Severus, *De Vita Beati Martini* 11, *PL* 20:166–167.

78. Philippus Jaffé et al., *Regesta Pontificum Romanorum* (Leipzig: Veit, 1885) no. 636, *PL* 56:694.

79. Theodoret, Φιλόθεος Ιστορία 3, *PG* 82:1335.

80. Sozomen, *Ecclesiastical History*, 7:15, *PG* 67:1453–1456.

81. Delehaye makes an interesting distinction, noting that while the emperor here is declaring that the fallen Christians *should* be honored as martyrs, he is not declaring that they *will* hereafter be venerated by the church as such. In this way, intentionally or not, the emperor publicly recognizes those Christians who died and yet avoids directly usurping the power of local church authorities. Delehaye, *Sanctus*, 179.

82. Theodoret, *Historia Ecclesiastica* 5, 26, *PG* 82:1255.

83. The Bollandists provide a detailed chronological list of the early calendars containing the name of Telemachus for his feast-day on January 1; *ASs* for January, vol. 1:31.

84. T. Mommsen, ed., *Codex Theodosianus* 7, 9, 17; vol. 1:466 (Berlin, 1905).

85. *Codex Iustinianus* 1, 3, 26, *Corpus Iuris Civilis*, vol. 1 (Berlin: Weidmann, 1884), 21.

86. *Monumenta Germaniae Historica, Capitularia regum Francorum*, vol. 1, 25, no. 5 (Hannover: Hahn, 1883).

87. *Capitularia regum Francorum*, vol. 1, 56, no. 42.

88. Ibid., 223, no. 25.

89. Canon 42, *Monumenta Germaniae Historica, Concilia*, vol. 2, *Concilia Aevi Karolini*, part 1:170 (Hannover: Hahn, 1906).

90. Ibid., 272.

91. This new law may very well have been a reaction to revelations of the spurious "relics" sold by the Roman deacon (i.e., a church official) Deusdona to some of Charlemagne's courtiers, who wished to place the remains of martyrs and other saints in various churches and monasteries throughout the newly Christianized kingdom. They included the alleged remains of Saint Tiburtius, which were quickly acknowledged to be fraudulent. At the same time, however, it appears that some of the relics obtained by the Franks through Deusdona's agency may be genuine, such as those of the martyrs Marcellinus and Peter, which were eventually translated to Seligenstadt (in modern-day Germany). See Patrick Geary, *Furta Sacra: Thefts of Relics in the Central Middle Ages* (Princeton, NJ: Princeton Univ. Press, 1978), and Jean Guiraud, *Questions d'histoire et d'archéologie chrétienne* (Paris: Victor Lecoffre, 1906), esp. chap. 7, "Les reliques romaines au IXe. siècle."

92. A. P. Lebedev, *Очерки внутренней истории византийско-восточной церкви в IX, X, и XI веках* (Moscow: Snegireva, 1902), 58.

93. Ibid., 79–80. Lebedev also notes parenthetically that the only concrete historical evidence we have is the fact that Basil built a church in honor of Constantine, and that other historians conclude that this constituted his canonization of his own son.

94. Vasiliev, *История канонизации русских святых*, 54.

95. Lebedev, *Очерки внутренней истории византийско-восточной церкви*, 80.

96. Giorgius Cedrenus, *Compendium historiarum* (Venice: Javarina, 1729), 519.

Notes to Chapter Two

1. Metr. Iuvenalii, *Канонизация святых: Доклад на освященном Поместном Соборе Русской Православной Церкви, посвященном 1000-летию крещения Руси* (Moscow: Izdanie Moskovskoi Patriarkhii, 1988), 18.

2. Vasiliev, *История канонизации русских святых*, 115. Unless specifically noted, all translations from Russian are my own.

3. Vasiliev, *История канонизации русских святых*.

4. E. E. Golubinskii, *История канонизации святых в русской церкви*, Moscow [undated].

5. As Paul Bushkovitch puts it, "The issue here is not that Golubinskii was careless or dishonest. His citations were accurate and his breadth of coverage exemplary, but his assumptions required him to read the sources in ways that were fundamentally misleading." *Religion and Society in Russia: The Sixteenth and Seventeenth Centuries* (Oxford: Oxford Univ. Press 1991), 75–77.

6. Vasiliev, *История канонизации русских святых*, 6. Or, to cite a more recent definition: "[Saints] ... live in a different world and there by the Holy Spirit see the glory of God and the beauty of the Lord. But in the same Holy Spirit, they also see our lives and our affairs.... They know our sorrows and hear our fervent prayers. Living on the earth, they learned the love of God by the Holy Spirit; and who has a love for the land, he goes with her to eternal life in the kingdom of heaven, where love grows and will be perfected. And if here on earth love cannot forget a brother, how much more will the Saints remember us and pray for us. Saints rejoice in our repentance, and they mourn when people turn from God and become like brute beasts. They feel sorry for the people in the world who live without knowing that if they loved each other, then the Earth would be free from sin; and where there is no sin, there is joy and gladness from the Holy Spirit. They are holy like the Lord ... [although] the Saints were ordinary people. Many of them committed great sins, but through their repentance they reached the kingdom of heaven. And everyone who reaches heaven, does so through repentance, which the merciful Lord has given us by virtue of His sufferings." "Святые," in *Настольная книга священнослужителя* (Moscow: Izdanie Moskovskoi Patriarkhii, 1988), 768.

7. "One particular category ... is that of the *strastoterptsy*, a term that can be translated as 'those who have undergone the Passion.' They are not martyrs for the faith properly so-called: their ascetic virtue consists in the acceptance of a violent death for the love of Christ, without offering resistance and identifying themselves with His Passion, in this way refusing to continue the circle of violence." I. Semenenko-Basin, "Chiesa Russa," in *Enciclopedia dei Santi: Le Chiese orientali* (Rome: Città Nuova, 1998), cxiv.

8. The *Сказание о свв. мучениках Борисе и Глебе*, which is the source most closely followed here, is believed to have been written by the eleventh-century monk Iakov Chernorizets. See G. Fedotov, *Святые древней руси* (New York, 1959), 20, for a discussion of the sources for information about these historical events.

9. "Vladimir had twelve sons, though not of the same wife.... Sviatopolk was Prince of Pinsk, Yaroslav of Novgorod, Boris of Rostov, and Glev of Murom." *Сказание о свв. мучениках Борисе и Глебе*, in Dmitrii Abramovich, ed., *Жития святых мучеников Бориса и Глеба и службы им* (Petrograd: Imperatorskaia Akedemiia Nauk, 1916), 27–28.

10. E.g., "Woe is me, light of my eyes, radiance of my face, punishment of my non-understanding! Woe is me, my lord Father! Where will I run to, if I find such evil everywhere around me ... ? Your honorable person has sent me, betrayed, to my grave ... remember me in thy chambers! My heart grieves ... my blood will be poured out and they will be glad of my death, I will be a martyr for my Lord." *Сказание о свв. мучениках Борисе и Глебе*, in Abramovich, ed., *Жития святых мучеников Бориса и Глеба*, 29.

11. *Сказание о свв. мучениках Борисе и Глебе*, in Abramovich, ed., *Жития святых мучеников Бориса и Глеба*, 37.

12. The words the chronicler puts into the mouth of Gleb are identical in tone to those of Boris. E.g., "O Lord, my Lord! As You said to Your apostles, 'For My name, for My sake, your relatives and friends will bind your hands, brother will hand over brother to death, and you will die for My name's sake.'" *Сказание о свв. мучениках Борисе и Глебе*, in Abramovich, ed., *Жития святых мучеников Бориса и Глеба*, 42.

13. Nikolai Barsukov, *Источники русской агиографии* (St. Petersburg, 1882), 70–72.

14. "Being in the Horde, he was slandered by some detractor: 'The Grand Prince Roman blasphemes you, Great Khan, and he berates your faith.' Then the Khan, believing the accuser, delivered him to the Tatars to be tormented ... but Grand Prince Roman, the Confessor of Christ, was unafraid ... 'I am a Christian, and the Christian Faith is truly holy; your Tatar faith is filthy and loathsome.'" *Степенная книга царского родословия по древнейшим спискам* for the year 6778 (i.e., 1270 AD) (Moscow: Iazyki slavianskikh kul'tur, 2007), 542.

15. "Saint Roman Olegovich, Prince of Ryazan', martyred by the Horde in 1270." *Верный месяцеслов всех русских святых чтимых молебнами и торжественными литургиями, общецерковно и место составленный по донесениям Святейшему Синоду преосвященных всех епархий в 1901–1902 годах* (Moscow: Sinodalnaia Tipografia, 1903), July 19.

16. For an interesting interpretation of Ivan's political motivations for persecuting Philip, see S. Tyszkiewicz, "Spiritualité et sainteté russe Pravoslave," *Gregorianum* 15 (1934): 355–356. Even if the author's analysis of the political situation and the thought-process of the tsar is true, it would not alter the fact that Philip was killed for his faith and the moral implications of it.

17. *Словарь исторический о святых, прославленных в российской церкви, и о некоторых подвижниках благочестия* (St. Petersburg, 1862), 235–238.

18. In one of the most recent liturgical calendars compiled for the Russian church, Philip is referred to on his first feast-day (January 9) as simply "Saint Philip, Metropolitan of Moscow, who died in 1569." On his second feast-day (July 3), commemorating the transfer of his relics to Moscow, the calendar notes, "The transfer of the relics of *Sviatitel'* Philip, Metropolitan of Moscow." *Верный месяцеслов всех русских святых*, 5 and 23. The issue of multiple feast-days, including celebration of the date of transfer of a saint's relics, will be addressed in the following section.

19. A good general discussion of the attitude of the Russian church toward the Old Believers with regard to the canonization of their own saints can be found in I. Semenenko-Basin, *Святость в русской православной культуре XX века: История персонификации* (Moscow, 2010), 36–47.

20. The prime example is of course the Archpriest Avvakum Petrov, executed in 1682 after enduring many years of imprisonment and other hardships for his refusal to accept the Nikonian reforms. The Old Believers' liturgical commemorations include a list of "Those Who Suffered for the Faith," upon whom the first one named is "Holy [or Saint] Archpriest Avvakum." A. Rurin, *Сводный Старообрядческий синодик по четырем рукописям XVIII-XIX в.* (St. Petersburg, 1883), 21.

21. A. Albani, ed., *Menologium graecorum iussu Basilii imperatoris graece olim editum, munificentia et liberalitate sanctissimi D.N. Benedicti XIII in tres partes divisum nunc primum praece et latine prodit studio et opera Annibalis tit. S. Clementis presb. Card. Albani* (Urbinum, 1727). It should be noted that, while the compilers of this calendar were establishing saints' feast-days for the entire church, they invariably included some saints who had been canonized for local churches only. In this way, and in keeping with the practice that had gradually developed in the first millennium of Christianity, they extended the cult of some local saints to the entire Greek church—a phenomenon taking place in other parts of the Christian world as well, as discussed in the preceding chapter.

22. Vasiliev, *История канонизации русских святых*, 42.

23. Ibid., 119.

24. Barsukov, *Источники русской агиографии*, 70–71.

25. See Golubinskii, who acknowledged that examples of calendars in which "a significant number" of Russian saints were included were rare, up until the mid-sixteenth century. Golubinskii, *История канонизации святых*, 309. With the unprecedented canonization councils of Metropolitan Makarii (discussed in more detail below), attempts were finally made to compile an accurate list.

26. Semenenko-Basin, *Святость в русской православной культуре*, 24–26.

27. "Calendars could serve as a means for determining the beginning of the church-wide veneration of saints, if we knew that they were under the strict supervision of the church and her hierarchs. If that had been the case, then obviously, the calendars of saints would all be uniform in their composition and volume.... Comparing extant church calendars not only from various centuries, but even those within the same century, we see total dissimilarity between them. This shows that the production of church calendars was not the work of the Church and her primates, but rather the work of private individuals, who included in them saints of their own choosing. Calendar copyists were guided by their own pious sentiments when drawing them up, leading them to include in the calendars as large a number of saints as possible." Vasiliev, *История канонизации русских святых*, 59.

28. Metr. Iuvenalii, *Канонизация святых*, 22.

29. The four cases he lists are Metropolitans Cyprian and Photius; Maxim, the Holy Fool of

Moscow; Princess Euphrosyne of Suzdal; and Archbishop Theodore of Rostov, Nicholas Kochanov, and Isidor Tverdislov. Vasiliev, *История канонизации святых*, 89–90.

30. P. Peeters, SJ, in "La canonisation des saints dans l'église russe," *Analecta Bollandiana* 33 (1914): 380–420, cites Golubinskii in support of his own assertion that there are some Russian saints "for whom this attestation [i.e., that ecclesiastical authorities formally established that they are to be venerated as saints] is lacking, and who thus may have been inscribed in the liturgical books either by involuntary error or by fraud." But Golubinskii says nothing about fraud in the passage cited by Peeters, instead noting simply (although at great length!) that there are in the Russian calendars some saints whose dates of canonization are unknown; and others who may never have been formally canonized at all and were included as a result of popular piety (*История канонизации святых*, 137–138). This confusion and lack of extant documentation is a far cry from the deception Peeters suggests may have occurred in some cases.

31. The role played by the Variag people in the Christianization of early Rus' is recounted in A. Kuz'min, "Варяги в хирстианизации Руси," in *Падение Перуна: Становление христианства на Руси* (Moscow: Molodaia gvardia, 1988).

32. See *Степпеная книга царского родословия по древнейшим спискам* for the year 6488 (i.e., 980 A.D.) (Moscow: Iazyki slavianskikh kul'tur, 2007), 237–240.

33. "Святых мучеников Феодора варяга и сына его Іоанна в Кіевѣ, в 983 году." *Верный месяцеслов всех русских святых*, July 12.

34. Metr. Platon, *Сборник древностей Казанской Епархии и других Приснопамятных обстоятельств* (Kazan: Universitetskaia Tipografiia, 1868), 75. Note that a *Panikhida*, or requiem, was to be said for these new saints—a good example of the blur between praying *to* them, and praying *for* them, discussed previously in both this and the first chapter.

35. "Освященного Архиерейского Собора Русской Православной Церкви о канонизации святителей Иова и Тихона, Патриархов Московских и всея Руси," *Журнал московской патриарха* 1990, no. 1:6–7.

36. "Житие святителя Тихона, Патриарха Московского и всея Руси," *Журнал московской патриарха* 1990, no. 6:56–68.

37. "A feast-day in honor of this or that saint, established with his canonization by the highest ecclesiastical authorities and with the participation of civil leaders, was meant to glorify the memory of the saint. This latter goal was achieved by drawing up an account of his life, which is necessary for the veneration of his memory on his feast-day. We see a similar phenomenon in the Greek church ... consequently, it is not unreasonable to assume that we adopted this custom from them. But there was no way to trace the relationship between the liturgical services on saints' feast-days and the stories of their lives—and so it was difficult to say whether a saint's life and the liturgical service in his honor were established together or not." Vasiliev, *История канонизации русских святых*, 121.

38. Vasilii Kliuchevskii, *Древнерусские жития святых как исторический источник* (Moscow, 1871), 3–7.

39. Ibid., 8 and 17.

40. Mikhail Tolstoi recounts an incident found in one of the later *zhitiia*, in which a group of pagans from Rostov sought out Leontii in order to kill him. When he came before them, holding a cross, they fell down as if dead and were subsequently baptized by him. Then, the author adds, "Since that time, the teachings and miracles of St. Leontii brought many inhabitants of Rostov to Christ, and although he died in peace (before 1077), he nonetheless earned a martyr's crown after the two Variags, who had suffered for the name of Christ in Kiev even earlier." Tolstoi, *Древния святыни Ростова-Великаго* (Moscow, 1860), 34.

41. This presumes, of course, that Leontii became a saint because of his manner of life/death. But Golubinskii, who does not even mention the possibility that Leontii died as a martyr, notes correctly that Leontii was declared a saint while his successor, Bishop Isaii, was not—and this even though the two tombs were uncovered at the same time. He concludes that Leontii was presumably canonized because of the documented miracles that took place at his tomb and presumes that Isaii was never made a saint because there were no miracles at his. This theory would be completely consistent with

the possible reasons for the failure to declare Boris and Gleb's brother Sviatoslav a saint, also suggested by Golubinskii and discussed below. Golubinskii, *История канонизации святых*, 61. If Golubinskii is correct, this would of course imply that Leontii was canonized solely because of subsequent miracles at his tomb and not because of his life and the manner of his death.

42. A. Kadlubovskii, *Очерки по истории древнерусской литературы житии святых* (Warsaw, 1902), 44ff.

43. Ibid., 48; see also 72–73.

44. "If we turn to other historical sources, and especially to the chronicles, we will find in them neither the story about Mercurius, nor that of the attack of the Tatars on Smolensk indicated. Among other things, the chronicles contain a detailed narrative about the invasion by Batievo [i.e., the Tatar khan] and list all the cities affected by it. . . . It is strange that the chronicles are silent about this attack of the Tatars on one of the main cities of what was then Russia, as is the absence of any written evidence about the event." Kadlubovskii, *Очерки по истории древнерусской литературы житии святых*, 48–49.

45. G. Golubovskii, *История Смоленской земли* (Kiev: Tipografiia Imperatorskago Universiteta Sv. Vladimira, 1895), 304.

46. Kadlubovskii, *Очерки по истории древнерусской литературы житии святых*, 53.

47. Kadlubovskii notes: "The acts of the canonization have not been preserved; it is very possible that they didn't even exist, and that the recognition has been effected through literature." Kadlubovskii, *Очерки по истории древнерусской литературы житии святых*, 81. Filaret notes that the cathedral in Smolensk, which was dedicated to Merkurii and contains his relics, was built in 1755. Filaret, *Жития святых, чтимых православною церковью: ноябрь* (St. Petersburg: Izdanie Knigoprodavtsa i L. Tuzova, 1900), 314.

48. Golubinskii, *История канонизации святых*, 42.

49. Ibid., 17–18. But with his typical inconsistency, soon after asserting this rule he acknowledges that, while the church in Russia followed the same procedural practices as that in Greece, there are definitely some examples of saints who are exceptions to the rule: "In the Greek church, there were several entire classes of ascetics, for whose elevation to the ranks of sainthood there were other grounds besides miracles" (ibid., 40). And later, he repeats his assertion that the Russian church "undoubtedly" adopted this practice from the Greeks but then frankly acknowledges that there is no evidence of this: "There is no doubt that we ourselves did not invent this custom of opening the relics in the expectation of a miracle on behalf of the deceased, but we borrowed it from the Greeks. [But] we cannot point to examples and evidence of this from the contemporary history of the Greek church" (ibid., 45–46). Thus, the only safe conclusion we might draw from the author's assertions is that it would be *logical* to think that the Russians received this practice from the Greeks, but there is no hard evidence that the Greeks had actually begun to regard miracles as a sine qua non for canonization.

50. Gordienko, a non-Christian historian of the Soviet era who does not attempt to conceal his negative opinion of the whole process of canonization in the Russian Orthodox Church, nevertheless cites accurately the historical facts to support his conclusion that "the Russian Orthodox Church glorifies and praises even the most distinguished persons among the number of its saints, not for their civic virtue or for their service to the community, but rather for the gift of 'miracles' received from God" and is consequently highly critical of the Canonization Commission established in the 1980s (which will be discussed in detail below). Gordienko, *Новые православные святые* (Kiev, 1991), 72; see also 85ff.

51. "The martyrs Boris and Gleb were our first saints. But there were not merely two martyrs who suffered a violent death at the hands of Sviatopolk, but three: a third brother, Sviatoslav, was also killed along with them. If all three of them were not numbered among the saints, that is because only the first two were glorified by God through miracles. Miracles soon began to take place on the tombs of Boris and Gleb in Vyshgorod, but the grave of Sviatoslav—where miracles could have been performed—was missing because he was killed somewhere in the Carpathian mountains while fleeing to Hungary. He was not brought to Russia, but rather was buried on the site of his death. There were no miraculous phenomena with him as with Boris and Gleb, and that is why, although he was a martyr just like them, he was not added with them to the list of the saints. . . . Consequently it is quite clear that they were canonized not as martyrs, but as miracle-workers; although insasmuch as

they were passion-bearers, this would imply that they were miracle workers." Golubinskii, *История канонизации святых*, 265.

52. Suvarov provides his own analysis of these events in the course of his lengthy review of Golubinskii's book: "We cannot make assumptions regarding the three princes, victims of a violent death at the hands of Sviatopolk, but it seems without a doubt that those who lived during their time were able to know, understand, and distinguish the nature, lifestyle, and circumstances of the deaths of Boris and Gleb on the one hand, and of Sviatoslav on the other." Suvarov, I., *Журнал министерства народнаго просвещения* 348 (July 1903): esp. 289–290.

53. N. Barsukov, *Источники русской агиографии*, 13–15.

54. Kliuchevskii notes that the historical evidence about Adrian is "corrupted by contradictions," particularly with regard to chronology. Another account about the same monk indicates that he died in 1619—sixty-nine years later! Kliuchevskii, *Древнерусские жития святых как исторический источник*. Since it does not seem possible to reconcile the conflicting accounts, one can only wonder whether in fact there were two different monks named Adrian who lived and died in this region of Russia. This may be yet another case of two separate biographies being conflated into one.

55. See, for example, Monakhinia Taisia, *Русские святие: 1000 лет русской святости* (St. Petersburg: Azbuka-klassika, 2001), 711. The *Верный месяцеслов всех русских святых*, however, makes no mention of martyrdom, simply noting in the calendar, "The suffering of the venerable Adrian of Poshekhonie, killed on March 5, 1550, by robbers." *Верный месяцеслов всех русских святых*, 11.

56. "*Criminals* threw the body of Abbot Adrian on the banks of the Ushloma River after he was killed." See Barsukov, *Источники русской агиографии*, 13 (emphasis added).

57. Makarii, *История русской церкви в период Монгольский*, vol. 5 (St. Petersburg: Golnik 1886), 419–420.

58. Any attempt to sort out the historical situation is further complicated by the fact that the bodies of both men were later transferred yet again in 1770, this time to Moscow, where they were placed inside one of the churches of the Kremlin (where they remain to this day). Golubinskii, *История канонизации святых*, 62–63n3. Regardless of how we interpret the first move to Chernigov, it seems undeniable that the second, to Moscow, did indeed constitute a formal translatio. If the first move is considered merely an informal move of the bodies back to their hometown from the place of martyrdom, this would imply that there was only one true translatio, which took place after miracles had already been happening at their burial site.

59. "In the year 6738, on March 9 . . . the martyr of Christ Avramii was brought out of the land of Bulgaria into the glorious city of Volodimir . . . on April 1 . . . the relics of the holy martyr Avramii were brought into Volodimer; Grand Prince Georgii met them a mile outside the city with great honor, with priests and the bishop Mitrofan with the entire choir and with abbots, with children and all the people; and they were laid in the Church of the Holy Mother of God." *Laurentian Chronicle* for the year 6738 (1230 AD), *Полное собрание русских летописей*, vol. 1 (St. Petersburg: Tipografia Eduarda Pratsa, 1846), 192–193.

60. Golubinskii asserts that "signs" had taken place at the site of Avramii's tomb immediately after his death, but the account contained in the chronicles, which he cites in support of this claim, makes no mention of this. He also asserts that "with full probability" a local liturgical commemoration was established for Avramii in Vladimir (or at least within the monastery, in whose church he was buried) after the translatio, but while it does seem likely, there is no evidence of this either. Golubinskii, *История канонизации святых*, 62.

61. Abramovich, ed., *Жития святых мучеников Бориса и Глеба*, 54–55.

62. Tolstoi, *Древния святыни Ростова-Великаго*, 35.

63. Subsequently, discussing the 1549 Canonization Sobor convened by Metropolitan Makarii, Golubinskii makes comparable suppositions regarding the verification of alleged miracles, but again without providing any specific evidence. Golubinskii, *История канонизации святых*, 41 and 102.

64. "An 'investigation into new miracle-workers,' carried out by the episcopal hierarchy, preceded the canonizations of 1549. Collecting the *zhitiia*, the canons, and the miracles of the local wonder-workers, they were guided by the testimonies of local residents. Descriptions of these investigations have not

survived." Kliuchevskii, *Древнерусские жития святых как исторический источник*, 423.

65. There is no evidence to support Golubinskii's thesis that it is "probable" that Mikhail was venerated as a saint locally in Tver immediately after his death. Golubinskii, *История канонизации святых*, 67. The earliest known action taken by the Russian hierarchy to declare Mikhail a saint took place in the seventeenth century, after the events described above.

66. Kliuchevskii, *Древнерусские жития святых как исторический источник*, 424.

67. "The elderly Aquilina asked to be brought to the tomb, and when she was brought to touch the incorrupt body ... she began to see as clearly as if she had not been blind. The priests and people who had witnessed such a divine healing of the blind praised God, for having given them such a doctor." *Историческия сказания о жизни святых подвизавшихся в Вологодской епархии прославляемых всею церковию и местно чтимых* (St. Petersburg: V. A. Gudkov-Beliakov, 1880), 368.

68. "A special diocesan commission that considered cases of miraculous healings sent to St. Petersburg, along with the petition, a book with records of miracles that occurred at the tomb of the matryed Metropolitan." Semenenko-Basin, *Святость в русской православной культуре*, 56.

69. It is a historical fact acknowledged even by the Canonization Commission established relatively recently by the Moscow Patriarchate: "Each of these saints was glorified above all by miracles, which constituted a sufficient condition for the inclusion of the servant of God in the lists of the saints. Even if the saint suffered for the faith (like Prince Mikhail of Chernigov and his boyar Theodore, or Grand Duke Mikhail of Tver), the chronicler focuses not on his confession of the faith [through his death], but rather on the working of miracles." Metr. Iuvenalii, *Канонизация святых*, 19.

70. Vasiliev, writing over a century ago, described this requisite and acknowledged frankly that it was not based on historical tradition in the Greek church. Vasiliev, *История канонизации русских святых*, 138.

71. A. Iu. Karpov, *Православные святые и чудотворцы* (Moscow: Vecha, 2005), 36.

72. As we saw above, Kliuchevskii traces the development of Leontii's *zhitie* and raises questions about the politicization of his cult; in the process, questions are simultaneously raised about the factual accuracy not only of his *zhitie* but also of accounts of his burial and reburial. Since the church in which Leontii had originally been buried and venerated collapsed in 1204, his tomb was subsequently moved into another church. This would imply that differing accounts of his burial in church may actually be the two separate incidents; or they may simply be the result of literary embellishment. Kliuchevskii, *Древнерусские жития святых как исторический источник*, 3ff.

73. Vasiliev, *История канонизации русских святых*, 140.

74. *Историческия сказания о жизни святых подвизавшихся в Вологодской епархии*, 366–367.

75. Golubinskii, *История канонизации святых*, 87–88.

76. See Gordienko, *Новые православные святые*, 13–14, where he ridicules the belief that finding a person's remains "incorrupt" constitutes a miracle; as well as I. Semenenko-Basin, "Belief in the incorruptibility (mummification) of the whole body (and not just some of the bones) of any and all saints became a peculiarity of Russian piety," Semenenko-Basin, *Святость в русской православной культуре*, 30.

77. Golubinskii recounts the burial practices of some monasteries, where bodies were buried in small aedicules akin to the Roman catacombs. Assuming that the atmosphere was sufficiently dry, it is quite possible that this type of burial, without tombs that completely enclosed the remains, inadvertently facilitated the mummification of bodies rather than their decomposition. See Golubinskii, *История канонизации святых*, 53n1.

In the case of the child Gavriil of Belostok, whose purported martyrdom will be discussed below, his body was also later found to be incorrupt—but since those who first discovered his dead body asserted that all the blood had been drained from it (a fact which had led them to conclude he had been killed in a ritual murder by Jews), this may have contributed to a natural mummification of his remains.

78. Golubinskii, *История русской церкви*, vol. 1 (Moscow, 1997), 839.

79. Vasiliev, however, seems to think that it does, and for this reason he is skeptical of the information in the chronicles: "We do not find confirmation of this anywhere except in the Nikon Chronicle,

which says that Bishop Ioann, together with the blessed Metropolitan Theodor, established the feast of St. Leontii. Among other things, in this case it is hardly possible to rely on the Nikon Chronicle, as at that time (like today) the right of canonization in the Russian church had already been transferred exclusively to the highest central authority." Vasiliev, *История канонизации русских святых*, 71. But it seems unnecessary to draw broad conclusions about general canonization practices from such a passing statement—which might simply be intended to indicate that the fame of Leontii's sanctity had spread throughout Russia, reaching even the highest levels of the Russian church hierarchy.

80. "Грамота патриарха Иоанна XIV митрополиту Феогносту об открытии мощей св. Петра митрополита," in *Памятиники древне-русскаго каноническаго права*, vol. 6 of *Русская историческая библиотека* (St. Petersburg, 1908), 11–13. Vasiliev notes, as do others, that there was probably some political motive for doing this. Vasiliev, *История канонизации русских святых*, 141. See also Golubinskii, *История канонизации святых*, 27 and 29.

81. But on occasion it is, nevertheless, erroneously cited as such: cf., for example, "It has been shown that the metropolitans of Kiev carried out the first canonizations of Russian saints only after the Patriarch of Constantinople had studied their cases; but starting in the fifteenth century, canonizations in Russia were happening already without the *placet* of Constantinople." Semenenko-Basin, "Chiesa Russa," in *Enciclopedia dei Santi*, 140. Upon further inquiry, the author cited the case of Saint Peter as his only evidence for the first part of this general statement.

82. As Temnikovskii noted, in canonizing new saints, the Russian hierarchy was limiting itself to association with a cult that had already been established and gave it a kind of confirmation after the fact. Temnikovskii, entry on the canonization of saints, in N. N. Glubokovskii, *Православная богословская энциклопедия* (Petrograd, 1907), as cited in Peeters, "La canonisation des saints dans l'église russe," 388–389.

83. P. Peeters, "La canonisation des saints dans l'église russe," 389.

84. Golubinskii compiled a long list of dozens of these informally venerated "non-saints," the majority of whom were founders and heads of various Russian monasteries down through the centuries. Golubinskii, *История канонизации святых*, 313ff. While it seems easy enough to imagine that individual monasteries might privately venerate a deceased monk without ever seeking his official canonization, the inclusion of some of the other names on Golubinskii's list is more questionable. Most incredible is Golubinskii's mention here of the martyrs Ioann, Stefan, and Petr (killed by Tatars in the sixteenth century and mentioned previously), even though the metropolitan of Kazan specifically requested—and obtained—the Moscow patriarch's approval of their veneration. Golubinskii's reason for insisting that the patriarch did not actually canonize this trio is that the wording of the metropolitan's request was not that they be "made saints" but simply that they be "honored." Ibid., 269. Since there is no reason to presume that in the sixteenth century (or in any subsequent century, for that matter), a precise, standardized formulation of such requests had been developed, it seems clear that this is in fact a distinction without a difference. There is absolutely no evidence to support Golubinskii's suggestion here that a separate category of non-saints, the honoring of whom had been approved by the supreme authority in the Russian church, has ever existed.

85. Golubinskii notes that his death must have occurred "before 1478," when Novgorod was still subject to Moscow. *История канонизации святых*, 150. The *Верный месяцеслов всех русских святых* (p. 20) lists his death as having occurred in 1427.

86. *Историческия сказания о жизни святых подвизавшихся в Вологодской епархии* contains a detailed account of events surrounding Kirill's cult, 366–375.

87. Leonid notes simply that Kirill was "not canonized." Leonid, *Святая Русь или Сведения о всех святых и подвижниках благочестия на Руси (до XVII века), обще и местно чтимых* (St. Petersburg: Tipografia M. Stasiulevicha, 1891), 88.

88. "The church burned down, and after the fire they gathered from it a few bones which were preserved in a box at the altar of the present stone Trinity Church. . . . Upon the formation of the city of Vel'sk, Kirill was no longer mentioned in church services; but to meet the demands of the people who came for the solemn celebration of his feast-day (June 9), one of the altars of the cemetery church was dedicated to St. Kirill." Barsukov, *Источники русской агиографии*, 306.

89. "After 1780, the year Vel'skii Posad was incorporated into the city of Vel'sk, the feast-day was suppressed by the Vel'sk clergy, who realized its illegality, i.e., its arbitrariness." Golubinskii, *История канонизации святых*, 150.

90. And while Golubinskii apologizes (*История канонизации святых*, 138–139), Peeters criticizes Golubinskii's excessively complex method of categorizing saints and compiling faulty lists of saints' names and asserts that the resulting confusion is a logical consequence of Golubinskii's broad definition of *saint* simply as one who is commemorated in the liturgy. Given the known problems with the liturgical calendars, thanks to copyists' errors and arbitrary decisions, there are undoubtedly feast-days in the calendar that do not in fact correspond to a person who was actually canonized by someone in the Russian hierarchy, as mentioned previously. Peeters, "La canonisation des saints dans l'église russe," 382–383.

91. Golubinskii, *История канонизации святых*, 92–93.

92. *Акты, собранные в библиотеках и архивах Российской империи археографическою экспедициею императорской академии наук* (St. Petersburg: Tipografia II-go Otdeleniia Sobstvennoi E.I.V. Kancheliarii, 1836), 203–204.

93. The text fails to specify the date for the feast of the latter two saints, who evidently were to be commemorated together. *Акты, собранные в библиотеках и архивах Российской империи*, 204.

94. Golubinskii documents in detail the complicating factor that there are discrepancies in the lists of saints' names contained in various manuscripts. Golubinskii, *История канонизации святых*, 99ff.

95. Vasiliev, *История канонизации русских святых*, 200.

96. A rather verbose account can be found in Metr. Platon, *Сборник древностей Казанской Епархии и других Приснопамятных обстоятельст* (Kazan: Universitetskaia Tipografiia 1868), 66–75.

97. "Устав церковных обрядов, совершавшихся в Московском Успенском соборе, около 1634 г.," *Русская историческая библиотека, издаваемая археографишескою коммиссиею*, vol. 3 (St. Petersburg, 1876), 54.

It is worth noting that the *Верный месяцеслов всех русских святых* does not describe Georgii as a martyr at all, instead stating simply that he "died in a battle with the Tatars on March 4, 1238." Interestingly, the calendar does not describe Mikhail as a martyr either. *Верный месяцеслов всех русских святых*, 9–10.

98. Golubinskii, *История канонизации святых*, 151. Golubinskii provides a list of over ninety different "saints" (or not), who fit into the very same category as Iakov and Ioann: persons from the post-Makarii period in the church in Russia whose veneration is definitely documented but for whom there is no evidence of a formal canonization with Moscow's approval, 139–159.

99. An official record of the consecration of the newly renovated church in Meniush, in the region of Novgorod, is found in *Церковныя Ведемости*, the organ of the Holy Governing Synod, which published all official documents of the Russian church during the period in which the synod was the supreme governing body of the church. It specifically mentions "consecration of the main altar in the church in honor of the youths Iakov and Ioann, whose relics rest in the northwestern part of the church." *Церковныя Ведемости* no. 45 (1895): 1583–1584.

100. Much has been made of the synod's proclamation of the canonization of (non-martyr) Seraphim of Sarov in 1903, which included a specific declaration that his body had been examined and found to be incorrupt (нетленными). Such a declaration followed the format of countless Russian canonizations before it; but this time word was leaked to the press that the true state of Seraphim's physical remains was in fact quite the opposite. The metropolitan of St. Petersburg ultimately released a statement acknowledging that "the skeleton of the deceased elder was found beneath the decayed remains of his monastic habit. The body underwent corruption." Yet at the canonization ceremony itself, formal mention was made once again of the new saint's relics as being "incorrupt." See, for example, Gordienko, *Новые православные святые*, 30–31.

101. A concise summary of the process during the Synodal period can be found in P. de Meester, OSB, "La canonizzazione dei santi nella chiesa russa ortodossa," *Gregorianum* 30 (1949): 402–403.

102. A scornful account of the whole affair, written during the Soviet period, can be found in *Святой отрок Гавриил* (Moscow: Ateist, 1923). Despite its blatant anti-Christian slant, it nevertheless contains much useful factual information, particularly 10ff.

103. See entry on "Гавриил" in the online *Православная Энсиклопедия* of the Moscow Patriarchate, http://www.pravenc.ru/text/161257.html (accessed April 26, 2011).

104. V. I. Dal', *Записка о ритуальных убийствах* (original title: *Розыскание о убиении евреями христианских младенцев и употреблении крови их*) (Moscow: Vitazh, 1995).

105. Ibid., no. 98.

106. I. Semenenko-Basin, *Святость в русской православной культуре*, 28. It is curious that Golubinskii did not seem to be aware of this group canonization; he makes no mention of it in his numerous lists of saints canonized during the various historical periods of the Russian church.

107. Isidor and his seventy-two companions were allegedly killed by German "latinizers"; but Fetisov outlines the suspiciously striking similarities between the language of Isidor's *zhitie* and that of Prince Mikhail Chernigovskii, killed two centuries earlier by the pagan Tatars (and discussed above). The language of the latinizing persecutors parallels that of the non-Christian Tatar Khan, while that of Isidor mirrors the speech of Prince Mikhail, strongly suggesting that the Latin killers were equivalent to pagans—all of which is sufficiently dubious that the author concludes that "the traits of one character were transferred to another." N. Fetisov, "К литературной истории повести о мученике Исидоре Юрьевском," in *Сборник статей в честь академика Алексея Ивановича Соболевского* (St. Petersburg: Izdatel'stvo Akademii Nauk SSSR, 1928), 218–221. Concurring with Fetisov, see also L. Sokolov, "Житие Исидора Юрьевского," in *Словарь книжников и книжности древней Руси*, vol. 2, pt. 1 (Leningrad, 1988), 284–285. There appear to be similarities between the dubious historicity of the *zhitie* upon which was based the canonization of Merkurii of Smolensk, discussed in detail previously, and that of Isidor: in each case, the *zhitie* was written long after the saint allegedly lived and died, and each appears to contain significant amounts of information copied from older accounts of the life of a completely different individual.

108. Semenenko-Basin, *Святость в русской православной культуре*, 49ff.

109. Quoted in Semenenko-Basin, *Святость в русской православной культуре*, 67–68.

110. Iosif's cause had been approved by the Holy Governing Synod in 1916, but a formal ceremony declaring his canonization was postponed because of the ongoing revolutionary activity, as well as disagreements between Moscow and the bishop of Astrakhan about financing it. By the time the issue was taken up again in 1918, the Holy Governing Synod had of course ceased to exist. The cause was reapproved and his sainthood was formally declared by the *sobor* under the newly restored patriarchate. See Semenenko-Basin, *Святость в русской православной культуре*, 56–57; Gordienko, *Новые православные святые*, 32.

111. Gordienko points out that no trace of this documentation remains; but given the political upheaval and active persecution of the Russian church at the time, it is hardly surprising that it went missing, and the disappearance of relevant documents does not mean that they never existed. Gordienko, *Новые православные святые*, 32.

112. An official description of the commission and the parameters of its authority can be found on the website of the Moscow Patriarchate, http://www.patriarchia.ru/db/text/65980.html (accessed April 15, 2011).

113. Technically, Tikhon was officially canonized as a sviatitel', and not as a *muchenik*, since (as was discussed earlier in this chapter) his status as a member of the hierarchy of the Russian church "outranked" his status as a new martyr. *Журнал московской патриарха*, no. 1 (1990): 6–7.

114. Ibid.

115. Ibid.

116. Ibid., 6.

117. Golubinskii, *История канонизации святых*, 126 and 199ff. Peeters ("La canonisation des saints dans l'église russe," 406) rightly points out that Golubinskii contradicts himself, providing the specifics regarding Simon's canonization in one chapter of his work while in a later chapter including Simon in a list of saints whose canonization is unknown.

118. Golubinskii, *История канонизации святых*, 159ff, esp. 164.

119. Cf., among others, Peeters, "La canonisation des saints dans l'église russe," 406, who notes that a statue of Anna near her tomb showed her giving a blessing with two fingers, instead of the three prescribed by Patriarch Nikon's reforms.

120. P. Peeters, "La canonisation des saints dans l'église russe," 407.

121. Interview republished in 2005 by P. Lanin, "Александр Мень и дело Бейлиса," in *Полемика и дискуссии*, accessed April 26, 2011, http://www.polemics.ru/articles/?articleID=6199.

122. The complete text of the official document, "Доклад Преосвященного митрополита Крутицкого и Коломенского Ювеналия, Председателя Комиссии по канонизации святых 'Об отношении Церкви к подвигу мученичества,' представленный на заседании Священного Синода Русской Православной Церкви 25 марта 1991 года," can be found in *Канонизация Святых в XX веке* (Moscow 1999), 96–126.

123. Particular reference is of course being made here to the many clerics who joined the schismatic Living Church, backed by the Soviet government, which in turn supported many aspects of the Communist political system. "Доклад Преосвященного митрополита Крутицкого и Коломенского Ювеналия," 123.

124. "Доклад Преосвященного митрополита Крутицкого и Коломенского Ювеналия," 114.

125. "Victims of political killings can be passion-bearer saints, because they were killed as symbols of Orthodox Russia. Moreover, it is known from history that the first of the well-known saints of the Russian church—Princes Boris and Gleb—fell as victims of political crimes, as they were killed by their brother Sviatopolk the Damned in princely strife. But the Church has glorified them as both martyrs and passion-bearers." "Доклад Преосвященного митрополита Крутицкого и Коломенского Ювеналия," 123.

126. Referenced in "Постановление Священного Синода Русской Православной Церкви от 1–2 октября 1993 года с одобрением представленного Комиссией порядка канонизации местночтимых святых и работе епархиальных комиссий по канонизации святых," in *Канонизация Святых в XX веке*, 147.

127. "Постановление Священного Синода Русской Православной Церкви от 1–2 октября 1993 года," 147.

128. Ibid.

129. The first text announcing the decision is found in *Журнал московской патриархa*, no. 6, (1991):9. Additional documentation is contained in *Канонизация Святых в XX веке*, 127–143.

130. "Деяние Освященного Юбилейного Архиерейского Собора Русской Православной Церкви о соборном прославлении новомучеников и исповедников Российских XX века," *Журнал московской патриархa*, no. 9 (2000): 56–68. Italian translation in I. Semenenko-Basin, *Eternamente fiorisce: I nuovi santi della chiesa ortodossa russa* (Milan: Edizioni La Casa di Matriona, 2005), 199–220.

131. Ibid., 56–57.

132. "Деяние Освященного Юбилейного Архиерейского Собора Русской Православной Церкви", 65. Note that the original text first describes the imperial family as *strastoterptsy*, while in the following sentence indicating that they died the deaths of *mucheniki*.

133. Much has been written on this topic, from both theological and political standpoints. See, among others, my three-part series of articles, "Ideology or Isolationism? Russian Identity and Its Influence on Orthodox–Catholic Relations," *Occasional Papers on Religion in Eastern Europe* 27, nos. 1–3 (2007). More specifically, with regard to the 2000 canonizations, see J. Burgess, "Retrieving the Martyrs in Order to Rethink the Political Order: The Russian Orthodox Case," *Journal of the Society of Christian Ethics* 34/2 (Fall/Winter 2014).

134. "Основания для канонизации Царской семьи из доклада Митрополит Крутицкого и Коломенского Ювеналия, Председателя Синодальной Комиссии по Канонизации Святых," accessed April 22, 2011, http://www.mospat.ru/archive/s2000r05.htm.

135. "Основания для канонизации Царской семьи из доклада Митрополит Крутицкого и Коломенского Ювеналия." While the commission declares them *strastoterptsy*, it elsewhere in the same document references the Romanovs as *mucheniki*, or martyrs—apparently intending these latter references in a loose sense.

136. The commission also noted that they, unlike the Romanov family, were not commonly being commemorated by the Russian people. "Основания для канонизации Царской семьи из доклада

Митрополита Крутицкого и Коломенского Ювеналия." In any case, the commission pointed out that two of the servants—a Catholic (footman Alexei Trupp) and a Lutheran (tutor Catherine Schneider)—were not members of the Russian Orthodox Church and thus could not be considered for canonization in any case; it thus criticized the Russian Orthodox Church Outside of Russia for its "unprecedented" canonization (not recognized by Moscow) of these persons who were not even members of the church. Ibid.

137. "The veneration of the Imperial Family, already begun by Patriarch Tikhon at the *panikhidi* for the murdered Tsar in the Kazan Cathedral in Moscow three days after the Ekaterinburg murders, continued—despite the dominant ideology—for decades during the Soviet period of our history. Both clergy and laity offered up prayers to God for the repose of the slain sufferers, members of the Imperial Family. . . . this demonstrates the growing reverence across all of Russia for the murdered Imperial Family." Ibid.

138. See also M. Pol'skii, *Новые Мученики Российские*, vol. 1 (Jordanville, NY: Holy Trinity Monastery, 1947), esp. 263.

139. In M. Shevchenko, "Прославление царской семьи—вопрос решенный: Член Синодальной комиссии по канонизации святых РПЦ протоиерей Георгий (Митрофанов)—о тех, кому будут молиться," accessed April 25, 2011, http://www.ng.ru/ideas/2000-05-31/8_tsar.html.

140. Ibid.

141. Igumen Damaskin, "Методология и практические особенности исследования подвига новомучеников и исповедников российских," accessed August 10, 2014, www.mepar.ru/documents/misc/2009/02/17/3069/.

142. Ibid.

143. Ibid.

144. "In the nineteenth to early twentieth centuries, many who became parish clergy of the church did so based on their social background [i.e., sons of Orthodox priests normally became priests themselves]. . . . For this very reason it is impossible to assess a person as a zealous Christian based solely on his social status as a member of the clergy. And therefore a rigorous study of the life of the martyr is required." Ibid.

145. Cited in "Постановление Священного Синода Русской Православной Церкви от 1–2 октября 1993 года," 147.

146. E.g., O. Platonov, *Жизнь за Царя: Правда о Григории Распутине*, St. Petersburg 1996.

147. See, for example, accessed April 26, 2011, http://www.themoscowtimes.com/news/article/orthodox-church-takes-on-rasputin/240577.html.

148. The document also addressed a separate push to canonize (as a non-martyr) Tsar Ivan the Terrible: "К вопросу о канонизации Царя Ивана Грозного и Г.Е. Распутина," "Приложение No. 2 к докладу митрополита Крутицкого и Комоненского Ювеналия, председателя Синодальной комиссии по канонизации святых," accessed April 26, 2011, http://www.patriarchia.ru/db/print/420877.html.

149. Ibid.

150. Ibid.

151. "Retrieving the Martyrs in Order to Rethink the Political Order: The Russian Orthodox Case," 9.

152. Metr. Iuvenalii, *Канонизация Святых*, 22.

Notes to Chapter Three

1. T. Aquinas, *Summa Theologiae*, II-II, q. 124 *De Martyrio*, art. 3.

2. T. Aquinas, *Com. In L. Sent.*, d. 49, q. 5, a. 3, sol. 2.

3. Benedict XIV (P. Lambertini), *De servorum Dei beatificatione et beatorum canonizatione*, l. 3, c. 8 (Rome: Academiae liturgicae Conimbricensis typographi, 1748), 227–231. A particularly clear exposition of the question can be found in A. Kleber, OSB, "A Soldier's Death, a Martyrdom?" *The American Ecclesiastical Review* 111 (1944): 281–290.

4. Benedict XIV (P. Lambertini), *De servorum Dei beatificatione et beatorum canonizatione*, l. 3, c. 11, 117. See also P. Gabriel de Sainte-Marie-Madeleine, "La béatification et la canonisation des martyrs," in *Limites de l'humain* (Paris: Desclée de Brouwer, 1953), esp. 227–229.

5. T. Aquinas, *Summa Theologiae*, II-II, q. 124 *De Martyrio*, art. 5.

6. *Beatificationis seu declarationis martyrii servae Dei Mariae Goretti virginis: Novissima positio super martyrio* (Rome: Guerra et Belli, 1944), 2.

7. "This year [978] was King Edward slain, at eventide, at Corfe-gate, on the fifteenth day before the calends of April. And he was buried at Wareham without any royal honour. No worse deed than this was ever done by the English nation since they first sought the land of Britain. Men murdered him but God has magnified him. He was in life an earthly king—he is now after death a heavenly saint. Him would not his earthly relatives avenge—but his heavenly father has avenged him amply. The earthly homicides would wipe out his memory from the earth—but the avenger above has spread his memory abroad in heaven and in earth. Those, Who would not before bow to his living body, now bow on their knees to His dead bones. Now we may conclude, that the wisdom of men, and their meditations, and their counsels, are as nought against the appointment of God." *The Anglo-Saxon Chronicle*, "Chronicle Years: 973–79" (London: Everyman Press, 1912), accessed May 13, 2011, http://www.britannia.com/history/docs/973-79.html.

8. André Vauchez, in *La sainteté en Occident aux derniers siècles du moyen age, d'après les procès de canonisation et les documents hagiographiques* (Rome: École Française de Rome, 1981), titles an entire section of his work "Kings and Princes: The 'Passion-Bearers'" and notes that while this phenomenon can be seen in both the East and the West in the medieval period, in Russian Orthodoxy "it survived longer than in the West." Vauchez, *La sainteté en Occident*, 191.

9. *Passio Sancti Kanuti Regis et Martiris*, in *Vitae Sanctorum Danorum* (Copenhagen: Kommission Hos, 1908), 68.

10. *MGHS*, vol. 29:19. It is true that the official bull of canonization, signed by Pope Alexander III in 1169 (*PL* CC, 603–604), nowhere describes Canute Lavard as a martyr; but in the Roman Martyrology for January 7 he is officially listed as such.

11. *MGHS*, vol. 12:619–623, as well as the contemporary *Vita Karoli comitis Flandrensis*, in *ASs* for March, vol. 1:163–179, esp. 174.

12. To be fair, Charles's already existing cult was confirmed in a case of equipollent beatification, which simply recognized that he had already been venerated for centuries as a martyr. See Congregatio de Causis Sanctorum, *Index ac status causarum* (Vatican City, 1999), 418. (The concept of equipollent beatification will be addressed at length later in this chapter.) But the fact remains that there was no obligation to confirm Charles's status as a martyr; his cult as such could equally have been suppressed if Vatican authorities had chosen to do so.

13. E. A. Peers, in *Ramon Lull: A Biography* (New York: MacMillan, 1929), notes that the condemnation is "now generally considered to have been a forgery. . . . Lull's descendants and followers caused the papal archives to be ransacked for the bull which Gregory was supposed to have issued—without result. Later, in the time of Martin V, the Lullists again raised the question of its spuriousness, and judgment was again given in their favour." Peers, *Ramon Lull*, 378–381.

14. John Paul II, Apostolic Constitution *Divinus perfectionis Magister*, *AAS* 75 (1983), 352.

15. Gratianus, *Decretum*, c. 1 de cons. D. 3, *PL* CLXXXVII, 1781–1782.

16. BonifaceVIII, *Sextus Decretalium liber* (Venetia, 1572), 313–314.

17. In the 1600s, the Spanish Dominican Dominic Banez thus argued against the Protestant reformers, who asserted that the pope had no authority over the veneration of saints: "The conclusion is therefore proven firstly by tradition, and by the perpetual usage of the Catholic Church, and by the common consensus of all Councils and of the Church Fathers from the beginning, and it has been believed and carried out by the Pope. And it is confirmed by the Council of Florence in the decree regarding the union of the Armenians, where the Armenians were instructed that most blessed Leo I is a saint." D. Bannes Mondragonensis, OP, *De Fide, Spe et Charitate: Commentaria in 2.2. D. Thomae, ibique Synopsis*, in I. Roccaberti, *Bibliotheca Maxima Pontificia* 8 (Rome: Typographia Ioannis Francisci Buagni), 333–334.

18. Pius V, *Quo primum*, in *Bullarum diplomatum et privilegiorum Sanctorum Romanorum Pontificum Taurinensis editio*, vol. 7 (Augustae Taurinorum: A. Vecco et sociis editoribus, 1878), 839–840.

19. The complete calendar can be found in M. Sodi, ed., *Missale Romanum, Editio Princeps (1570)* (Vatican City: Libreria Editrice Vaticana, 1998), 39–50.

20. Full text of the pope's original canonization decree in *ASs* for May 7, vol. 2:259ff.

21. *Calendarium Romanum ex decreto Sacrosancti Oecumenici Concilii Vaticani II instauratum auctoritate Pauli PP. VI promulgatum* (Vatican City: Typis polyglottis Vaticanis, 1969), 122.

22. Complete Latin text of the Congregation's decree in G. Ippolito, *Memorie e culto S. Filomena V. e M.* (Naples: Stabilimento Tipografico dell'Italia, 1870), 122–123.

23. Sacra Congregatio Rituum, *Instructio de calendariis particularibus et Officiorum ac Missarum propriis ad normam et mentem codicis rubricarum revisendis*, February 14, 1961, *AAS* 53 (1961), 174.

24. M. Toynbee, *S. Louis of Toulouse and the Process of Canonization in the Fourteenth Century* (Farnborough: Gregg, 1966), 210.

25. See *ASs* for October 3, "the feast of Saint Gerard, who was the abbot who translated the body of Saint Eugenius," vol. 2:304ff.

26. Gratianus, *Decretum*, c. 37 de cons. D. 3, 1717.

27. See S. Kuttner: "Into the last part of his book, Gratian had inserted a canon of the Synod of Mainz of 813, which concerned *translatio*, ruling that it could not be carried out 'without permission of the prince or the bishops of the holy Synod.'" Kuttner, "La réserve papale du droit de canonisation," *Revue historique de droit français et étranger* 4, series 17 (1938): 200.

28. Kuttner, "La réserve papale du droit de canonisation," 186.

29. Two different but consistent historical accounts of these events can be found in *ASs* for October 30, vol. 8:291 and 294.

30. Full text of the inscription in ibid., 292.

31. E.g., Saint Douceline (1214–1274) was not a martyr but rather a French mystic who eventually became superior of a community of Beguines in Marseilles. Her remains were formally translated on two separate occasions in the 1270s. It is unclear which (if either) of these two occasions was connected to her canonization; although she is known as Sainte Douceline in France, it is possible that she was never formally canonized. See Kemp, *Canonization and Authority*, 127.

32. "Die Chronik der Böhmen des Cosmas von Prag," in *MGHS Rerum Germanicarum*, Nova series, vol. 2 (Berlin: Weidmann, 1923), 84ff. (Irregular Latin spelling in original.) Kuttner, without challenging the overall historical truthfulness of the account, casts doubt on the veracity of the wording of this papal condemnation: "One sentence that Cosme [i.e., the author of "Die Chronik," cited above] has made Pope Benedict IX pronounce would have been absurd: neither in 1039, nor at the time of Cosme himself, had there ever been 'canons' or 'decrees of the fathers' that would have defended translations by bishops." Kuttner, "La réserve papale du droit de canonisation," 189.

33. Alexander III, *Epistola 1023, Ad capitulum Cantuariense—De canonizatione beati Thomae archipraesulis, PL* CC, 901.

34. It is of interest that Alexander III's letter to the clergy of Canterbury, noted above, makes no mention of Thomas Becket having died a martyr's death, referencing only his meritorious life and the miracles attributed to his intercession after his death. Alexander III, *Epistola 1023, Ad capitulum Cantuariense—De canonizatione beati Thomae archipraesulis*, 901. But in an earlier letter confirming the interdict imposed on England because of Thomas Becket's murder, the same pope pointedly described Thomas as a martyr: "By his precious martyrdom he lives with the saints in heaven." Alexander III, *Epistola 790, Ad Joscium archiepiscopum Turonensem et eius suffraganeos—Confirmat sententiam interdicti latam in cismarinam terram regis Angliae propter vim illatam S. Thomae Cantuariensi archiepiscopo, PL* CC, 727.

35. Kemp, *Canonization and Authority*, 50–51.

36. The anonymous *Controversia de S. Joanne Nepomuceno* (Vienna: Typis et sumpt. L. Mayer [undated]) provides descriptions of the extant historical sources and suggests possible theories that would explain what has ultimately become a virtually inextricable tangle of two biographical accounts. Their basis in great part on a Latin translation of the *Annales Bohemorum* may have included a copyist's error in the date of martyrdom, which eventually led to the confusion. The situation was unfortunately complicated further by the publication in the 1600s of a dramatic "biography," presumably fanciful at least in part, by the Jesuit Bohuslav Balbinus, which includes many unverifiable details about the presumed life and death of Saint John Nepomucene. It was subsequently included in the *ASs* for May 16, vol. 3:668ff.

37. Urban VIII, *Caelestis Hierusalem cives*, in *Bullarum diplomatum et privilegiorum Sanctorum*

Romanorum Pontificum Taurinensis editio, vol. 14 (Augustae Taurinorum: A. Vecco et sociis editoribus, 1878), 436–437.

38. L. Hertling, SJ, "Materiali per la storia del processo di canonizzazione," *Gregorianum* 16 (1935): 187.

39. For a detailed discussion of canonization during this period, see G. Papa, *La cause di canonizzazione nel primo periodo della Congregazione dei Riti (1588–1634)* (Rome: Urbaniana University Press, 2001).

40. Vauchez, *La sainteté en Occident*, 56–57. Vauchez notes that, despite all the testimony submitted at Cacciafronte's process, he was not in fact canonized (p. 61). For the developing need for witnesses to miracles as well as to the deceased's virtuous life, see also Hertling, SJ, "Materiali per la storia del processo di canonizzazione," esp. 187–191.

41. Full text can be found at http://www.vatican.va/roman_curia/congregations/csaints/documents/rc_con_csaints_doc_20070517_sanctorum-mater_en.html (accessed August 4, 2011).

42. The actual criteria used by local bishops, toward the end of the first millennium, to determine whether a *non-martyr* should be canonized or not remain largely unknown to this day. See Agostino Amore, "La canonizzazione vescovile," *Antonianum* 52 (1977): 266.

43. One does, however, encounter early collections of miracles that occurred through a martyr's intercession *after* already being venerated as a saint. Such miracles obviously had no effect on the martyr's status; but they naturally constituted confirmation (not that any was necessary!) of the authenticity of the church's belief that these persons were indeed saints. See, for example, "Les miracles des SS. Cosme et Damien," in Hippolyte Delehaye, *Les recueils antiques de miracles des saints* (Brussels: Bollandistes, 1925), 8ff.

44. *Casus S. Galli: Continuatio II*, in *MGHS* vol. 2:156; see also *ASs* for May 2, vol. 1:283.

45. *PL* 214, 483.

46. *Bulla Innocentii III de canonizatione sanctae Cunegundis, PL* 140, 220.

47. *Epistola Innocentii III Papae, de nece B. Petri de Castro-Novo*, in *ASs* for March 5, vol. 1:415.

48. See chap. 4, "Ultima beatificazione decretata da Urbano VIII," in Fabijan Veraja, *La beatificazione: storia, problemi, prospettive* (Rome: S. Congregazione per le Cause dei Santi, 1983), 80ff, for a discussion of the issues involved in Jozafat's cause, especially as they were affected by the new legislation that had coincidentally just been published by Urban VIII on canonization procedure (this will be addressed below).

49. Cited in Benedict XIV (P. Lambertini), *La beatificazione dei servi di Dio e la canonizzazione dei beati*, vol. 1, chap. 30 (Vatican City: Libreria Editrice Vaticana, 2010), 618–619.

50. Cited in Benedict XIV (P. Lambertini), *La beatificazione dei servi di Dio e la canonizzazione dei beati*, vol. 1, chap. 30, 619–620.

51. Innocent III, "Rescriptum Domini Papae super inquisitione morum vitae et miraculorum," in *Thesaurus novus anecdotorum*, vol. 3, ed. E. Martene (Paris, 1717), 1842–1843.

52. Quoted in Vauchez, *La sainteté en Occident*, 63.

53. The relevant canon was actually even more complicated, for it also factored in the evidentiary weight of testimony about the candidate's virtuous life: "Can. 2117. For the beatification of Servants of God only two miracles are required, if eyewitnesses can bring forward proof of virtues in both the informative and the apostolic processes, or if witnesses examined in the apostolic process at least had heard or seen them; three miracles, if there were eyewitnesses in the informative process, and witnesses in the apostolic process who had heard about it; four miracles, if in each process it is established only through non-eyewitnesses and through documents." A complicated, almost mathematical formula had thus been devised, in which the evidence of witnesses and that of miracles were to be weighted in such a way that when combined, they equalled one single complete, convincing case for beatification.

54. In a case of equipollent beatification—which will be discussed extensively later in this chapter—*three* more miracles were required for canonization.

55. Fabijan Veraja, *Le cause di canonizzazione dei santi* (Vatican City: Libreria Editrice Vaticana, 1992), 83.

56. E. Piacentini, OFM Conv., *Il martirio nelle cause dei santi* (Rome: Libreria Editrice Vaticana, 1979), 151.

57. See Veraja, *Le cause di canonizzazione dei santi*, 83.

58. *ASs* for March 5, vol. 1:416–417. The account goes on to say that another miracle (at least in the view of the anonymous author) was the fact that Pierre's killer, the count of Toulouse, was so shunned by all from that time forward that even dogs refused to accept food from his hand. It is evident that this was not accepted as a miracle justifying Pierre's canonization. See also Benedict XIV (P. Lambertini), *La beatificazione dei servi di Dio*, vol. 1, chap. 29, 607.

59. J. Susza, *Cursus vitae et certamen martyrii B. Josaphat Kuncevicii* (Paris: Victor Palmé, 1863), contains accounts of no less than eighty-three miracles, mostly medical cures, alleged to have taken place through Jozafat's intercession; interestingly, number 84 and last on the list is a mention of the discovery that Jozafat's body was still incorrupt fifteen years after his death (pp. 129–130). While there is no mention of which of these miracles were accepted by Rome as authentic, it is obvious that the promotors of Jozafat's canonization were not emphasizing the state of his remains as a key miracle supporting his cause.

60. "De miraculis post obitum," in *Beatificationis et canonizationis servi Dei Andreae Bobola, sacerdoti professi Societatis Jesu*, vol. 1: *Super signatura commissionis introductionis causae* (Rome, 1726), 8–12.

61. *Beatificationis et canonizationis servi Dei Andreae Bobola, sacerdoti professi Societatis Jesu*, vol. 4, *Positio super miraculis* (Rome: Typ. Pont. Universitatis Gregorianae, 1936).

62. See, among others, A. P. Frutaz, "*Auctoritate . . . beatorum apostolorum Petri et Pauli*: Saggio sulle formule di canonizzazione," *Antonianum* 42 (1967): 438.

63. The original text, dated 6 July 1171, identifies the addressee simply as "K." Kol Sverkerson reigned as king of Sweden from 1167 to 1173, which is wholly consistent with the date of the letter. But L. Porsi, in his "Collectio legum ecclesiae de beatificatione et canonizatione a saeculo decimo usque ad praesens," *Monitor Ecclesiasticus* 111 (1986): 359, holds that the letter was addressed to "Canute, king of the Swedes and of the Goths," a fact that could only be true if the letter was actually written no earlier than 1173, when Canute Eriksson succeeded Kol as king of Sweden. Since Pope Alexander III reigned from 1159 to 1181, it is theoretically possible that the date on the extant copies of the letter is incorrect.

64. Latin text in L. Porsi, "Collectio legum ecclesiae," 359.

65. *Decretales Gregorii Noni Pont. Max.*, vol. 3, title 25 (Venice, 1572), 822.

66. Kuttner, "La réserve papale du droit de canonisation," 197.

67. Norman Tanner, ed., *Decrees of the Ecumenical Councils*, vol. 1 (Washington, DC: Georgetown University Press, 1990), 263.

68. *BSs* vol. 11 (Rome: Città Nuova, 1990), 1184ff.

69. A long list of fifteenth-century miracles attributed to Simoncino's intercession is included in the *ASs* for March 24, vol. 3:501–502.

70. Latin text in Benedict XIV (P. Lambertini.), *La beatificazione dei servi di Dio e la canonizzazione dei beati*, vol. 1, chap. 14, 326.

71. Interestingly, Jewish scholar Ariel Toaff reached different conclusions in the first edition of his *Pasque di Sangue: Ebrei d'Europa e omicidi rituali* (2007), which is now out of print.

72. *BSs* vol. 11 (Rome: Città Nuova, 2000), 1186–1187.

73. Even if adequate evidence of Simoncino's martyrdom had really existed, questions about the suitability of canonizing the boy would nevertheless have been raised because of his young age. In fact, Benedict XIV discusses this very case, not because of the questions raised about its truthfulness, but solely in the context of a discussion as to whether it was possible to canonize small children: "It is a matter of children dying below the age of reason having received the baptism not of water, but of blood, who were killed out of hatred of Christ and the Faith." Benedict XIV, *La beatificazione dei servi di Dio*, vol. 1, chap. 14, 323.

74. Cases like that of Simoncino were presumably also the impetus for the subsequent legislation of Pope Urban VIII prohibiting the initiation of canonization procedures for anyone who had

died less than ten years previously. In 1627 the same pope amended the law to *fifty* years—so that the emotional enthusiasm of the faithful had sufficient opportunity to calm down, enabling the process to then take place in a more objective, rational atmosphere. See Urban VIII, Decree of November 20, 1627, in L. Porsi, *Leggi della Chiesa su beatificazione e canonizzazione dall'anno 993 all'anno 2000* (Rome: Nova Res, 2006), 131.

75. Canon 2038.1.

76. John Paul II, Apos. Const. *Divinus perfectionis Magister*, sec. 1, *De inquisitionibus ab Episcopis faciendis, AAS* 75 (1983): 349–355.

77. Ibid., 352.

78. Ibid., 355.

79. Henricus de Segusio, Cardinalis, "*De reliquiis, et veneratione sanctorum,*" cap. 1, *In tertium decretalium librum commentaria* (Torino: Bottega d'Erasmo, 1965), 172a.

80. Thomas Netter, *Doctrinale antiquitatum fidei catholicae ecclesiae Dei de sacramentalibus*, tit. 14 "De canonizatione sanctorum," col. 764.

81. See, for example, Tullio Citrini, "Memoria, riconoscimento e canonizzazione dei santi," *La Scuola Cattolica* 108 (1981): 326.

82. H. Leclercq, OSB, notes in his entry "Ampoules de sang," in the *Dictionnaire d'archéologie chrétienne et de liturgie* (Paris: Librairie Letouzey et Ané, 1924), (1747 ff) that "these vials probably were merely containers of fragrances. The widespread practice in ancient times of burying a body with a certain amount of spices is well known." If this is the case with the vial found in Philomena's tomb, a chief piece of objective evidence arguing in favor of her status as a martyr for the faith is instantly removed.

83. A particularly appalling piece of "scholarship" was *Sulla lapide sepolcrale di S. Filomena vergine e martire, con le animadversioni critiche sulle di lei memorie* (Rome: Tipografia delle belle arti, 1837), authored by S. Santucci; it dissected in painstaking detail the narrative of the dream as reported by the religious from Naples and ultimately established, e.g., that Philomena "was scourged only once, and not twice," but "was subjected to shooting by arrows three times, and not twice" (pp. 68–69). The entire work is based on the apparent assumptions that (a) the sister's account of her dream is to be accepted as inspired and constitutes documentary evidence of undeniable historical facts; and (b) that the arrows, anchor, and other carvings on Philomena's tomb were carved as a literal record of the different methods whereby her Roman persecutors repeatedly tried in vain to martyr her, before she finally was successfully beheaded.

84. The writings of F. di Lucia, a priest associated with the shrine in Mugnano, Italy, where Philomena's remains are now kept, are replete with accounts of what he asserts unequivocally are not only miracles but miracles performed through the intercession of Philomena; see di Lucia, *Relazione istorica della traslazione del sagro corpo e miracoli di santa Filomena vergine e martire da Roma a Mugnano del Cardinale* (Benevento: Presso Pietro Paolo Paternó, 1834), 1:88 ff; 2:105 ff; 3:19 ff, among many others. Although the author protests at the very start of each volume that he submits "to the decrees of the Supreme Roman Pontiff, especially to those of Urban VIII, as an obedient son of the holy Catholic Apostolic Church," it is clear that these "miracles" have not been established as such by the Holy See. Despite his protests, therefore, di Lucia repeatedly violates the norms of Urban VIII's *Caelestis Hierusalem cives*, which (as discussed above) forbid anyone to declare without the authorization of the Holy See that a cure has been truly "miraculous" and is attributable to the intercession of a particular individual.

85. *Bulla Sixti IV Papae de Sanctorum Martyrum veneratione*, full text in the *ASs* for January 16, vol. 2:71.

86. Fabijan Veraja believes that because this was clearly a case "of a *concession* made to the Friars Minor, we are within the ambit of beatification." Veraja, *La beatificazione*, 27 (emphasis in original).

87. *Bullarum diplomatum et privilegiorum Sanctorum Romanorum Pontificum Taurinensis editio*, vol. 13 (Augustae Taurinorum: A. Vecco et sociis editoribus, 1878), 593–596.

88. Veraja, *La beatificazione*, 66.

89. Urban VIII, *Caelestis Hierusalem cives*, in *Bullarum diplomatum et privilegiorum Sanctorum Romanorum Pontificum Taurinensis editio*, vol. 14 (Augustae Taurinorum: A. Vecco et sociis editoribus, 1878), 437.

90. While this wording is commonly cited as a part of Urban VIII's *Caelestis Hierusalem cives*, it in fact was appended to the document as a logical addendum at an unspecified later date. See Porsi, *Leggi della Chiesa su beatificazione e canonizzazione*, 153 (no. 92). The pope's original decree is technically a separate document, 146–150 (no. 88).

91. *ASs* for July 9, vol. 2:747–748.

92. Benedict XIV (P. Lambertini), *La beatificazione dei servi di Dio*, vol. 1, chap. 31, 632.

93. Veraja, *La beatificazione*, 117.

94. The bewildering confusion of the presentation by Veraja, who describes the step-by-step evolution of the beatification process, is due more to the complexity of the historical situation than to any fault of the author; Veraja, *La beatificazione*, esp. 69–128.

95. Benedict XIV (P. Lambertini), *De servorum Dei beatificatione et beatorum canonizatione*, l. 2, c. 17, 110.

96. Piacentini, *Il martirio nelle cause dei santi*, 141.

97. "Pope Francis signs canonization decrees for John XXIII and John Paul II," Vatican Radio, accessed August 20, 2014, http://www.news.va/en/news/pope-francis-signs-canonization-decrees-for-john-x.

98. "Promulgazione di Decreti della Congregazione delle Cause dei Santi," Holy See Press Office, December 12, 2013, accessed August 20, 2014, http://press.vatican.va/content/salastampa/en/bollettino/pubblico/2013/12/17/0849/01906.html.

99. With Pope Benedict XVI came a change in praxis, at least regarding the beatification ceremony itself: "While it should be understood that the Holy Father will preside at a Canonization, which attributes the devotion of the whole Church to the Blessed, a Beatification, nonetheless a Pontifical act, will be celebrated by a representative of the Holy Father who will normally be the Prefect of the Congregation for the Causes of Saints." "Communique by the Congregation for the Causes of Saints," September 29, 2005, accessed August 1, 2011, http://www.vatican.va/roman_curia/congregations/csaints/documents/rc_con_csaints_doc_20050929_comunicato_en.html. Note that the communique indicates clearly that beatification still remains a papal prerogative.

100. Writing in 1983, Veraja lists some of the possible changes to the beatification process that have been suggested, including its complete elimination: Veraja, *La beatificazione*, 110–111. It is interesting that one of the suggestions he discusses, "that the actual solemnity of the beatification in the Vatican basilica be simply eliminated, thus returning to the praxis prior to 1662," is exactly what Pope Benedict XVI subsequently did, as discussed in the preceding note.

Notes to Chapter Four

1. Schweigl finds four different schools of thought: (a) the Russian church was Catholic until the Council of Florence; (b) Russia was Catholic from its original conversion until 1104, and from 1104 to 1461 it was for the most part separated from Rome; (c) Russia was Catholic throughout the entire eleventh century, but some hierarchs became questionable in the twelfth century, in the thirteenth all the metropolitans became suspect, in the fourteenth none was certainly Catholic, and in the fifteenth the church split into two parts, of which one broke with Rome at the Council of Florence while the other remained Catholic until 1520; and (d) Russia was Catholic until the thirteenth century, but in the early 1200s it began to distance itself from the West in political matters, and consequently it separated from the West in religious affairs as well. The wide differences between these theories—all held by respectable scholars with historical evidence to buttress their opinions—are obvious. Schweigl, "De Menologio graeco-slavico post annum 1054," *Periodica* 1941: 222–223.

2. To complicate the issue further, what would the Russian Orthodox Church think of accepting as saints those Catholics who were martyred by Orthodox attackers? The question is not merely theoretical, as martyrs such as Jozafat and Andrew Bobola were, according to historical accounts, killed by Orthodox because of their Catholic faith. To suggest that the church in Russia should automatically accept them as genuine martyrs presents, to say the least, a thorny theological dilemma.

3. Not surprisingly, there is no provision in the Catholic Church's official procedural rules outlining circumstances when one should *not* canonize a saint. There are, nonetheless, a number

of causes that are unofficially said to have been at least temporarily sidelined for political reasons. For example, the canonization of Pope Pius XII (d. 1958) has occasionally been protested because of allegations that he failed to do enough to save Jews from the Nazis during World War II; there are rumors that the cause had consequently been slowed because the pope at that time, John Paul II, wished to canonize Pius XII together with his successor, John XXIII, so as to achieve a sort of ideological balance. K. Woodward, *Making Saints: How the Catholic Church Determines Who Becomes a Saint, Who Doesn't, and Why* (New York: Touchstone, 1996), 290–292. See also Dennis Sadowski, *National Catholic Reporter*, "Scholars Ask Pope [Benedict XVI] to Slow Pius XII's Canonization," accessed November 20, 2014, http://ncronline.org/news/vatican/updated-scholars-ask-pope-slow-pius-xiis-canonization. And John Paul II is also said to have been opposed to the canonization of Archbishop Oscar Romero of San Salvador, gunned down by a right-wing assassin in 1980, because "Archbishop Romero has become a [political] banner because they say he was a guerrilla. So long as that is so . . . we should not think to canonize him as a saint" (*Making Saints*, 44). Subsequently, first Benedict XVI and then Francis stated that the cause had been "unblocked" and should proceed. Andrea Tornelli, "Romero's Beatification Cause was 'Unblocked' by Two Popes," *Vatican Insider*, accessed November 20, 2014, http://vaticaninsider.lastampa.it/en/the-vatican/detail/articolo/romero-romero-romero-25531/.

Selected Bibliography

Primary Sources

Acta Apostolicae Sedis, Commentarium Officiale. Vatican City: Libreria Editrice Vaticana, 1909–. (Hereafter cited as *AAS*.)
Acta Sanctorum. Antwerp/Brussels, 1643–1940. (Hereafter cited as *ASs*.)
Aleksei II. "К вопросу о канонизации Царя Ивана Грозного и Г. Е. Распутина," "Приложение No. 2 к докладу митрополита Крутицкого и Комоненского Ювеналия, председателя Синодальной комиссии по канонизации святых." At Русская Православная Церковь, official site of the Moscow Patriarchate, http://www.patriarchia.ru/db/text/420877.html.
The Anglo-Saxon Chronicle. London: Everyman Press, 1912. At Britannia History, http://www.britannia.com/history/docs/973-79.html. (Accessed May 13, 2011.)
Beatificationis et canonizationis servi Dei Andreae Bobola, sacerdoti professi Societatis Jesu. Vol. 1, *Super signatura commissionis introductionis causae*. Rome, 1726.
———. Vol. 4, *Positio super miraculis.* Rome: Typ. Pont. Universitatis Gregorianae, 1936.
Boniface VIII. *Sextus Decretalium liber.* Venetia, 1572.
Bullarum diplomatum et privilegiorum Sanctorum Romanorum Pontificum Taurinensis editio, ed. Augustae Taurinorum, A. Vecco, et al., 1878–.
Calendarium Romanum ex decreto Sacrosancti Oecumenici Concilii Vaticani II instauratum auctoritate Pauli PP. VI promulgatum. Vatican City: Typis polyglottis Vaticanis, 1969.
Capitularia regum Francorum. Hannover: Hahn, 1835.
Casus S. Galli: Continuatio II. In *MGHS,* vol. 2. Berlin: Weidmann, 1923.
Chronica Minora, Saec. IV, V, VI, VII. In *MGHS,* vol. 9. Berlin: Weidmann, 1892.
"Die Chronik der Böhmen des Cosmas von Prag." In *Monumenta Germaniae Historica Scriptores Rerum Germanicarum,* Nova series, vol 2. Berlin: Weidmann, 1923.
Codex Iustinianus, vol. 1 in *Corpus Iuris Civilis.* Berlin: Weidmann, 1884.
Concilia Magnae Britanniae et Hiberniae, ab anno MCCCL ad annum MDXLV, ed. David Wilkins. Brussels: Culture and Civilisation, 1964.
Congregatio de Causis Sanctorum. *Index ac status causarum.* Vatican City, 1999.
———. *Instructio Sanctorum Mater* 2007. At http://www.vatican.va/roman_curia/congregations/csaints/documents/rc_con_csaints_doc_20070517_sanctorum-mater_en.html. (Accessed August 4, 2011.)
Corpus Christianorum: Series Latina. Turnhout: Brepols Publishers, 1953–. (Hereafter cited as *CCSL*.)
Corpus Scriptorum Ecclesiasticorum Latinorum. Vindobonae: C. Gerold, 1866–. (Hereafter cited as *CSEL*.)
Decretales Gregorii Noni Pont. Max. Venice, 1572.
Innocent III. "Rescriptum Domini Papae super inquisitione morum vitae et miraculorum." In *Thesaurus novus anecdotorum,* ed. E. Martene, vol. 3. Paris, 1717, 1842–1843.
Ioann XIV, Patriarch. "Грамота патриарха Иоанна XIV митрополиту Феогносту об открытии мощей св. Петра митрополита." In *Памятиники древне-русскаго каноническаго права,* vol. 6 of *Русская историческая библиотека.* St. Petersburg, 1908.
Iuris ecclesiastici graecorum historia et monumenta, ed J. Pitra. Rome: Typis Collegii Urbani, 1868.
John Paul II. *Divinus perfectionis Magister. AAS* 75 (1983): 349–355.
Журнал московской патриархии. Moscow, 1931–.
Le Liber Pontificalis: Texte, introduction et commentaire, ed. L. Duchesne. Paris: E. de Boccard, 1955.
Martyrium Polycarpi. In *Ausgewählte Märtyrerakten,* ed. Knopf D. Rudolf. Tubingen: Mohr, 1929.
Migne, Jacques-Paul, ed. *Patrologia Graeca.* Paris: Migne, 1857–1866. (Hereafter cited as *PG*.)
———. *Patrologiae Cursus Completus: Series Latina.* Paris: Migne, 1841–. (Hereafter cited as *PL*.)
Missale Romanum, Editio Princeps (1570), ed. M. Sodi. Vatican City: Libreria Editrice Vaticana, 1998.

Monumenta Germaniae Historica, Scriptorum. Hannover: Hahn, 1826—. (Hereafter cited as *MGHS*.)
"Основания для канонизации Царской цемьи из доклада Митрополита Крутицкого и Коломенского Ювеналия, Председателя Синодальной Комиссии по Канонизации Святых." At Русская Православная Церковь, archive of the official site of the Moscow Patriarchate, http://www.mospat.ru/archive/s2000r05.htm. (Accessed April 22, 2011.)
Passio Sancti Kanuti Regis et Martiris. In Vitae Sanctorum Danoru, Copenhagen: Kommission Hos, 1908.
Pius V. *Quo primum. In Bullarum diplomatum et privilegiorum Sanctorum Romanorum Pontificum Taurinensis editio,* vol. 7, 839–840. Augustae Taurinorum: A. Vecco et sociis editoribus, 1878.
Полное собрание законов российской Импери. St. Petersburg, 1885.
Полное собрание русских летописей. St. Petersburg: Tipografia Eduarda Pratsa, 1846.
Православная Энциклопедия of the Moscow Patriarchate. At http://www.pravenc.ru/text/161257.html. (Accessed April 26, 2011.)
Sacra Congregatio Rituum. Instructio de calendariis particularibus et Officiorum ac Missarum propriis ad normam et mentem codicis rubricarum revisendis. February 14, 1961, *AAS* 53 (1961): 168–180.
Степенная книга царского родословия по древнейшим спискам. Moscow: Iazyki slavianski kultur, 2007.
Церковныя Ведемости, 1895.
Urban VIII. *Caelestis Hierusalem cives. In Bullarum diplomatum et privilegiorum Sanctorum Romanorum Pontificum Taurinensis editio.* Vol. 14. Augustae Taurinorum: A. Vecco et sociis editoribus, 1878.
Верный месяцеслов всех русских святых чтимых молебнами и торжественными литургиями, общецерковно и место составленный по донесениям Святейшему Синоду преосвященных всех епархий в 1901–1902 годах. Moscow: Sinodalnaia Tipografia, 1903.

Secondary Sources

Abramovich, Dmitrii, ed. *Жития святых мучеников Бориса и Глеба и службы им.* Petrograd: Imperatorskaia Akademiia Nauk, 1916.
Акты, собранные в библиотеках и архивах Российской империи археографическою экспедициею императорской академии наук. St. Petersburg: Tipografia II-go Otdeleniia Sobstvennoi E.I.V. Kantseliarii, 1836.
Albani, A., ed. *Menologium graecorum iussu Basilii imperatoris graece olim editum, munificentia et liberalitate sanctissimi D. N. Benedicti XIII in tres partes divisum nunc primum praece et latine prodit studio et opera Annibalis tit. S. Clementis presb. Card. Albani.* Urbinum, 1727.
Alekseeva, Svetlana I. *Святейший Синод в системе высших и центральных государственных учреждений пореформенной России.* St. Petersburg: Nauka 2003.
Amore, Agostino. "La canonizzazione vescovile." *Antonianum* 52 (1977): 231–266.
———. "Culto e canonizzazione dei santi nell'antichita' cristiana." *Antonianum* 52 (1977): 38–40.
———. *I martiri di Roma.* Rome: Edizioni Antonianum, 1975.
———. "Vindicatio." In *Dizionario Storico Religioso,* ed. Pietro Chiocchetta. Rome: Studium 1966, 1139.
Apeciti, E. "L'evoluzione storica delle procedure ecclesiastiche di canonizzazione." *Quaderni di diritto ecclesiale* 15 (2002).
———. "Le nuove norme per le cause di canonizzazione." *La Scuola Cattolica* 119 (1991): 113–118.
Bannes Mondragonensis, D., OP. *De Fide, Spe et Charitate: Commentaria in 2.2. D. Thomae, ibique Synopsis.* In *Bibliotheca Maxima Pontificia,* ed. I Roccaberti, vol. 8, 333–334. Rome: Typographia Ioannis Francisci Buagni.
Barsukov, Nikolai. *Источники русской агиографии.* St. Petersburg, 1882.
Bastiaensen, A.A.R. *Atti e passioni dei martiri.* Milan, 1987.
Benedict XIV. *See* Lambertini, P.
Bescòs Ricardo, Q., ed. *El milagro en las causas de canonización.* Barcelona: Scire, 2004.
Bibliotheca Sanctorum. Rome: Città Nuova, 1990–2000. (Hereafter cited as *BSs*.)

Blaher, Damian. *The Ordinary Process in Causes of Beatification and Canonization: A Historical Synopsis and a Commentary.* Washington, DC: CUA Press, 1949.
Bois, J. "Canonisation dans l'église russe." In *Dictionnaire Théologique*, vol. 2, cols. 1659–1672.
Brown, Peter. *The Cult of Saints: Its Rise and Function in Latin Christianity.* Chicago: University of Chicago Press, 1981.
Buida, Iurii. "'В них мы ищем откровения нашего собственного духовного пути': Заметки по поводу возможной канонизации Николая II." *Независимая газета*, July 7, 1993.
Burgess, John. "Retrieving the Martyrs in Order to Rethink the Political Order: The Russian Orthodox Case." *Journal of the Society of Christian Ethics* 34/2 (Fall/Winter 2014): 177–201.
Bushkovitch, Paul. *Religion and Society in Russia: The Sixteenth and Seventeenth Centuries.* Oxford: Oxford Univ. Press, 1992.
Butler, Alban. *The Lives of the Fathers, Martyrs and Other Principal Saints.* Dublin, 1833.
Bynum, Caroline Walker. *The Resurrection of the Body in Western Christianity 200–1336.* New York: Columbia Univ. Press, 1995.
Casieri, Antonio. "Attuale prassi procedurale da seguirsi nelle diocesi per le cause di beatificazione e canonizzazione." *Monitor Ecclesiasticus* 100 (1975): 169–182.
———. "Iter processus beatificationis et canonizationis iuxta constitutionem apostolicam 'Sacra Rituum Congregatio' et 'Sanctitas Clarior.'" *Monitor Ecclesiasticus* 98 (1973): 244–259.
Castelli, Elizabeth. *Martyrdom and Memory: Early Christian Culture Making.* New York: Columbia Univ. Press, 2007.
Cedrenus, Giorgius. *Compendium historiarum.* Venice: Javarina, 1729.
Christo, Gus George. *Martyrdom according to John Chrysostom: "To Live Is Christ, To Die Is Gain."* Lewiston, NY: Edwin Mellen Press, 1997.
Citrini, Tullio. "Memoria, riconoscimento e canonizzazione dei santi." *La Scuola Cattolica* 108 (1981): 325–352.
Congar, Yves. "A propos des saints canonisés dans les églises orthodoxes." *Revue des Sciences Religieuses* 22 (1948): 240–259.
Controversia de S. Joanne Nepomuceno. Vienna: Typis et sumpt. L. Mayer [undated].
Dal', V. I. *Записка о ритуальных убийствах* (original title: *Розыскание о убиении евреями христианских младенцев и употреблении крови их*). Moscow: Vitazh, 1995.
Damaskin, Ieromonaco. *Мученики, исповедники и подвижники благочестия Российской Православной Церкви XX столетия.* Tver: Bulat, 1992.
Daniel-Rops, Henri. *The Church of Apostles and Martyrs.* New York: E. P. Dutton, 1960.
de Gaiffer, B. "Réflexions sur les origines du culte des martyrs." *Maison Dieu* 52 (1957): 19–43.
Dehandschutter, Boudewijn. *Polycarpiana: Studies on Martyrdom and Persecution in Early Christianity.* Leuven: University Press, 2007.
de Labriolle, P. "Martyr et confesseur." *Bulletin d'ancienne littérature et d'archéologie chrétienne* 1 (1901): 50–54.
Delehaye, Hippolyte, S. J. "L'Amphithéâtre flavien et ses environs dans les textes hagiographiques." *Analecta Bollandiana* 16 (1897): 209–252.
———. "Hagiographie napolitaine." *Analecta Bollandiana* 57 (1939): 5–64.
———. "Martyr et confessor." *Analecta Bollandiana* 39 (1921): 20–49.
———. *Les origines du culte des martyrs.* Brussels, 1933.
———. *Les passions des martyrs et les genres littéraires.* Brussels: Bollandistes, 1966.
———. "Les recueils antiques de miracles des saints." *Analecta Bollandiana* 43 (1925): 5–85.
———. "Saint Almachius ou Télémaque." *Analecta Bollandiana* 33 (1914): 421–428.
———. *Sanctus: Essai sur le culte des saints dans l'antiquité.* Brussels, 1927.
Dell'Oro F. *Beatificazione e canonizzazione. Excursus storico-liturgico.* Rome, 1997.
Delooz, Pierre. *Glossarium Mediae et Infimae Latinitatis.* Paris: Librairie des Sciences et des Arts, 1938.
———. *Sociologie et canonisation.* Liège: Faculté de droit, 1969.

de Meester, Placido, OSB. "La canonizzazione dei santi nella chiesa russa ortodossa." *Gregorianum* 30 (1949): 393–407.
de Rossi, Giovanni, and L. Duchesne, eds. *Martyrologium Hieronymianum ad fidem codicum adiectis prolegomenis*. Brussels [undated].
de Sainte-Marie-Madeleine, P. Gabriel. "La béatification et la canonisation des martyrs." In *Limites de l'humain*. Paris: Desclée de Brouwer, 1953, 225–234.
di Lucia, F. *Relazione istorica della traslazione del sagro corpo e miracoli di santa Filomena vergine e martire da Roma a Mugnano del Cardinale*. Benevento: Presso Pietro Paolo Paternó, 1834.
du Cange, Charles du Fresne. *Glossarium ad scriptores mediae et infimae latinitatis*. Paris: Osmont, 1733.
Dufourcq, Albert. *Étude sur les Gesta Martyrum romains*. Paris: Fontemoing, 1900.
Duluman, E. K., and A. S. Glushak. *Введение Христианства на Руси: Легенды, события, факты*. Simferopol: Tavriia, 1988.
Fedotov, G. P. *Святые древней руси (X–XVII Ct.)*. New York, 1959.
Fetisov, N. "К литературной истории повести о мученике Исидоре Юрьевском." In *Сборник статей в честь академика Алексея Ивановича Соболевского*. St. Petersburg: Izdatel'stvo Akademii Nauk SSSR, 1928.
Filaret, Bishop. *Жития святых, чтимых православною церковью*. St. Petersburg: Izdanie Knigoprodavtsa i L. Tuzova, 1900.
Filipazzi, Antonio G. *La prova del martirio nella prassi recente della Congregazione delle Cause dei Santi*. Rome, 1992.
Foreville, Raymonde. *Un procès de canonisation à l'aure du XIIIe siècle: Le livre di saint Gilbert de Sempringham*. Paris: Bloud and Gay, 1943.
Frend, William Hugh Clifford. *Martyrdom and Persecution in the Early Church*. New York: Doubleday, 1967.
Frere, Walter H. *Studies in Early Roman Liturgy I: The Kalendar*. Oxford: Oxford Univ. Press, 1930.
Frutaz, A. P. "*Auctoritate . . . beatorum apostolorum Petro et Pauli*: Saggio sulle formule di canonizzazione." *Antonianum* 42 (1967): 435–501.
———. "Elementi costitutivi delle cause di beatificazione e di canonizzazione." *Rivista di Vita Spirituale* 30 (1976): 362–375.
Gagna, Ferdinando. *De processu Canonizationis a primis Ecclesiae saeculis usque ad codicem iuris canonici*. Rome, 1940.
Galassi, Italus. "Quaestiones de processibus beatificationis et canonizationis." *Ephemerides Iuris Canonici* 3 (1947): 150–153.
Gasquet, Francis. *La vita religiosa di re Enrico VI*. Florence: Libreria Editrice Fiorentina, 1924.
Geary, Patrick. *Furta Sacra: Thefts of Relics in the Central Middle Ages*. Princeton, NJ: Princeton Univ. Press, 1978.
Gelin, A. "Origines biblique de l'ideé du martyre." *Lumière et Vie* 36 (1958): 123–129.
Golubinskii, E .E. *История русской церкви*, vol. 1. Moscow, 1997.
———. *История канонизации святых в русской церкви*. Moscow, 1903.
Golubovskii, G. *История Смоленской земли*. Kiev: Tipografiia Imperatorskago Universiteta Sv. Vladimira, 1895.
Goodich, Michael. *Miracles and Wonders: The Development of the Concept of Miracle, 1150–1350*. Burlington, VT: Ashgate, 2007.
Gordienko, N. S. *Новые православные святые*. Kiev, 1991.
Gordon, Ignacio. "De Conceptu Theologico-Canonico Martyrii." In *Ius Populi Dei: Miscellanea in honorem Raymundi Bidagor*, vol. 1, 485–521. Rome: Pontificia Università Gregoriana, 1972.
Gori, Antonio. *Thesaurus veterum diptychorum consularium et ecclesiasticorum*. Florence, 1759.
Guiraud, Jean. *Questions d'histoire et d'archéologie chrétienne*. Paris: Victor Lecoffre, 1906.
Gutierrez, J. L. *Studi sulle cause di canonizzazione*. Milan: Giuffre Editore, 2005.
Haddan, Arthur W., and William Stubbs, eds. *Councils and Ecclesiastical Documents Relating to Great Britain and Ireland*. Oxford: Clarendon Press, 1871.
Hertling, Ludwig. "Materiali per la storia del processo di canonizzazione." *Gregorianum* 16 (1935): 171–195.

Indelicato, Salvatore. *Le basi giuridiche del processo di beatificazione*. Rome: Officium Libri Catholici, 1944.
———. "Miracolo." In *Enciclopedia Cattolica*. Città del Vaticano: Ente per l'Enciclopedia Cattolica e per il Libro Cattolico, 1951.
Ippolito, G. *Memorie e culto S. Filomena V. e M*. Naples: Stabilimento Tipografico dell'Italia, 1870.
Исторические сказания о жизни святых подвизавшихся в Вологодской епархии прославляемых всею церковию и местно чтимых. St. Petersburg: V.A. Gudkov-Beliakov, 1880.
Iuvenalii, Metr. Krutitskogo i Kolomenskogo. *Канонизация святых: Поместный Собор Русской Православной Церкви, посвященнии июбилею 1000-летия Крещения Руси*. Moscow: Izdanie Moskovskoi Patriarkhii, 1988.
———. *К канонизации новомучеников российских*. Moscow, 1991.
Jaffé, Philippus, et al. *Regesta Pontificum Romanorum*. Leipzig: Veit et Comp., 1885.
Jaros, Joannes. "Sacra congregatio Rituum: Normae servandae in construendis processibus ordinariis super causis historicis." *Apollinaris* 12 (1939): 451–459.
Joannou, Périclès-Pierre, ed. *Discipline générale antique (IVe–IXe s.)*. Grottaferrata: S. Nilo, 1962.
Kadlubovskii, Arsenii. *Очерки по истории древне-русской литературы житий святых*. Warszawa, 1902.
Kahla, Elina. "The New Martyrs of Russia: Regeneration of Archaic Forms or Revival?" *Ortodoksiia* 51 (2010): 193–208.
Канонизация святых в XX веке. Moscow, 1999.
Karpov, A. Iu. *Православные святые и чудотворцы*. Moscow: Vecha, 2005.
Kemp, Eric A. *Canonization and Authority in the Western Church*. London: Oxford Univ. Press, 1948.
Kephala, E. "The Martyr-Patriarch Gregory V's Canonization: The Canonization of Saints in the Orthodox Church." *Christian East* 2 (1921): 67–68.
Kleber, A., O.S.B. "A Soldier's Death, a Martyrdom?" *American Ecclesiastical Review* 111 (1944): 281–290.
Kliuchevskii, Vasilii. *Древнерусские жития святых как исторический источник*. Moscow, 1871.
Kuttner, S. "La réserve papale du droit de canonisation." *Revue historique de droit français et étranger* 17 (1938): 172–228.
Kuz'min, A. "Вариаги в хирстианизации Руси." In *Падение Перуна: Становление христианства на Руси*. Moscow: Molodaia gvardiia, 1988.
Lambertini P. (later Benedict XIV). *La beatificazione dei servi di Dio e la canonizzazione dei beati*, vol. 1. Vatican City: Libreria editrice vaticana, 2010.
———. *De servorum Dei beatificatione et beatorum canonizatione*, vol. 3. Rome: Academiae liturgicae Conimbricensis typographi, 1748.
Lanin, P. "Александр Мень и дело Бейлиса." At *Полемика и дискуссии*, http://www.polemics.ru/articles/?articleID=6199&hideText=0&itemPage=1. (Accessed April 26, 2011.)
Lebed, A. P. *Греческие церковные историки: IV, V и VI веков*. Moscow: Snegireva, 1890.
———. *Очерки внутренней истории Византийско-восточной Церкви в IX, X и XI веках*. Moscow: Snegireva, 1902.
Leclercq, H., OSB. "Ampoules de sang." In *Dictionnaire d'archéologie chrétienne et de liturgie*. Paris: Librairie Letouzey et Ané, 1924, 1747.
Leemans, J., ed. *More than a Memory: The Discourse of Martyrdom and the Construction of Christian Identity in the History of Christianity*. Leuven: Peeters, 2005.
Leemans, J., and Wendy Mayer, *"Let Us Die That We May Live": Greek Homilies on Christian Martyrs from Asia Minor, Palestine and Syria c. AD 350–AD 450*. London: Routledge, 2003.
Leonid. *Святая Русь или Сведения о всех святых и подвижниках благочестия на Руси (до XVII века), обще и местно чтимых*. St. Petersburg: Tipografia M. Stasiulevicha, 1891.
Mabillon, Jean, ed. *Vetera Analecta, sive collectio veterum aliquot operum*. Farnborough: Gregg, 1967.
Mai, Angelo, ed. *Veterum Scriptorum nova collectio*. Rome: Typis Vaticanis, 1825–1838.
Makarii, *История русской церкви*, vol. 5. St. Petersburg: Golnik, 1886.
Martigny, Joseph-Alexandre. "Diptyques." *Dictionnaire des antiquités chrétiennes*, ed. Joseph-Alexandre Martigny, 249. Paris: Librairie Hachette, 1877.

Martinov, Joannes M. *Annus ecclesiasticus graeco-slavicus editus anno millenario Sanctorum Cyrilli et Methodii slavicae gentis apostolorum seu commemoratio et breviarium rerum gestarum eorum qui fastis sacris graecis et slavicis illati sunt.* Brussels: H. Goemaere, 1863.
Maulucci, Vincenzo. *La santitá eroica presso i cristiani non cattolici.* Rome, 1968.
Mazzocchi, Alessio. *In vetus marmoreum sanctae neapolitanae ecclesiae Kalendarium commentarius.* Naples: Novelli de Bonis, 1744.
Melinsky, A. H. *Healing Miracles: An Examination from History and Experience of the Place of Miracle in Christian Thought and Medical Practice.* London: Mowbray, 1968.
Mikhail, Arkhiepiskop Vologodskii i Velikoustyuzhskii. "Святость, освящение, святые." *Журналъ Московской Патриархии* 12 (1987): 68–70.
Misztal, Henryk. *Le cause di canonizzazione: Storia e procedura.* Rome: Vaticana, 2005.
Morcelli, Stefano. *Menologion ton Euangelion heorstastikon, sive Kalendarum Ecclesiae Constantinopolitanae.* Rome: Monaldini e Giunchi, 1788.
Moss, Candida. *The Myth of Persecution: How Early Christians Invented a Story of Martyrdom.* NY: HarperCollins, 2014.
Musurillo, Herbert, ed. *The Acts of the Christian Martyrs.* Oxford: Clarendon Press, 1972.
Nedungatt, George, and Michael Featherstone, eds. *The Council in Trullo Revisited.* Rome: Pontificio Istituto Orientale, 1995.
Netter, Thomas, O. Carm. *Doctrinale antiquitatum fidei catholicae ecclesiae Dei.* Farnborough: Gregg, 1967.
Osimo, Agostino da. *Storia dei diciannove martiri gorcomiesi.* Rome: Tipografia Monaldi, 1867.
Paciocco, R. "Per un 'carisma' del diritto: Canonizzazioni, procedura processuale e agiografia (secoli XI–XIII)." *Studi Storici* 40 (1999): 1009–1037.
Palmieri, Norberto. *Relazione della gloriosa morte de' sette martiri gorcomiensi.* Rome: Tipografia Monaldi, 1868.
Papa, G. *La cause di canonizzazione nel primo periodo della Congregatione dei Riti (1588–1634).* Rome: Urbaniana Univ. Press, 2001.
Pargoire, J. *L'église byzantine de 527 à 847.* Paris: V. Lecoffre 1923.
Peers, E. Allison. *Ramon Lull: A Biography.* New York: MacMillan, 1929.
Peeters, P., SJ. "La canonisation des saints dans l'église russe." *Analecta Bollandiana* 33 (1914): 380–420; 38 (1920): 172–176.
Pellegrino, Michele, ed. *Vita e martirio di san Cipriano/Pontius: Introduzione, testo critico, versione e note.* Alba: Paoline, 1955.
Perham, Michael. *The Communion of Saints.* London: Alcuin Club, 1980.
Piacentini, Ernesto, OFM Conv. *Il martirio nelle cause dei santi.* Vatican: Libreria Editrice Vaticana, 1979.
Pini, Giovanni. *Panarion di Epifanio di Salamina,* vol. 1. Brescia: Morcelliana, 2010.
Platon, Metr. *Сборник древностей Казанской Епархии и других приснопамятных обстоятельст.* Kazan: Universitetskaia Tipografiia, 1868.
Platonov, O. *Жизнь за Царя: Правда о Григории Распутине.* St. Petersburg, 1996.
Pokrovskii, N., ed. *Степенная книга царского родословия по древнейшим спискам: Тексты и комментарии в трех томах.* Moscow: Iazyki slavianskikh kul'tur, 2007.
Pol'skii, M. *Новые мученики российские,* vol. 1. Jordanville, NY: Holy Trinity Monastery, 1947.
Porsi, L. "Collectio legum ecclesiae de beatificatione et canonizatione a saeculo decimo usque ad praesens." *Monitor Ecclesiasticus* 110 (1985): 530–559; 111 (1986): 235–239, 345–366; 113 (1988): 405–430.
———. *Leggi della chiesa su beatificazione e canonizzazione dall'anno 993 all'anno 2000.* Rome: Nova Res, 2006.
Prokhorov, G. M., ed. *Святые князья-мученики Борис и Глеб.* St. Petersburg: Izdatel'stvo Olega Abyshko, 2006.
Quentin, Henri. *Martyrologes historiques du moyen age: Etude sur la formation du martyrologe romain.* Paris: J. Gabalda, 1908.

Rordorf, W. "Aux origines du culte des martyrs." *Irénikon* 45 (1972): 315–331.
Rosweyde, Heribert, SJ, ed. *Vitae patrum: de vita et verbis seniorum sive historiae eremiticae libri X*. Antwerp: Plantiniana, 1628.
Ruinart, Thierri. *Acta Primorum Martyrum Sincera et Selecta*. Paris: Muguet, 1689.
Rurin, A. *Сводный Старообрядческий синодик по четырем рукописям XVIII–XIX в*. St. Petersburg, 1883.
Santucci, S. *Sulla lapide sepolcrale di S. Filomena vergine e martire, con le animadversioni critiche sulle di lei memorie*. Rome: Tipografia delle belle arti, 1837.
Schlafke, Jacobus. *De competentia in causis sanctorum decernendi a primis post Christum natum saeculis usque ad annum 1234*. Rome: Catholic Book Agency, 1961.
Schultze, Bernardo. "Santità e santi fuori della chiesa cattolica." *Unitas* 17 (1962): 112–129.
Schweigl, P., SJ. "De Menologio graeco-slavico post annum 1054." *Periodica* (1941): 221–228.
Segusio, Henricus de. *In primum [-sextum] decretalium librum commentaria*. Torino: Bottega d'Erasmo, 1965.
Semenenko-Basin, I. "Chiesa Russa." In *Enciclopedia dei santi: Le chiese orientali*. Rome: Città Nuova, 1998.
———. *Eternamente fiorisce: I nuovi santi della Chiesa Ortodossa Russa*. Milan: Edizioni La Casa di Matriona, 2005.
———. *Святость в русской православной культуре XX века: История персонификации*. Moscow, 2010.
Sergei, Archbishop. *Польный месяцеслов востока*. Vladimir: Tserkovno-nauchnii tsentr "Pravoslavnaia ensiklopediia," 1997.
Shevchenko, M. "Прославление царской семьи—вопрос решенный: Член Синодальной комиссии по канонизации святых РПЦ протоиерей Георгий (Митрофанов)—о тех, кому будут молиться." *Независимая газета*, March 31, 2000.
Словарь исторический о святых, прославленных в российской церкви, и о некоторых подвижниках благочестия. St. Petersburg, 1862.
Société des Bollandistes, ed. *Bibliotheca hagiographica graeca*. Brussels: Société des Bollandistes, 1909.
Sokolov, L. "Житие Исидора Юрьевского." In *Словарь книжников и книжности древней Руси*. Leningrad, 1988.
Špidlík, T., SJ. "La santità nella chiesa orientale." In *Santitá cristiana: Dono di Dio e impegno dell'uomo*, ed. E. Ancilli. Rome: Teresianum, 1980.
Steeves, Paul. "Canonization of Saints (Orthodox)." In *The Modern Encyclopedia of Religions in Russia and the Soviet Union*. Gulf Breeze, FL: Academic International Press, 1997.
Susza, J. *Cursus vitae et certamen martyrii B. Josaphat Kuncevicii*. Paris: Victor Palmé, 1863.
Suvarov, I. *Журнал министерства народнаго просвещения* 348 (1903): 263–308.
"Святые." In *Настольная книга священнослужителя*. Moscow: Izdanie Moskovskoi Patriarkhii 1988, 768.
Taft, Robert F. *The Diptychs*. Rome: Orientalia Christiana Analecta 238 (1991).
———. "Praying to or for the Saints? A Note on the Sanctoral Intercessions/Commemorations in the Anaphora." In *Ab Oriente et Occidente (Matt. 8:11): Kirche Ost und West: Gedenkschrift für Wilhelm Nyssen*, ed. M. Schneider, 439–455. St. Ottilien, 1996.
Taisia, Monakhinia. *Русские святые: 1000 лет русской святости*. St. Petersburg: Azbuka-klassika, 2001.
Temnikovskii, Yevgeny. "Канонизация святых." In "Православная богословская енсикопедия, или, Богословский енсиклопедический словарь," ed. N. N. Glubokovskii, fasc. 19. Petrograd, 1907.
Thiel, Andreas, ed. *Epistolae Romanorum Pontificum genuinae et quae ad eos scriptae sunt a S. Hilaro usque ad Pelagium II*. Brunsberg: E. Peter, 1868.
Thunduparampil, Cherian J. *The Role of Miracle in the Process of Canonization in the Light of the New Legislation*. Rome, 2001.
Tolstoi, Mikhail. *Древния святыни Ростова-Великаго*. Moscow, 1860.

Toynbee, Margaret R. *Saint Louis of Toulouse and the Process of Canonization in the Fourteenth Century*. Farnborough: Gregg, 1966.
Trombley, F. R. *Hellenic Religion and Christianization, c. 370–529*. Leiden: Brill, 1993.
Tuchkova, Alla. "Новомученику Николаю II поставили новый памятник." http://www.ng.ru/style/2000-08-22/8_canonization.html.
Tyszkiewicz, S. "La sainteté de l'église." *Nouvelle Revue Théologique* 63 (1936): 449–479.
———. "Spiritualité et sainteté russe pravoslave." *Gregorianum* 15 (1934): 349–376.
Vasiliev, Vasilii. *История канонизация русских святых*. Moscow, 1893.
Vauchez, André. *La sainteté en Occident aux derniers siècles du Moyen Age: D'après les procès de canonisation et les documents hagiographiques*. Rome, 1981.
Veraja, Fabijan. *La beatificazione: Storia, problemi, prospettive*. Rome: S. Congregazione per le Cause dei Santi, 1983.
———. *Le cause di canonizzazione dei santi: Commento alla legislazione e guida pratica*. Vatican City, 1992.
———. *Commento alla nuova legislazione per le cause dei santi*. Rome, 1983.
Williams, D. H. *Ambrose of Milan and the End of the Arian-Nicene Conflicts*. Oxford: Clarendon Press, 1995.
Woodward, Kenneth L. *Making Saints: How the Catholic Church Determines Who Becomes a Saint, Who Doesn't, and Why*. New York: Touchstone, 1996.
Zachariae, Carolus Eduardus a Lingenthal. *Collectio librorum juris graeco-romani ineditorum. Ecloga Leonis et Constantini, Epanagoge Basilii Leonis et Alexandri*. Leipzig: J. A. Barthius 1852.

Index

A
acta martyrum, 28, 30, 44
Adalbert of Egmond, 35
Adalbert of Prague, 113
Adrian of Poshekhonie, 65–66
Aeschylus, 12
Aleksandr Men', Father, 83
Alexander III, Pope, 112, 113, 128–129, 131, 132, 152
Ambrose of Milan, 33–34, 40
Andrew Bobola, 127
Anna Kashinskaia, 82
Aquinas, Thomas, 102–103, 122
Arians, 39
Armenia, 108
Arsenii of Tver, Bishop, 75
Assembly of Russian New Martyrs and Confessors of the Twentieth Century, 86
Athanasius of Alexandria, Bishop, 16
Augustine of Canterbury, 114
Augustine of Hippo, 14, 15, 22, 29
Avramii of Bulgaria, 66

B
Babylas, 16
Basil I "The Macedonian," Emperor, 42
Becket, Thomas, Archbishop, 113
Benedict IX, Pope, 113
Benedict XIV, Pope (Prospero Lambertini), 6, 102, 103, 138, 139
Bertolf FitzErembald, 105
Bolshevik Revolution (1917), 7, 80, 85, 96
Boniface, Archbishop, 27
Boniface of Mainz, 114
Boniface VIII, Pope, 118
Boris and Gleb, 49–50, 55, 64–65, 67, 72, 84, 93, 104

C
Caelestis Hierusalem cives, 116, 136–139
Calendar, liturgical, 3, 4, 5, 20, 22–28, 32, 40, 42, 44, 47, 52, 54–58, 71–72, 74–75, 77–78, 81–82, 93–94, 96, 99, 106–113, 115, 117, 124, 131, 133–135, 146–148, 155, 161
Callistus, Pope, 23

Canonization Commission of the Moscow Patriarchate, 47, 80, 84
Canterbury, Archbishop of, 27, 113
Canute IV of Denmark, King, 104, 105, 149
Canute Lavard of Denmark, Prince, 104–105, 149, 159
Cappadocia 34
Carloman, King of the Franks, 41
Carthage, calendar of, 24, 25
Carthage, Councils of, 14, 27, 29, 30, 37, 51
Charlemagne, Emperor, 30, 41–42, 128
Charles the Good, 105
Chronology of 35423
Chrysanthus and Daria, 26
Chudotvortsy, 52, 81
Claudius, Lupercus, and Victoricus, 112–113
Clement I, Pope, 18, 24, 28
Clement II, Pope, 122
Code of Canon Law (1917)119–120, 125, 131
Congregation for Causes of Saints, 119, 120, 140–141
Congregation of Rites, 110, 119, 124, 126, 134, 139
Constance, Council of, 133
Constantia, City of, 18
Constantine, Son of Basil I, 42
Constantine the Great, Emperor, 17, 157
Constantinople, City of, 75, 101, 152
Constantinople, Patriarch of, 43, 72, 103
Council of _____, *see location*
Cremona, 119
Cunegunda of Luxemburg, Empress, 123
Cyprian, 17, 20, 23, 24, 29
Cyril of Jerusalem, 21

D
Damaskin of Moscow, Hegumen 90–91, 97–98
decanonization, 82, 83, 110, 133, 135, 148, 153
Decius, Emperor, 15
depositio, 32
Depositio Episcoporum, 23, 25, 26
Depositio Martyrum, 23, 24
Dies natalis, 17, 18, 24, 28, 44, 110
Diocletian, Emperor, 134
Diptychs, 20–24, 26–27, 28, 44, 48, 54, 147

Divinus Perfectionis Magister 131
Donatism, 13–14, 15, 105

E
Edmond of Canterbury, 125
Edward the Confessor, 2
Edward the Martyr, 104
Equipollent Beatification, 138
Eugenius, 111
Eusebius of Caesarea, 13, 19, 32, 35, 69

F
Fabian, Pope, 23
Filaret of Moscow, Patriarch, 65
Filioque, 4
Florence, Council of, 108, 153
Francis, Pope, 140–141, 143–144
Francis of Assisi, 109
Franciscan martyrs of Morocco, 135
Frankfurt, Council of, 41, 42

G
Gangra, Council of, 20
Gavriil of Belostok, 78, 83, 84, 89, 130
Gelasius I, Pope, 30, 38
Gaza, 18
Genocide, 1
George, 30, 31
Georgii, Archpriest, 89–90
Georgii Vsevolodovich of Vladimir, Prince, 77
Georgetown University, 1
Gervase and Protase, 33–34, 40
Ghent, 114
Gorkum, Martyrs of, 138
Gratian, 108, 111
Gratus, Bishop, 14, 25
Great East-West Schism of 1054, *see* Schism
Gregory IX, Pope, 129
Gregory XI, Pope, 106
Gregory XVI, Pope, 110, 134
Gregory Nazianzen, 16
Gregory of Tours, 28

H
Hadrian I, Pope, 30
Henry of Segusio, 132
Hermogen of Kazan, Metropolitan, 76
Holy Governing Synod of the Russian Orthodox Church, 56, 68, 77, 96
Homobonus, 123
Honorius, Emperor, 40
Hyacinth, Cardinal, 112

I
Iakov of Borovich, 70–71, 133
Iakov Chernorizets, 67
Iakov and Ioann Meniushskie, 77
Iaroslav, brother of Boris and Gleb, 72
Imperial Family, *see* Romanov Family
Innocent III, Pope, 123–124, 127
Innocent IV, Pope, 109
Ioann, Stefan, and Peter, 58
Ioann of Nizhny Novgorod, 76
Ioann I, Metropolitan, 72
Ioann Konchurov, Archpriest, 79
Ioachim, Patriarch, 82
Iosif of Astrakhan, 68, 80
Iov, Patriarch, 58, 76, 81, 88
Isidor of Iur'ev, 78, 84
Iuvenalii, Metropolitan, 87, 97
Ivan the Variag, 58, 60
Ivan IV "the Terrible," Tsar, 52, 103

J
Januarius of Naples, Bishop, 25, 26
Japanese Martyrs, 136
Jerome, 24
Jeron, 35, 111
John XV, Pope, 128
John XXIII, Pope, 134, 140
John the Baptist, 24
John the Evangelist, 13
John Cassian, 22
John Chrysostom, 16, 50
John Nepomucene, 115
John Wycliffe, 133
John Paul II, Pope, 5, 131
John Sordi Cacciafronte of Vicenza, Bishop, 119
Jozafat Kuncewicz of Polotsk, Bishop, 124, 127

K
Kirill of Vel'sk, 68, 70, 149
Kirill Vel'skii of Novgorod, 73–74
Kol of Sweden, King, 128

L
Lambertini, Prospero, *see* Benedict XIV, Pope
Lateran Council, Fourth, 129–130
Laodicea, Council of, 15
Lawrence of Rome, 24, 26
Leo I, Emperor, 41
Leo I, Pope, 108
Leo VI, Emperor, 42–43
Leon, City of, 112
Leontii of Rostov, 55, 59–60, 67, 70, 72, 76

Liberian Catalogue, 32
Liberius, Pope, 23
Livinius, 114
Llull, Ramon, 105
Luke the Evangelist, 24

M
Mainz, Council of, 42
Makarii of Moscow, Metropolitan, 68, 74–78, 96, 152
Marble calendar of Naples, 25–26
Marcellus I, Pope, 16
Marcion, 19
Maria Goretti, 103
Mark, Liturgy of Saint, 21
Martin of Tours, Bishop, 15, 37–38
Martyrdom, definition, 2, 5, 44, 102, 146, 154, 160–161
Martyrologium Hieronymianum, 24, 33
Matthew the Evangelist, 12
Maximian, Emperor, 16
Menologium of Basil II, 55
Mensurius, Bishop of Carthage, 14
Mercurius of Caesarea, 60–61
Merkurii of Smolensk, 60–61, 95, 149
Metrodorus, 19
Michael the Archangel, 42
Mikhail Chernigovskii, Prince, 66, 77
Mikhail Iaroslavich of Tver, Grand Prince, 68, 82
Miltiades, Pope, 14
Missale Romanum, 108, 109
Moscow, Patriarch of, 2, 9, 78, 81, 86, 92, 99, 139
Mucheniki, definition, 49–50, 93

N
Necrology, 23
Nero, Emperor, 6, 14, 157
Nemessianus of Numidia, Bishop, 25
Nicephorus II Phocas, Emperor, 43, 103
Nicholas Eymeric, 106
Nicomedia, 35, 68
Nikon, Patriarch, 52

O
Old Believers, 52, 82, 155
Oprichnina, 52, 103
Optatus of Milevis, Bishop, 14, 37
Origen, 13, 35

P
Panikhida, 65–66
Passion-bearers, *see* Strastoterptsy

Passio Cypriani, 29
passiones martyrum, 28, 44
Patriarch of _____, *see location*
Paul the Apostle, 12, 33, 42
Paul of Constantinople, 26
Perpetua and Felicity, 23, 24
Peter, Apostle, 23, 33, 42
Peter Faber, 140
Peter the Great, Tsar, 78
Peter of Moscow, Metropolitan, 72
Philip II of Moscow, Metropolitan, 52, 103
Philomena, 110, 133–135, 148
Phocas, 26
Pierre de Castelnau, 123–124, 126–127
Pionius, 19
Pitrim of Nizhny Novgorod, Bishop, 82
Pius V, Pope, 108–109, 110
Plato, 12
Polycarp, 13, 17, 19, 20, 23, 28, 32, 69
Pomponius, Bishop, 26
Pontian, Pope, 23
Pontianus, Deacon, 29

Q
Quiritus and Julitta, 30, 31

R
Rasputin, Grigori, 92
Ratzinger, Cardinal Joseph, *see* Benedict XVI, Pope
Raymond of Pennafort, 129
Roman of Ryazan', Grand Prince, 50
Romanov family, 2, 4, 87–88, 92, 97, 122, 139, 150, 155
Rome, Council of, 30
Rostov Chronicle, 60

S
Sabbas, 34
Sanctorum Mater, 120
Schism, Great East-West (1054)6, 8, 11, 45, 101, 106, 107, 111, 122, 135, 152, 155
Scythia, 35
Septimia of Carthage, 25
Severus, Bishop, 26
Simon of Iurevits, 82
Simon of Vladimir, Bishop, 60
Simone of Trent, 130–131, 159
Sixtus I, Pope, 23, 24
Sixtus IV, Pope, 130, 135, 159
Sixtus V, Pope, 119, 131
Sluzhba, 58, 60, 72, 74, 82, 85

Smolensk, 60–61, 95, 149
Smyrna, Church of, 13, 23
Soviet Union, 5, 7, 81, 84, 87, 96
Sozomen, 18, 39
Spanish Inquisition, 1
Stanislaw of Krakow, Bishop, 109–110
Stefan and Peter, 76
Stephen, Bishop, 26
Stephen, Protomartyr, 29
Strastoterptsy, 49–50, 52, 65, 84, 87–88, 89–90, 93, 146
Sulpicius Severus, 15, 38
Sviatitel', 51
Sviatopolk, Prince, 49–50, 64–65
Sviatoslav, brother of Boris and Gleb, 65

T
Tatars, 50–51, 58, 61, 68, 77, 95, 149, 158
Telemachus, 40
Tertullus, 18
Theodor of Chernigov, 66
Theodor the Variag, 58, 60
Theodoret, Bishop, 38, 40
Theodosius I, Emperor, 39, 40
Theofania, Empress, 42–43
Theognost of Moscow, Metropolitan, 72
Thomas Aquinas, *see* Aquinas, Thomas
Thomas Becket, *see* Becket, Thomas
Thomas Netter of Walden, 133
Tikhon of Moscow, Patriarch, 58–59, 80–81, 85, 88

translatio of relics, 31, 33, 34, 35, 40, 41, 45, 55, 62, 66–67, 111–113, 114, 115, 116
Trent, Council of, 108, 136
True Calendar of All Russian Saints, 56, 77
Trullo, Council of, 30, 31
Tsar Nicholas Romanov, *see* Romanov family

U
Ukraine, 3–4
Ukrainian Greek Catholic Church, 4
Ulric of Augsburg, Bishop, 128
Union of Brest, 4
Urban VIII, Pope, 116, 124, 127, 136–139, 154
Ustav, 77

V
Valerian, Emperor, 33
Vatican Council II, 140
Vincent of Spain, 24
vindicatio, 37
Vladimir, Prince of Rus', 46, 49
Vladimir of Kiev, Metropolitan, 79, 85

W
Wenceslaus of Bohemia, King, 115
Wiborada of Swabia, 122–123

Z
zhitie, 58–61, 67, 78, 79, 81, 82, 85, 94, 114, 149
Zoe, Empress, 42–43